ROAD RAGE

ROAD RAGE

Assessment and Treatment of the Angry, Aggressive Driver

Tara E. Galovski, Loretta S. Malta, and Edward B. Blanchard

American Psychological Association • Washington, DC

Published by
American Psychological Association
750 First Street, NE
Washington, DC 20002
www.apa.org

To order
APA Order Department
P.O. Box 92984
Washington, DC 20090-2984
Tel: (800) 374-2721
Direct: (202) 336-5510
Fax: (202) 336-5502
TDD/TTY: (202) 336-6123
Online: www.apa.org/books/
E-mail: order@apa.org

In the U.K., Europe, Africa, and the Middle
East, copies may be ordered from
American Psychological Association
3 Henrietta Street
Covent Garden, London
WC2E 8LU England

Typeset in Goudy by World Composition Services, Inc., Sterling, VA

Printer: United Book Press, Baltimore, MD
Cover Designer: Naylor Design, Washington, DC
Technical/Production Editor: Harriet Kaplan

The opinions and statements published are the responsibility of the authors, and such
opinions and statements do not necessarily represent the policies of the American
Psychological Association.

Library of Congress Cataloging-in-Publication Data

Galovski, Tara E.
    Road rage : assessment and treatment of the angry, aggressive driver / Tara E. Galovski,
Loretta S. Malta, and Edward B. Blanchard.—1st ed.
        p. cm.
    Includes bibliographical references and index.
    ISBN 1-59147-305-5
    1. Automobile drivers—Mental health. 2. Road rage. 3. Aggressiveness—Treatment.
4. Anger—Treatment. 5. Automobile driving—Psychological aspects. I. Malta, Loretta S.
II. Blanchard, Edward B. III. Title.

    RC451.4.A98G34 2006
    363.12'51—dc22   2005006927

British Library Cataloguing-in-Publication Data
A CIP record is available from the British Library.

Printed in the United States of America
First Edition

To my husband, Jim; my colleague and friend, Connie Veazey,
who kept me laughing through it all;
and to my daughters, Saige and Hope,
just because they are such treasures.
—*Tara E. Galovski*

To my husband, Dennis McFarland, and my parents,
Joseph and Maria Malta, with thanks and gratitude
for their love and support.
—*Loretta S. Malta*

To my wife, Cris, with thanks
for tolerating my work habits over the years.
—*Edward B. Blanchard*

CONTENTS

PREFACE

Although a large amount of psychological literature on driving has been produced over the past 50 to 60 years, much of the early research was focused on two broad areas: (a) psychological factors associated with motor vehicle accidents and (b) psychological factors related to driving while intoxicated. Work on aggressive driving has lagged noticeably behind. This book seeks to remedy this relative lack by summarizing the existing literature on the aggressive or angry driver and by presenting in detail our own recent work on the assessment and treatment of angry and aggressive drivers, with a focus on the clinical application of this work.

This book has three parts. The first three chapters (Part I) provide background information, including a summary of what is known about aggressive driving and our effort to integrate this knowledge with the literature on the general topics of anger and aggression. The initial chapter summarizes the survey research that seeks to determine the magnitude of the problem presented by aggressive driving. Chapter 2 offers a discussion of the interrelated concepts of anger, hostility, and aggression, focusing especially on how driving aggression and driving anger fit within the broader framework of anger and aggression. Chapter 3 examines theories of aggressive driving that have emerged over the past 55 years.

In Part II, we switch from background information to a summary of our assessment information on court-mandated and self-referred aggressive drivers. Chapters 4 through 7 summarize our assessment methodologies, including a structured interview to begin the assessment of an aggressive driver (chap. 4). In chapter 5, we present data on psychiatric comorbidity, especially the understudied intermittent explosive disorder (IED).[1] In chapter 6, we describe dimensional assessment with psychological tests and include norms from our sample of treatment-seeking aggressive drivers and from a large sample of undergraduates. Chapter 7 describes our work on psychophysiological assessment.

In Part III, we shift the focus to treating the angry and aggressive driver. Chapter 8 reviews current evidence-based treatments for aggressive drivers. In chapter 9, we discuss the results of our treatment research at the Center for Stress and Anxiety Disorders. Chapter 10 presents Galovski and Blanchard's (2002a) detailed manual for cognitive–behavioral group treatment of aggressive drivers. In chapter 11, we offer suggestions for working with the criminal justice system to obtain treatment and research participation referrals of aggressive drivers and provide summary conclusions and directions for future research.

We hope to serve two audiences with this book. First, we seek to provide information of clinical value to the mental health practitioners who are called on to assess and treat the angry or aggressive driver. To help meet this goal, throughout the book we provide "Clinical Hints" on topics for which firm research data are missing but for which we have ideas based on our clinical experience. Second, we seek to provide a summary and integration of the available information on aggressive drivers to guide the design of future research studies on assessment, treatment, and prevention.

---

[1] As we discuss in detail in chapters 4 and 5, we found ourselves with a noticeable sample of aggressive drivers who met criteria for IED. Because this is an understudied disorder that affects as many as one third of treatment-seeking aggressive drivers, we have done two things: First, we present in chapter 5 a brief summary of descriptive research and diagnostic issues regarding IED as well as our own approach to diagnosis, and second, we present separate analyses of our own assessment data (chaps. 5–7) comparing drivers who meet criteria for IED with those who do not. In chapter 9, we also separate the treatment outcome results for this subgroup.

ACKNOWLEDGMENTS

First and foremost, we acknowledge the assistance of Jim Murphy, District Attorney of Saratoga County, New York, for his assistance in recruiting the court-referred aggressive drivers. Without his assistance, much of this work could not have been done.

We also recognize the efforts and achievements of the aggressive drivers who participated in our research. We hope their own safety and well-being and that of those around them have improved as a result of their experience in our program.

We also acknowledge the assistance of several University at Albany graduate students who provided assessment and treatment services or helped with data analysis: Connie Veazey, Brian Freidenberg, Mark Sykes, and Tiffany Fusé. Finally, we acknowledge the help of Sandy Agosto in preparing the manuscript.

I

BACKGROUND INFORMATION

1

AGGRESSIVE DRIVING: SIGNIFICANCE AND SCOPE OF THE PROBLEM

When you think of an aggressive driver, what sort of individual do you imagine? A young, "macho" man in a sports car? A hard-driving executive on a cell phone, darting through traffic to make an important meeting? An antisocial thug? A stressed-out "soccer mom" rushing through suburban streets? Consider the following popular media interview excerpts of aggressive drivers and, as you read, try to imagine the identity of each speaker.

> "I'm not even thinking of other cars," *** admits cheerfully [and] lays on the horn. An oldster in an econo-box ahead has made the near fatal mistake of slowing at an intersection with no stop sign or traffic light. *** swears and peels off around him . . . "I don't think I'm an aggressive driver. . . . But there are a lot of bad drivers out there." (Ferguson, 1998, pp. 64, 66)

> "People on the road were an impediment to my progress . . . on the road, you were in my way." (Ferguson, 1998, p. 67)

Before the identities of the individuals are revealed, take a moment to consider the sort of people you imagined as you were reading. Now see if you guessed correctly.

The first interview subject was described as a "prosperous, well-adjusted," 40-year-old, "loving" mother of three. She was interviewed for

Time magazine as she drove her Chevy Suburban through a residential neighborhood with her children in the car. In the interview, the children were also described as shouting "Make him move over!" when their mother was stuck behind a slow driver in the left lane. The second *Time* interview subject was described as a 47-year-old "soft-spoken salesman" from a small city in the Northeast. Were you surprised, or did you guess correctly?

These examples were chosen to illustrate the diversity of individuals who drive aggressively. Mizell's (1997) review of more than 10,000 reported aggressive driving incidents revealed that perpetrators ranged from men with criminal records to a former state legislator to Academy Award–winning actor Jack Nicholson:

> There is no one profile of the so-called "aggressive driver" ... the majority of aggressive drivers are relatively young, relatively poorly educated males who have criminal records, histories of violence, and drug or alcohol problems. ... But hundreds of aggressive drivers— motorists who have snapped and committed incredible violence—are successful men and women with no known histories of crime, violence, or alcohol and drug abuse. (p. 1)

Who is the aggressive driver? Why do people drive aggressively? These are not new questions. Understanding the nature of aggressive driving has intrigued social scientists for more than 50 years, and the earliest publications describing aggressive drivers date back to the late 1940s (e.g., Tillmann & Hobbs, 1949). Even earlier references can be found in the popular literature. James and Nahl (2000) noted that a reference to "furious driving" can be found in Gilbert and Sullivan's 1893 play "Mr. Jericho." However, the proliferation of media reports of so-called "road rage" incidents throughout the past decade has more recently brought aggressive driving to the attention of the general public and legislators. There are several reasons to revisit the issue of aggressive driving, the most salient of which is the enormous toll of motor vehicle accidents (MVAs) on the health and safety of individuals in the United States and worldwide.

MVAs are the leading cause of accidental death and injury in the United States and the leading cause of death of people ages 5 to 29 years (U.S. Department of Transportation [DOT], Bureau of Transportation Statistics, 2002). According to the DOT, MVAs were responsible for more than 42,000 deaths and more than 3 million injuries in the United States in 2001 (U.S. DOT, Bureau of Transportation Statistics, 2002). International estimates of the annual incidence have ranged from 300,000 to 500,000 deaths and 10 million to 15 million injuries worldwide (U.S. DOT, Bureau of Transportation Statistics, 1999). Because MVAs occur more frequently than other types of traumatic events, they are also one of the more common precipitants of posttraumatic stress disorder (Norris, 1992). The health and economic impact of MVAs underscores the importance of investigating aggressive driving, which has been identified as a risk factor for MVAs.

SCOPE OF THE PROBLEM OF AGGRESSIVE DRIVING

The DOT reported in 1998 that approximately 21% of MVAs involved speeding, 9% involved failure to yield the right of way, and 5% involved reckless and careless driving (U.S. DOT, Bureau of Transportation Statistics, 1998). The National Highway Traffic Safety Administration (2001) estimated that 67% of MVA fatalities and 33% of injuries involved aggressive driving. However, the actual prevalence of aggressive driving has not been well studied. One difficulty with ascertaining the prevalence of aggressive driving is that, as we discuss in chapter 2 of this volume, there is currently no consensus on what constitutes aggressive driving or road rage. Fumento (1998) criticized the media, the U.S. DOT, and the American Automobile Association (Mizell, 1997) for exaggerating the prevalence of road rage incidents. Mizell (1997) reviewed 10,037 reports from 30 newspapers and 16 police departments as well as an unspecified number of reports from insurance companies from 1990 through 1996. Fumento noted that the 218 deaths Mizell found to be related to reported road rage incidents constituted only a small percentage (0.08%) of approximately 280,000 deaths during the same period. Moreover, Mizell's estimate of at least 1,500 annual injuries related to aggressive driving also constitutes only a fraction of the approximately 3 million annual injuries, an amount (like fatalities) that has been fairly consistent throughout the 1990s (U.S. DOT, Bureau of Transportation Statistics, 2002). However, it should be noted that Mizell's report was restricted to aggressive driving incidents that were severe enough to warrant news coverage and police involvement, that is, those that involved some sort of personal or vehicular assault. Although such extreme incidents appear to be rare, the few studies that have examined the prevalence of aggressive and risky driving behaviors suggest that relatively milder, but potentially endangering, aggressive driving behaviors are more common.

Data from studies that have examined the prevalence of aggressive driving in large samples of drivers in the United States are shown in Table 1.1. As shown in the table, verbal and gestural aggression (making obscene gestures, cursing, yelling, honking) is the most common form of driving aggression. In one of the earliest studies, Novaco (1991) surveyed 412 drivers in Orange County, California, who participated in a court-approved program for traffic violators seeking to avoid fines and insurance company notification of violations. He found that 34% endorsed some form of verbal or gestural aggression (obscene gestures, threatening arguments). Although the sample consisted of traffic violators, this prevalence rate is similar to that of three

TABLE 1.1
Summary of Aggressive Driving Prevalence Studies—U.S. Drivers

Study	N	Location	Method	Time period	Verbal/gestures	Tailgate or block	Physical aggression	Other
							Sample with behavior	
Clifford (1989)	2,032	Southern CA	Newspaper poll	Lifetime	38% gestures 12% arguments			31% give chase
Novaco (1991)	412	Orange County, CA	Questionnaire	Lifetime	34% gestures 34% violent threats		12% throw object 8% physical assault 5% bump/ram vehicle 1% threaten with gun <1% weapon assault	
Hemenway & Solnick (1993)	1,802	Southern CA	Telephone survey	Lifetime	38% gestures 12% arguments			47% speed 20% run lights
Miller et al. (2002)	790	Arizona	Telephone survey	Past year	34% gestures or cursing	28%	<1% threaten with gun	
Wells-Parker et al. (2002)	1,382	United States	Telephone survey	Current driving	20% honk or yell 7% gestures	16%	<1% bump/ram vehicle	7% speed past cars in anger 1% threatening driving moves <1% each: give chase, cut car off road, leave car to confront, leave car to hurt other driver

other studies of general population drivers. Two surveys of drivers in southern California revealed that 38% of drivers endorsed having ever made obscene gestures, and 12% reported having an argument with another driver in the past year (Clifford, 1989; Hemenway & Solnick, 1993). In a more recent telephone survey, M. Miller, Azrael, Hemenway, and Solop (2002) also found that 34% of drivers in Arizona endorsed obscene gesturing or cursing at other drivers within the past year. Wells-Parker et al. (2002) found a lower prevalence of verbal and gestural aggression in a national telephone survey in which drivers reported on the frequency of current aggressive driving. The prevalence of behaviors endorsed at a frequency of at least "sometimes" or more often was 20% for honking or yelling but only 7% for obscene gesturing.

A lower prevalence has been reported for vehicular forms of aggression. The prevalence of tailgating and blocking other vehicles has ranged from 6% and from 10% for tailgating and blocking, respectively (Wells-Parker et al., 2002), to 28% for either tailgating or blocking (M. Miller et al., 2002). Hemenway and Solnick (1993) found that 47% of drivers in southern California endorsed speeding frequently, and 20% reported having run at least one red light during the past month. However, Wells-Parker et al. (2002) found that only 6% of U.S. drivers reported speeding past cars specifically for the purpose of expressing anger. An even lower prevalence has been reported for more extreme forms of driving aggression, such as assault. Although 31% of the traffic offenders surveyed by Novaco (1991) reported having given chase to other drivers, less than 0.05% of general population drivers reported this (Wells-Parker et al., 2002). In Wells-Parker et al.'s study, only 1% of U.S. drivers reported sometimes making sudden or threatening driving moves, and less than 0.05% reported sometimes trying to cut a car off the road or leaving their vehicle to confront another driver. In Novaco's sample of traffic offenders, the prevalence of physical aggression ranged from 12% (throwing objects) to 0.7% (shooting another driver). However, in general population drivers the prevalence of physical confrontations is 0.1% or less (Clifford, 1989; Wells-Parker et al., 2002). Only 2% of U.S. drivers reported carrying a weapon in case it would be needed for a driving incident (Wells-Parker et al., 2002), and only 0.5% of drivers in Arizona reported having ever brandished a gun at another driver (M. Miller et al., 2002).

To summarize the U.S. prevalence data, excluding Novaco's (1991) sample of traffic violators, the research reveals a variable current (within the past year, current driving habits) prevalence of verbal and gestural driving aggression that has ranged from 7% to 34% (M. Miller et al., 2002; Wells-Parker et al., 2002), with two reports (Clifford, 1989; Hemenway & Solnick, 1993) of a lifetime prevalence of 38% for making obscene gestures and 12% for having arguments with other drivers. The current prevalence of tailgating, blocking other vehicles, or both has ranged from 16% to 28% (M. Miller et al., 2002; Wells-Parker et al., 2002), and extreme forms of driving aggression have been endorsed by only 1% or less of drivers.

As shown in Table 1.2, international studies have also found a variable prevalence of aggressive driving. The prevalence of drivers in the United Kingdom who endorse committing some form of aggressive driving has ranged from 20% to 88% across three studies, depending on methodology. The highest overall prevalence (88%) was reported from Parker, Lajunen, and Stradling (1998), who conducted a mail survey of English drivers in which participants reported on the frequency of specific aggressive driving behaviors. The authors did not report the prevalence of each behavior but found that only 11% of their drivers endorsed never giving chase, indicating hostility to other drivers, or honking the car horn in annoyance. Gulian, Debney, et al. (1989) found a much lower prevalence: 20% of English drivers (assessed using questionnaires and 1-week driving diaries) endorsed using aggressive strategies ("cut in front of cars, take any opportunity to get out") to cope with traffic. In Joint's (1995) survey of motorists throughout the United Kingdom, 88% of drivers reported being on the receiving end of road rage incidents (the definition of *road rage* was unspecified) during the past year, including aggressive tailgating (62%), headlight flashing (59%), rude or aggressive gestures (48%), deliberate blocking of vehicles (21%), verbal abuse (16%), and physical assault (1%). It is interesting that, as shown in Table 1.1, when the same drivers were asked about the types of aggressive driving behaviors they had committed within the past year, they reported a much lower prevalence. A total of 60% of drivers endorsed engaging in at least one of the behaviors sampled in contrast to the 88% of drivers who reported being on the receiving end of driving aggression. It is possible that the disparity reflects differential exposure to aggressive driving by individuals who themselves do not drive aggressively; however, it also suggests that people may underreport their own aggressive driving, overreport that of other drivers, or both.

Three other studies from Europe suggest a cross-cultural aggressive driver prevalence of approximately 25%. In a mail survey of Greek drivers, Kontogiannis, Kossiavelou, and Marmaras (2002) found that 26% of drivers endorsed engaging in aggressive driving behaviors that included hostile gestures, speeding, tailgating, unsafe passing out of impatience, giving chase, excessive accelerating when lights turn green to "show off," and engaging in "unofficial races" with other drivers. In an early study that directly observed drivers in the Netherlands, Hauber (1980) assessed aggressive driving responses (failing to stop, honking, making gestures, yelling) to delays created by a confederate pedestrian and found that 25% of drivers made some sort of aggressive response. Most of the responses were verbal or gestural in nature, but Hauber also reported that experimenters occasionally had to

TABLE 1.2

Summary of Aggressive Driving Prevalence Studies—International Drivers

Study	N	Location	Method	Time Period	Verbal/gestures	Sample with behavior		Other
						Tailgate or block	Physical aggression	
Hauber (1980)	966	Netherlands	Observation	Current driving				25% display variety of aggressive driving behaviors
Gulian et al. (1989)	209	England	Questionnaire and driving diary	Current driving				20% cut in front of drivers in traffic/take any opportunity to get out
Joint (1995)	526	United Kingdom	Survey	Past year	45% flash lights 22% gestures 12% verbal abuse	11%	<1% assault	60% endorse at least one aggressive driving behavior
Parker et al. (1998)	270	England	Mail survey	Current driving				Only 11% endorse never giving chase, indicating hostility, or honking horn in annoyance
Kontogiannis et al. (2002)	1,425	Greece	Mail survey	Current driving				26% endorse variety of aggressive driving behaviors
Shinar & Compton (2004)	7,200	Tel Aviv, Israel	Observation	Current driving	5% honk horn			22% cut off vehicles to pass 3% cut across multiple lanes or drove on shoulder to pass 30% at least one aggressive driving behavior

run to escape drivers who failed to stop, despite the pedestrian having the legal right of way. In what appears to be the only other study that directly observed drivers, as well as the prevalence study with the largest sample (N = 7,200; see Table 1.2), Shinar and Compton (2004) found that 22% of Tel Aviv drivers cut off other vehicles to pass, 5% honked horns, and 3% cut across multiple lanes or drove on the shoulder of the road to pass vehicles.

The international research suggests an overall current aggressive driving prevalence of 20% to 25% of drivers, with two reports of a prevalence ranging from 60% to 88% (Joint, 1995; Parker et al., 1998). It is not possible to estimate a total prevalence of aggressive drivers in the United States, because all of the studies sampled the frequency of specific behaviors, some of which may have been committed by the same driver, and none of the studies reported a total number of aggressive drivers (i.e., those who had endorsed any of the behaviors). However, three consistent findings emerge from all of the studies: (a) Milder forms of aggression are a fairly common occurrence, (b) extreme driving aggression is rare, and (c) verbal and gestural driving aggression (yelling, honking, making obscene gestures, flashing the headlights) is the most common type of aggression. Although there is much variability across studies, there is also some concordance. For example, the U.S. verbal and gestural aggression current prevalence range of 20% to 34% is similar to Joint's (1995) finding of 22% to 45%. Similarly, the 12% U.S. lifetime prevalence of arguing with other drivers (Clifford, 1989; Hemenway & Solnick, 1993) mirrored Joint's report of a current prevalence of 12% for verbal abuse, although it is not clear that these represented the same behavior. Both the United States (Wells-Parker et al., 2002) and Joint reported a current prevalence of 6% for tailgating, although Wells-Parker et al. (2002) found a prevalence of 10% for blocking vehicles, compared with Joint's 5%. The U.S. studies did not survey whether respondents ever cut off other drivers, but the studies by Gulian, Debney, et al. (1989) and Shinar and Compton (2004) suggest that the prevalence may be approximately 20% to 25% of drivers. Studies in the United States and Joint's U.K. survey have also consistently found a prevalence of extreme driving aggression of 1% or less of drivers.

It should be noted that there are significant limitations to the epidemiological research. In particular, with the exception of the observational studies by Hauber (1980) and Shinar and Compton (2004), all of the prevalence data are based on self-report. This is problematic, because study samples may have been biased toward respondents who (a) were willing to participate in surveys and (b) were willing to report undesirable driving behaviors. As noted, Joint (1995) found a much higher prevalence of aggressive driving when drivers were asked to report how often they had been the recipient of aggression rather than the perpetrator. Novaco (1991) found a similar disparity in his sample of traffic violators. Part of the problem may be that aggressive driving is in the "eye of the beholder"; that is, some drivers may not recognize their own driving as aggressive. Recall the interview excerpt from the suburban American mother at the beginning of this chapter, who was described as swearing, tailgating, and "peeling off" around other drivers. She nonetheless insisted that *she* was not an aggressive driver but asserted, "There are a lot of bad drivers out there." It is also possible that drivers who frequently drive aggressively, and those who commit the most extreme aggression, are unwilling to participate in surveys or may underreport such behavior when they do.

Moreover, it is difficult to estimate the prevalence of aggressive driving from studies whose methods differ, and the research indicates variability in the reported prevalence of aggressive driving, depending on the behaviors, time period, and region sampled. For example, M. Miller et al. (2002) found that 28% of their Arizona sample endorsed tailgating or blocking vehicles, whereas Wells-Parker et al. (2002) found that only 16% (6% tailgating, 10% blocking) of their national U.S. sample endorsed either of these behaviors. Because these studies sampled different populations as well as different driving time periods (within the past year in Miller et al.'s [2002] study vs. a frequency scale of current driving habits in Wells-Parker et al.'s [2002] study), it is not possible to determine the nature of the variability in prevalence.

More precision is clearly needed in epidemiological aggressive driving research. Future research studies should use direct observation of driving behaviors as well as standardized self-report instrumentation and should sample different driving time periods (both lifetime and current driving habits). However, despite the limitations, the research suggests that although extreme driving aggression does indeed appear to be rare, mild to moderate driving aggression is a common occurrence on roadways, with a conservative estimated prevalence of approximately 20% to 25% of drivers who at least occasionally engage in verbal and gestural aggressive driving behaviors as well as tailgating or blocking other vehicles.

IS AGGRESSIVE DRIVING ON THE INCREASE?

Joint (1995) reported that 62% of the motorists he surveyed thought that the behavior of motorists had changed for the worse in recent years. In his review of reported aggressive driving incidents culled from the news media, police departments, and insurance companies, Mizell (1997) found a 60% increase in reports of aggressive driving incidents from 1990 to 1996. However, whether the prevalence of aggressive driving has actually increased is unknown at present. As noted, it is difficult to ascertain the prevalence of aggressive driving across studies that use different criteria for aggressive driving, sample different time periods of driving, and rely primarily on self-report. Regarding Mizell's finding, it is important to note that an increase in the report of a phenomenon is not synonymous with an increase in the actual behavior. It is not atypical for the news media to latch onto what they consider a new trend and print a spate of stories before dropping the issue. The perceptions of the driving public are also susceptible to the media's influence. Greater attention from the media could produce a greater awareness among drivers and increase their tendency to notice aggressive driving behaviors, resulting in the perception that aggressive driving is on the increase.

It is noteworthy that, as shown in Tables 1.1 and 1.2, the prevalence studies reviewed in this chapter, which spanned 1980 through 2003, do not appear to indicate an increase in the prevalence of aggressive driving behaviors. For example, Hemenway and Solnick (1993) found the same lifetime prevalence of obscene gestures and arguments in southern California drivers as did a *Los Angeles Times* poll (Clifford, 1989) conducted 5 years earlier. Also, as Novaco (1991) noted, some of his findings with Orange County, California, drivers were similar to those reported by Clifford (1989) 2 years earlier. In addition, although they sampled drivers in different countries, Gulian, Debney, et al.'s (1989) report that 20% of their English drivers cut off cars or forced their way out of traffic was also consistent with Shinar and Compton's (2004) finding that 22% of drivers observed in Tel Aviv cut off other drivers to pass, and Hauber's (1980) finding that 25% of drivers in the Netherlands responded aggressively to a pedestrian delay was similar to Kontogiannis et al.'s (2002) finding of an aggressive driving prevalence of 26% of Greek drivers. These studies do not suggest an obvious increase in aggressive driving; moreover, as noted, there is variability in the methodology used to gather prevalence data, and the majority of studies have relied on self-report. Therefore, it is difficult to draw strong conclusions regarding the current prevalence of aggressive driving, let alone any increase in the phenomenon.

Mizell's (1997) study also has limitations. As Fumento (1998) noted, Mizell examined a relatively small number of sources. Another problem with Mizell's analysis is that he did not control for any increase in the number of drivers on the road from 1990 to 1996, which could produce an increase in the number of incidents but not necessarily the prevalence of aggressive driving (i.e., the proportion of aggressive drivers to nonaggressive drivers). In their observational study of aggressive driving in Tel Aviv, Shinar and Compton (2004) found a significant linear relationship ($R^2 = .81$) between the frequency of observed aggressive driving behaviors and the number of cars on the road during different observation periods and at different locations, suggesting that the increase in the prevalence of aggressive driving behaviors was due to the increase in the number of vehicles rather than a change in the rate of increase itself. The authors did find that *time urgency* (defined in this study as driving during rush hour) was associated with increased aggressive driving, even after controlling for the number of vehicles.

Shinar and Compton's (2004) study highlights the importance of examining confounding variables, such as increases in the number of vehicles, when investigating any change in the prevalence of aggressive driving behaviors. From 1990 to 1996, urban and rural road mileage in the United States increased from a total of 3,866,926 miles in 1990 to 3,919,652 miles in 1996, an increase of 1.36% (U.S. DOT, Bureau of Transportation Statistics, 2002). During that same period, the number of registered vehicles increased from 193,057,376 in 1990 to 210,441,249, an increase of 9% (U.S. DOT, Bureau of Transportation Statistics, 2002). The percentage increase in the number of vehicles was nearly seven times that of the increase in road mileage, which suggests that U.S. roads became more congested from 1990 through 1996. This suggests the possibility that Mizell's (1997) finding of an increase in the number of reported aggressive driving incidents was due at least in part to an increase in the number of vehicles on the road rather than to an increase in the prevalence of aggressive driving. Thus, the question of whether aggressive driving is on the increase remains unanswered; a definitive answer awaits more rigorous longitudinal prevalence research.

AGGRESSIVE DRIVING AS A RISK FACTOR FOR MOTOR VEHICLE ACCIDENTS

Regardless of whether aggressive driving is actually increasing, more than 40 years of descriptive and experimental research studies have supported a reliable association between aggressive driving and increased risk of MVAs. In an early descriptive study, Parry (1968) observed an arithmetically higher prevalence of MVAs in individuals who reported driving aggressively. In two descriptive studies reviewed by MacMillan (1975), Goldstein and Mosel (1958, cited in MacMillan, 1975) and Golby and Crawford (1963, cited in MacMillan, 1975) found that driving in an aggressive and competitive fashion was associated with arithmetically greater numbers of traffic violations and MVAs. MacMillan's early cluster analysis of driving behaviors appears to be the first well-controlled study to specifically test and demonstrate that aggressive driving directly increases the risk of MVAs, in that he used statistical analyses, the sample selection was unbiased, and he controlled for driver mileage in his analyses. MacMillan administered a questionnaire about driver attitudes and behaviors to a sample of more than 800 drivers. He found that drivers in the "competitive" cluster (i.e., irritation at being passed by other cars, fondness for speeding) and those in the "aggressive" cluster had a significantly greater number of MVAs and traffic convictions.

More recent research has also supported an association between an increased risk of MVAs and aggressive driving. Hemenway and Solnick (1993) found that the self-reported frequency of arguments with other drivers and a positive endorsement of having ever made obscene gestures at other drivers were significantly correlated with MVAs, speeding, and running red lights. Blanchard, Barton, and Malta (2000); Chliaoutakis et al. (2002); Dula and Ballard (2003); and Wells-Parker et al. (2002) have all found that self-reported aggressive driving was significantly correlated with MVAs. The fact that each of these studies used a different measure of aggressive driving offers further support for the reliability of the association between aggressive driving and an increased risk of MVAs.

SUMMARY

Aggressive driving may not necessarily be on the increase, and more rigorous research on its prevalence is needed. However, to the extent that aggressive driving increases the risk of MVAs, it continues to pose a serious public health risk. Thus, as recognized by social scientists for more than 50 years, aggressive driving is a significant societal problem. The fatalities, injuries, and psychological impact of MVAs and the potential physical and psychological toll of daily stress associated with commutes on congested highways (Novaco, Stokols, Campell, & Stokols, 1979; Schaeffer, Street, Singer, & Baum, 1988) as well as the relatively rare but extremely dangerous road rage incidents all make aggressive driving a relevant societal issue and a topic worth continued social and clinical scientific study.

2

DEFINING DRIVING AGGRESSION
AND RELATED CONSTRUCTS

In discussing the general literature on aggression, anger, and hostility, Spielberger and his colleagues (Spielberger, Jacobs, Russel, & Crane, 1983; Spielberger et al., 1985) have noted that the definitions of these constructs are inconsistent and that the terms are often used interchangeably. By extension, the same tendency exists in the literature on aggressive driving, in which the constructs of driving anger, aggression, and road rage are inconsistently defined and often blended together. As we discuss in this chapter, there currently is no consensus within the general literature, much less within driving research literature, on definitions of *hostility*, *anger*, and *aggression*. The merging of these constructs is likely due in part to the inherent difficulty of defining and distinguishing among them.

HOSTILITY

The definition of the construct of hostility appears to be the least disputed among theorists. There is a consensus that hostility is, in essence, a set of cognitive behaviors that include assigning pejorative verbal labels and negative evaluations and that hostility is associated with a concurrent negative emotional state. Buss (1961) regarded hostility as a conditioned verbal response that becomes automatic and "implicit" over time, acquired through pairings of anger-evoking stimuli and negative labeling. Spielberger et al. (1983, 1995) have characterized hostility as a combination of a negative attitude and angry feelings that may function to motivate aggression. Other researchers have specified an interpersonal element, that is, that hostility involves appraisals of individuals and expectations of harm from others (Berkowitz, 1993; Eckhardt, Norlander, & Deffenbacher, 2004; G. T. Smith, 1994). Berkowitz (1993) defined a hostile individual as someone who is quick to indicate a negative attitude toward others, and G. T. Smith (1994) defined hostility as a cognitive–behavioral tendency that includes negative evaluations, expectations of harm from others, an oppositional stance, and malicious intent toward others. Eckhardt et al. (2004) described the central features of hostility as mistrust, cynicism, and denigration of others.

DRIVING HOSTILITY

Driving anger and aggression scales typically contain items that may imply driving hostility on the basis of the assumption that driving anger and aggression involve appraising the behavior of drivers or pedestrians in a manner that potentially provokes an angry and aggressive response. For example, the Driving Anger Scale (Deffenbacher, Oetting, & Lynch, 1994), the Driving Vengeance Questionnaire (Wiesenthal, Hennessy, & Gibson, 2000), and the Driver's Stress Profile (Larson, 1996a) assess anger directed at other drivers; the Driving Anger Scale also measures anger directed at pedestrians and the police. However, few researchers have attempted to define or measure driving hostility as a construct distinct from driving anger or aggression. Some driving instruments do include a few items that assess hostile attitudes; these include the Dangerous Driving Index (Dula & Ballard, 2003); the Driver Behaviour Questionnaire (Reason, Manstead, Stradling, Baxter, & Campbell, 1990); and James and Nahl's (2000) Range of Hostility Checklist, which includes behaviors ranging from denigrating other drivers to confrontations and assault. One instrument, the Driver's Angry Thoughts Questionnaire (Deffenbacher, Petrilli, Lynch, Oetting, & Swaim, 2003; Deffenbacher, White, & Lynch, 2004), assesses a wide range of hostile (and angry) thoughts, including pejorative labeling, thoughts of revenge and retaliation, and judgmental attitudes. Its creators found that such thoughts significantly correlate with general (non-driving-related) hostility and anger as well as with driving anger.

Assessing driving hostility is germane to cognitive–behavioral treatments of driving anger and aggression that target maladaptive cognitions (Deffenbacher, Filetti, Lynch, Dahlen, & Oetting, 2002; Deffenbacher, Huff, Lynch, Oetting, & Salvatore, 2000; Galovski & Blanchard, 2002a; James & Nahl, 2000; Larson, 1996b; Larson, Rodriquez, & Galvan-Henkin, 1998), because many aggressive drivers denigrate other drivers as stupid or inept and believe that their own superiority as drivers justifies their aggressive driving (Deffenbacher et al., 2004; Deffenbacher, Petrilli, et al., 2003; James & Nahl, 2000; Larson, 1996b; Parry, 1968). Deffenbacher and his associates (Deffenbacher et al., 2004; Deffenbacher, Petrilli, et al., 2003) found that hostile attitudes and thoughts of aggression toward other drivers were significantly correlated with aggressive and reckless driving and that different classes of thoughts (i.e., pejorative labeling, retaliation, etc.) were differentially related to specific aggressive driving behaviors. Moreover, the Driver's Angry Thoughts Questionnaire significantly increased the amount of variance in driving aggression predicted by driving anger and general hostility.

These findings underscore the usefulness of conceptualizing and assessing driving hostility as a construct that is distinct from anger and aggression. To proffer a definition that integrates extant definitions and has utility for treatment, we define *hostility* as learned cognitive behaviors consisting of the assignment of negative labels, appraisals, and evaluations of individuals who are perceived as potentially harmful or oppositional; hostility's function is to facilitate the planning and selection of behaviors that will reduce or thwart the threat or effects of harm or opposition. Because *driving hostility* appears to be somewhat distinct from general hostility (Deffenbacher, Petrilli, et al., 2003), we define it as hostility that is specific to the context of driving (i.e., is directed toward other drivers, pedestrians, or traffic law enforcement).

ANGER

Spielberger et al. (1983, 1995) have offered a descriptive definition of *anger* as an emotional state that varies along a continuum ranging from irritation to rage or fury. Most theorists also characterize anger as a negative arousal state that is maintained through its consequences. Where theorists tend to differ is regarding the nature of the response. Behaviorists such as Buss (1961) characterized anger as a *respondent* (an unconditioned or conditioned response). Salzinger (1995) described anger as an attenuated attack respondent and suggested that the expression of anger could become an *operant* (a response conditioned by its consequence) through *reinforcement* (positive consequences of the response). Most cognitive–behavioral theorists conceptualize anger as a complex syndrome. Averill (1982, 1983), Bandura (1973), Berkowitz (1993, 1994), and Kassinove and Sukhodolsky (1995) have all suggested that anger is an integrated experience involving negative arousal, contextual cues, cognitive behaviors (labeling and appraisals), and maintenance through positive consequences. Kassinove and Sukhodolsky included in their definition of anger the involvement of action tendencies to engage in "socially-constructed and reinforced, organized behavioral scripts" (p. 7). Averill (1982, 1983), Bandura (1973), and Kassinove and Sukhodolsky also emphasized the socially constructed aspects of anger as functioning to maintain societal standards of conduct.

These definitions appear to reflect the phenomenological experience of anger, in which negative labeling and appraisal (i.e., hostility) occur with changes in mood, physiological arousal, and tendencies toward overt behavioral responses. However, although the integrated percept of anger may include several cognitive, affective, and behavioral elements that moderate its perceived intensity, multicomponent definitions may be overly inclusive. It is, granted, very difficult to parse the many components involved in an integrated anger response. However, although negative appraisals may moderate anger responses, their inclusion in the definition of anger blurs the distinction between anger and hostility. Similarly, although it is important to include the activation of behavioral tendencies as a function of anger, a distinction should be made between an individual's feeling of anger and the expression of that anger. The function of a feeling-state, which may act as an interoreceptive stimulus for the individual experiencing it, differs from the function of an expression of that feeling-state, which acts on the environment. Thus, as Salzinger (1995) suggested, it is the *expression* of anger, rather than the *feeling* of anger, that is maintained by consequences. This distinction has implications for treatment, because altering the consequences of anger expression without addressing conditions that evoke the feeling-state could result in someone who continues to experience strong feelings of anger, although he or she might have learned to suppress its expression. To integrate the various theoretical perspectives and provide a definition that has treatment utility, we define *anger* as a respondent to stimuli that evoke hostility or inherently signify attack or opposition that is characterized by an interoreceptive, negatively valenced arousal state that functions to facilitate the planning and selection of behaviors to reduce or thwart attack or opposition.

DRIVING ANGER

Deffenbacher and his associates (Deffenbacher, Deffenbacher, Lynch, & Richards, 2003; Deffenbacher, Filetti, Richards, Lynch, & Oetting, 2003) have proposed a state–trait model of driving anger in which a general proclivity to become angered while driving (trait driving anger) predicts situation-specific (state) driving anger, and their research has demonstrated that trait driving anger correlates with state driving anger as well as with aggressive and reckless driving (Deffenbacher, Deffenbacher, et al., 2003; Deffenbacher et al., 2000; Deffenbacher, Filetti, et al., 2003; Deffenbacher,

Lynch, Deffenbacher, & Oetting, 2001; Deffenbacher, Lynch, Filetti, Dahlen, & Oetting, 2003; Deffenbacher, Lynch, Oetting, & Yingling, 2001). Research also suggests a broader trait–state model in which people who are generally angry also tend to be high in driving anger and aggression (Deffenbacher, Deffenbacher, et al., 2003; Deffenbacher et al., 1994, 2000, 2004; Deffenbacher, Filetti, et al., 2003; Deffenbacher, Lynch, et al., 2003; Deffenbacher, Lynch, Oetting, & Swaim, 2002; DePasquale, Geller, Clarke, & Littleton, 2001; Dula & Ballard, 2003; Lawton & Nutter, 2002; Malta, 2004; Malta & Blanchard, 2004; Malta et al., 2001). However, like driving hostility, driving anger appears to be a construct that is distinct from general (non-driving-related) anger (Deffenbacher, Deffenbacher, et al., 2003 Deffenbacher et al., 2004; Deffenbacher, Filetti, et al., 2003). Thus, we define *driving anger* as a context-specific form of anger that occurs in response to driving-related stimuli encountered while operating a vehicle or riding in one as a passenger.

AGGRESSION

Aggression is another construct whose definition has been hotly debated. Spielberger et al. (1983; Spielberger et al., 1995) have defined *aggression* simply as punitive or destructive behavior; however, most theorists include in the definition the goal of injuring or harming another person (Averill, 1982; Dollard, Doob, Miller, Mowrer, & Sears, 1939; Kassinove & Sukhodolsky, 1995). Buss (1961) and Bandura (1973) rejected the inclusion of intent in definitions, because it was difficult to ascertain, and they considered it superfluous to defining the antecedents and consequences associated with aggression. They also recognized that some aspects of aggression are socially defined. For example, Buss stated that the delivery of aversive stimuli (e.g., dental procedures), "within the context of a recognized social role and with socially desirable, long-run consequences" (p. 4), is not aggressive, and Bandura (1973), in his definition of aggression, included the notions of both harmful behavior and the violation of social norms.

Berkowitz (1993) noted problems and contradictions with the proposed definitions of aggression. Although intent to harm may be difficult to determine, without its inclusion accidental injury could be considered aggressive. Reliance on socially defined norms makes it difficult to consistently classify aggression, because norms vary. Berkowitz (1993) chose instead to distinguish between *hostile aggression*, which he described as impulsive, automatic aggression with the goal of inflicting harm, and *instrumental aggression*: premeditated, unemotional aggression with the goal of access to some reward. Buss (1961) had earlier made the same distinction, but both he and Bandura (1973) stated that both forms of aggression were instrumental in that they were directed toward achieving some goal. Dodge and his colleagues (Dodge & Coie, 1987; Dodge, Lochman, Harnish, Bates, & Pettit, 1997; Dodge, Price, Bachorowski, & Newman, 1990) later renamed these constructs *reactive aggression* (hostile) and *proactive aggression* (instrumental). More recently, Bushman and Anderson (2001) proposed dispensing with the hostile–instrumental aggression distinction and proposed instead a "knowledge structure" approach to conceptualizing aggression in which aggression is viewed as involving learned cognitive scripts that include appraisal, motivation, and automatic and controlled responses. They also questioned the impulsive–premeditated aggression distinction and suggested that many aggressive behaviors that appear impulsive may instead represent overlearned scripts that become automatized. Tedeschi and Felson (1994) replaced the construct of aggression with that of *coercive actions*, those "taken with intention of imposing harm or forcing compliance" (p. 168). Tedeschi and Felson also distinguished between *proactive coercion* (gaining status, dominance) and *reactive coercion* (responding to attacks).

DRIVING AGGRESSION

As with general aggression, there is no current consensus on a definition of *aggressive driving* or *road rage*. The latter term, coined by the media in the late 1980s (Fumento, 1998), is defined in the 1997 *Oxford English Dictionary of New Words* as "a driver's uncontrolled aggressive behavior, apparently caused by the stresses of modern driving" (Knowles & Elliott, 1997, p. 264). Shinar (1998) defined *road rage* as a form of hostile aggression (i.e., committed with harmful intent) directed toward other drivers. Wells-Parker et al. (2002) stated that *road rage* implies intentional acts of anger and aggression, with extreme forms involving confrontation and assault.

Fumento (1998) was critical of the media's tendency to use the term *road rage* to describe relatively benign behaviors, such as tailgating or using cell phones while driving, and his point is well taken. Although, as Wells-Parker et al. (2002) noted, the extent to which road rage is distinct from aggressive or reckless driving is unclear, applying the term to all forms of aggressive or reckless driving is problematic. It is, at the very least, inaccurate to equate horn honking and tailgating with assault. Moreover, in defining a potential treatment population, an individual who commits vehicular or personal assault during an aggressive driving episode is likely to have far more severe psychiatric or behavioral problems than a driver who limits aggressive outbursts to horn honking and tailgating. In addition, labeling all aggressive or dangerous driving incidents as *road rage* assumes that they are all provoked by anger, when in some cases the driving may represent sensation seeking or joyriding. Thus, from a clinical, scientific standpoint, it is preferable to either eschew the term *road rage* (and its sensationalistic connotation) or restrict its use to refer to the most extreme cases of driving aggression, that is, those that involve assault or attempted assault.

The National Highway Traffic Safety Administration (1999) defined *aggressive driving* as "the operation of a motor vehicle in a manner which endangers or is likely to endanger persons or property" (Introduction, ¶3). The definition included a broad array of behaviors, ranging from moving violations such as speeding, weaving, unsafe lane changes and passing, running stop signs and lights, failure to yield, and tailgating; to hostile hand and facial gestures, screaming, and honking; to, at the extreme end of the spectrum, violent confrontations. However, many researchers believe this definition lacks precision. Galovski and Blanchard (2002b) noted the need, when defining *driving aggression*, to distinguish between behaviors committed as a result of errors or lapses and those committed with intent. Deffenbacher (1999) criticized definitions that do not distinguish between *aggressive* driving (i.e., committed with harmful intent) and *reckless* driving (which is not necessarily committed with malicious intent). He suggested that these constructs be kept conceptually and empirically separate. He and his associates (Ellison-Potter, Bell, & Deffenbacher, 2001) more recently defined *aggressive driving* as behavior that "intentionally (whether fueled by anger or frustration or as a calculated means to an end) endangers others psychologically, physically, or both" (p. 432). Unlike Ellison-Potter et al. (2001), Shinar (1998) proposed distinguishing between *instrumental* driving aggression and *hostile* driving aggression. As noted above, Shinar defined *road rage* as hostile aggression directed toward other drivers. He defined *instrumental driving aggression* as frustration-evoked behaviors manifested by inconsideration or annoyance toward other drivers and deliberately driving dangerously for the purpose of saving time.

The definitions described above are problematic for several reasons. As noted, the National Highway Traffic Safety Administration's (1999) topographical description does not sufficiently distinguish between driving behaviors that may be the result of error or lapses and the intentional commission of such behaviors. Shinar's (1998) characterization of all instrumental driving aggression as frustration driven ignores positively reinforcing functions such as thrill and competition seeking. Moreover, as Buss (1961) and Bandura (1973) suggested, hostile aggression is also instrumental in that it is goal directed. Deffenbacher's (1999) proposed separation of intentionally harmful and risky driving, as well as the definition proposed by Ellison-Potter et al. (2001), are also troublesome because of the inclusion of intent to harm or endanger. As we have discussed, it may be difficult to objectively ascertain intent in aggression. Moreover, some aggressive drivers may lack insight into how their driving affects others.

Clinical Hint

In our clinical experience, aggressive drivers not only frequently deny any intent to actually harm others, they also often do not appear to realize that their driving endangers others. In many cases, they simply want other drivers to move out of their way and, as Shinar (1998) suggested, may be motivated primarily by time urgency. In this respect, the goal of such drivers appears to be coercion rather than a wish to harm or endanger. Similarly, a driver who treats the highway like a slalom course or who races other drivers may simply be seeking thrills and may also be unaware that such driving endangers others. However, as other researchers (e.g., Dula & Ballard, 2003; James & Nahl, 2000) have noted, the examples cited above may be considered aggressive driving by virtue of both their potential to harm and their disregard for the safety and rights of other drivers.

As Deffenbacher (1999) himself noted, aggressive driving and high-risk driving are often combined in the same act. Moreover, many individuals who drive aggressively also drive in a risky fashion (Deffenbacher, Deffenbacher, et al., 2003; Deffenbacher, Filetti, et al., 2002; Dula & Ballard, 2003; Malta, 2004; Wells-Parker et al., 2002). On the one hand, an empirical separation of aggressive versus risky driving may have utility in elucidating the function of the driving behavior and so better target the intervention. However, an empirical distinction might also logically lead to the development of separate interventions for aggressive and reckless drivers, which may present a practical problem for clinicians.

In our experience in treating court-mandated drivers, the courts have not distinguished between aggressive driving and reckless driving. At our aggressive driving treatment program (at the Center for Stress and Anxiety Disorders, University at Albany, State University of New York), we have assessed and treated self-referred and court-mandated drivers whose driving was primarily risky, primarily anger evoked and aggressive, or both. For example, one driver was a very mild-mannered man (i.e., who endorsed low anger and aggression scores on all instruments) who had been mandated to treatment because he and his fellow motorcyclists were speeding (100 mph) and forced the police to chase them when the police signaled the group to pull over. Another court-referred driver, who was in his 30s, no longer generally drove in a risky fashion, although he admitted to having done so when younger. However, he had been mandated to treatment because he had used his vehicle to ram his girlfriend's car into an intersection after an argument. Yet another court-mandated driver endorsed both reckless and aggressive driving. He reported that he liked to drive fast in his sports car and did not feel the need to stop at stop signs because of his knowledge of local roads. He also tailgated slow drivers and then "peeled off" in front of them when passing to "punish" them. We treated these drivers (and others like them) in a group treatment modality using a manualized treatment developed by Galovski and Blanchard (2002a); delivering separate interventions for these three very different types of drivers would have rendered this impossible.

Rather than designing separate interventions for different types of drivers, a more practical approach might be to examine the full range of behaviors involved and to design comprehensive treatments that can address different aspects of aggressive driving. Such an approach requires a conceptualization that can speak to the heterogeneity of aggressive drivers. Thus, to adopt definitions that have utility for the treatment of aggressive driving, we define *aggression* as behaviors whose function is attack or coercion or that inherently contain both the potential to harm and a disregard for the rights and safety of others, and *driving aggression* is defined as aggression committed within the context of driving. Because commissions of driving errors would not involve disregard for the safety of others, such lapses would not constitute aggressive driving.

THE RELATIONSHIP OF AGGRESSION, ANGER, AND HOSTILITY

In a chapter section entitled "The Banality of Evil," Zimbardo (1978) described an analysis conducted by the San Francisco Police Department that found that the principal motive for 131 homicides was "a trivial argument" that triggered a violent response, including "stepping on a man's foot at a party, missing a billiard shot, taking someone's seat, and having mustard instead of the requested catsup put on a steak" (pp. 159–160). Berkowitz (1993) cited similar accounts of trivial arguments leading to murder. Reports of aggressive driving contain many similar anecdotes of trivial disputes escalating to extreme aggression, including a parking space dispute that led to a stabbing, a car being rammed in response to an obscene gesture from a child passenger, a driver who was shot because he honked at another driver, and another confrontation over honking that led to one driver smashing the knees of another driver with his car (James & Nahl, 2000). Mizell (1997) catalogued the following triggers for aggressive driving incidents, each of which was associated with at least 25 incidents that resulted in death or injury: parking disputes; being honked at, blocked from passing, tailgated, or cut off; and anger at drivers who changed lanes without signaling, blocked traffic, or drove too slowly.

Although these anecdotes suggest that anger and hostility can trigger aggression, the relationship of anger and hostility to aggression is not clear. Anger and hostility are generally believed to promote aggression

(Spielberger, Reheiser, & Sydeman, 1995), but anger does not typically lead to aggression (Averill, 1983). Most behavioral approaches propose that hostility, anger, and aggression are produced by the same environmental contingencies and that anger and hostility facilitate, but do not necessarily mediate, aggression (Buss, 1961; Salzinger, 1995). Buss (1961) made the following useful distinctions: *Hostility* is a conditioned implicit verbal response, *anger* is a respondent, and *aggression* is an attack behavior. Buss also noted that although anger and hostility could intensify aggression, they both can occur in the absence of aggression, and aggression can occur in the absence of anger or hostility.

Cognitive–behavioral conceptualizations have tended to suggest that anger either mediates or moderates aggression. Zillman (1994) proposed that anger and cognitive processes moderate aggression such that, under conditions of high arousal, cognitive functions become impaired, making the individual more likely to aggress. Berkowitz (1989, 1993, 1994) initially suggested that anger merely accompanies aggression, but later he presented models in which it appeared to function as a mediator of aggression. Buss and Perry (1992) also later suggested that anger might mediate the relationship between hostility and aggression. In a factor analysis, they found strong correlations between anger and both hostility and aggression but only moderate correlations between hostility and aggression. After controlling for the relationship of anger to aggression, correlations between hostility and aggression were markedly reduced and nonsignificant. These findings were replicated by Archer, Kilpatrick, and Bramwell (1995).

Driving anger is also a robust and reliable correlate of driving aggression (Deffenbacher, Deffenbacher, et al., 2003; Deffenbacher et al., 1994, 2000; Deffenbacher, Filetti, et al., 2003; Deffenbacher, Lynch, Deffenbacher, & Oetting, 2001; Deffenbacher, Lynch, et al., 2003; Deffenbacher, Lynch, Oetting, & Yingling, 2001; Knee, Neighbors, & Vietor, 2001; Lajunen & Parker, 2001; Malta, 2004; Malta & Blanchard, 2004; Malta et al., 2001; Neighbors, Vietor, & Knee, 2002). Fewer studies have specifically examined the relationship between driving hostility and driving aggression; however, as mentioned, Deffenbacher and his associates have found that hostile thoughts about other drivers significantly correlated with aggressive driving (Deffenbacher et al., 2004; Deffenbacher, Petrilli, et al., 2003) and, like general (non-driving-related) anger, general hostility has been associated with aggressive driving (Deery & Fildes, 1999; Deffenbacher et al., 2004; Deffenbacher, Petrilli, et al., 2003; DePasquale et al., 2001; D. M. Donovan, Umlauf, & Salzberg, 1988; Malta, 2004; Malta & Blanchard, 2004; Wilson, 1991).

These studies all suggest that general and driving anger and hostility may promote aggressive and risky driving. However, in some studies, high levels of driving anger and hostility have not fully accounted for driving aggression. For example, although drivers may be more likely to speed when in an angry mood (Arnett, Offer, & Fine, 1997), high-anger drivers tend to speed and drive in a risky fashion even when their reported level of state driving anger is low (Deffenbacher, Deffenbacher, et al., 2003). Driving simulator studies have found that aggressive driving is not always related to driving anger (Deffenbacher, Deffenbacher, et al., 2003; Ellison-Potter et al., 2001), and the frequency of driving anger does not fully account for the variance in aggressive driving scores (Blanchard, Barton, & Malta, 2000). Driving anger also does not fully mediate the relationship between driving aggression and variables such as physical aggression (Lajunen & Parker, 2001; Malta, 2004; Malta & Blanchard, 2004); sensitivity to attacks on self-esteem (Neighbors et al., 2002); and traits such as sensation seeking, narcissism, and impulsiveness (Malta, 2004; Malta & Blanchard, 2004).

Moreover, although driving anger appears to be quite common (Parker, Lajunen, & Summala, 2002; Underwood, Chapman, Wright, & Crundall, 1999), driving anger does not always lead to an intention to retaliate (Dukes, Clayton, Jenkins, Miller, & Rodgers, 2001), most of the reactions are relatively mild (Novaco, 1991; Parker et al., 2002), and many drivers find constructive ways to manage their anger (Deffenbacher, Lynch, et al., 2002). As Deffenbacher, Lynch, et al. (2002) noted, what appears to be key is not only the intensity of driving anger but also the form of its expression. Moreover, they found that different types of driving anger expression showed specificity in their ability to predict individual aggressive driving behaviors.

The collective driving research is consistent with Averill's (1983) finding that for most people anger does not result in aggression and with Buss's (1961) assertion that aggression can occur in the absence of anger. Thus, the answer to the question of whether anger and hostility mediate aggression (driving or general) appears to be "somewhat." This answer is likely to be unsatisfactory, and so perhaps a more useful way to understand the relationship of anger, hostility, and aggression is to consider these behaviors in terms of their functions. As we have proposed, feeling states (anger) and cognitions (hostility) act on the individual. When the individual expresses hostility and anger, the behavior may take the form of aggression (verbal or physical), which acts on the environment. Because the actual behavior selected would depend on the reinforcement history, current contingencies, and the presence of other behavioral tendencies that may also moderate aggression, anger and hostility may facilitate aggression, but they will not necessarily lead to aggression. Thus, anger and hostility may perhaps be most accurately characterized as partial mediators of aggression. They are among several types of response tendencies that may collectively increase the probability of aggression.

SUMMARY

In this chapter, we have discussed some of the issues involved in defining general hostility, anger, and aggression and their specific counterparts related to driving. Although defining constructs may appear to be a philosophical exercise with little practical utility, the manner in which we define and conceptualize constructs informs the design of assessment instruments and treatments and the formulation of theoretical models. For example, the lack of a distinction between *driving anger* and *driving hostility* has led to a paucity of instruments measuring driving hostility, despite its potential as a target of treatment in cognitive therapy. Similarly, the exclusion of dangerous driving motivated by thrill seeking from definitions of *aggressive driving* could potentially narrow the focus of aggressive driving interventions to teaching anger management techniques that may not adequately address problem behaviors such as poor judgment and impulsiveness. Equating driving aggression with anger or the feeling of anger with its expression could result in interventions that do not sufficiently address driving anger and hostility; such is the case with programs that consist of increased law enforcement and penalties for aggressive driving but omit interventions that target driving anger and hostility.

It is difficult to formulate definitions that are broad enough to span theoretical differences yet are precise enough to clarify our thinking, and it is likely that some readers will take issue with our definitions. However, we propose the definitions from a clinical scientific perspective, with the goal of elucidating issues relevant to the assessment and treatment of aggressive drivers. We hope that the conceptual issues discussed here will stimulate thought and discussion and encourage researchers and clinicians to more fully examine their theoretical assumptions and conceptualizations of aggressive driving.

3

THEORIES OF AGGRESSIVE DRIVING

The literature describing reckless and aggressive driving is extensive and dates as far back as the late 1940s. Although this early literature focused primarily on motor vehicle accident (MVA) risk, the characteristics and driving behaviors of at-risk drivers are strikingly similar to those of today's aggressive drivers. For example, Tillmann and Hobbs's (1949) profile of accident-prone taxi drivers as irritable, impatient drivers with hostile and competitive attitudes toward other motorists is similar to descriptions of aggressive drivers offered by Parry (1968), MacMillan (1975), Larson (1996b), and James and Nahl (2000). The early MVA risk literature can provide information relevant to the understanding of modern-day aggressive and reckless drivers; thus, the objective of this chapter is to review and integrate findings from the early literature with more recent research to promote the formulation of a comprehensive model of aggressive driving.

Attempts to identify drivers at risk for MVAs developed from industrial research on accident-prone munitions workers (Greenwood & Woods, 1919). Noting that the population distribution of MVA frequency reliably demonstrated that a small portion of the population had a high frequency of MVAs, Ross (1940) was one of the earliest to suggest that this nonnormal distribution was due to driver characteristics. Although the concept of the "accident-prone" driver was subsequently rejected on the basis of little empirical support (McFarland, 1968), the early literature produced three main theories (Mayer & Treat, 1977): (a) social maladjustment theory, which views risky and aggressive driving as an extension of general antisocial tendencies; (b) personal maladjustment theory, which proposes that psychological problems and stress contribute to MVA risk; and (c) impulse noncontrol theory, which posits that individuals with poor impulse control are more likely to express aggressive and risk-taking tendencies while driving.

During the 1980s, researchers proposed MVA risk behavior syndrome theory (Beirness, 1993; Beirness & Simpson, 1988; Jessor, 1987; Jonah, 1986), which views reckless and aggressive driving as a manifestation of a generalized proclivity toward risk taking and deviance. During the past decade, as reports of road rage incidents have proliferated, researchers have applied the frustration–aggression hypothesis (Berkowitz, 1989; Dollard, Doob, Miller, Mowrer, & Sears, 1939; N. E. Miller, 1941) to aggressive driving (Novaco, 1991; Shinar, 1998). As we discuss in the following sections, there is evidence to support each of the theories; however, each is also limited in its ability to fully account for aggressive driving. The review begins with social maladjustment theory, which represents the oldest attempt to ascertain driver characteristics that predict MVA involvement.

SOCIAL MALADJUSTMENT THEORY

Social maladjustment theory is exemplified by Tillmann and Hobbs's (1949) frequently quoted maxim, "A man drives as he lives" (p. 329). The main finding from this pioneer study was that high-MVA-risk taxi drivers and general population drivers had a significantly greater history of contact with criminal justice and social service agencies, a finding that was replicated in a study of truck drivers (McFarland, 1968; McFarland & Moseley, 1954). Research throughout the 1970s continued to support the association between antisocial tendencies and MVA risk (Harano, 1975; Mayer & Treat, 1977; McGuire, 1976; Michalowski, 1975). In one study that specifically examined aggressive driving, MacMillan (1975) also found that aggressive drivers and drivers with a history of contact with the courts and social agencies had a significantly greater number of traffic convictions, and traffic convictions were significantly correlated with scores on a social problems scale. More recent studies of aggressive drivers have found that they exhibit a significantly greater prevalence of antisocial personality disorder compared with nonaggressive drivers (Galovsky, Blanchard, & Veazey, 2002; Malta, Blanchard, & Freidenberg, in press).

Even mild levels of social deviance and tolerant attitudes toward deviance correlate with MVA frequency (West, Elander, & French, 1993) and reckless driving (Hartos, Eitel, & Simons-Morton, 2002; Hilakivi, Veilahti, Asplund, Sinivuo, & Laitinen, 1989; Iversen & Rundmo, 2002; Lawton, Parker, Stradling, & Manstead, 1997; Meadows, Stradling, & Lawson, 1998;

Ulleberg, 2002; Ulleberg & Rundmo, 2003; West et al., 1993; West & Hall, 1997) as well as driving anger (Underwood, Chapman, Wright, & Crundall, 1999). One limitation of this line of research is its reliance on self-reported driving behaviors: It is possible that drivers who endorse tolerance of deviance may be more likely to report reckless driving because they may be less concerned with making socially desirable responses. However, drivers with positive attitudes toward violations also drive more recklessly (Ulleberg & Rundmo, 2003; West & Hall, 1997), which provides further evidence of the association between deviance tolerance and reckless driving.

Collectively, research over the last 50 years has consistently supported associations between aggressive and reckless driving and antisociality, traffic violations, and MVA risk. However, reports of aggressive drivers are replete with descriptions of individuals who, at least when not driving, appear to be law-abiding citizens, such as lawyers, legislators, and educators (James & Nahl, 2000; Mizell, 1997). It is possible that some of these individuals have mild levels of social deviance that primarily manifest during driving. However, because most people are not socially deviant or criminal, social maladjustment theory might account for only a minority of aggressive drivers. Although it is possible that this segment is responsible for the more severe acts of driving aggression, especially those involving weapons, this theory may not adequately account for mild to moderate driving aggression that has been observed in drivers who are otherwise law abiding.

PERSONAL MALADJUSTMENT THEORY

Personal maladjustment theory posits that acute and chronic stressful life events, psychopathology, or both, increase MVA risk. A few early studies suggested that acute and chronic stress were associated with MVA involvement (Brenner & Selzer, 1969; Mayer & Treat, 1977; Selzer, Rogers, & Kern, 1968; Selzer & Vinokur, 1974); however, these studies were limited in that reports of stressors were obtained post MVA and thus could have been biased. Later studies found no relationship between the presence of negative life events and MVA risk (Isherwood, Adams, & Hornblow, 1982) or aggressive driving (Fong, Frost, & Stansfeld, 2001). Thus, the overall evidence in support of personal maladjustment theory is weak.

PSYCHOPATHOLOGY

The literature regarding psychopathology and MVAs dates back to studies that compared driving records of psychiatric patients with those of the general public and found significantly higher rates of MVAs in the patients, especially those diagnosed with personality disorders or alcoholism (Crancer & Quiring, 1969; Eelkema, Brosseau, & Koshnick, 1970; Selzer & Payne, 1962; Waller, 1965). General population drivers also show an association between elevated MVA risk and alcoholism (cf. Tsuang, Boor, & Fleming, 1985); symptoms of antisocial and borderline personality disorder (cf. McGuire, 1976); and psychological problems such as belligerence, hostility, and poor tolerance of stress (Conger et al., 1959). Some early research reported an association between suicidal tendencies and MVA risk (MacDonald, 1964; Selzer et al., 1968; Shaw, 1956), but later studies challenged this finding (e.g., Isherwood et al., 1982).

The U.S. Department of Transportation Federal Highway Administration has cited attention-deficit/hyperactivity disorder (ADHD) as a risk factor for problem driving (cf. Barkley, Guevremont, Anastopoulos, DuPaul, & Shelton, 1993), and longitudinal research has demonstrated an association between ADHD and increased risk of MVAs (Weiss & Hechtman, 1986; Weiss, Hechtman, Perlman, Hopkins, & Wener, 1979). Compared with control participants, adolescents and young adults with ADHD drive more poorly in a simulator and have more MVAs, traffic citations, and suspended and revoked licenses, despite having a knowledge of driving skills and experience comparable to that of control participants (Barkley et al., 1993; Barkley, Murphy, & Kwasnik, 1996; Murphy & Barkley, 1996; Nada-Raja et al., 1997). College students with ADHD symptoms also endorse higher levels of aggressive and reckless driving, driving anger, and hostile and aggressive expressions of driving anger than do control participants (Richards, Deffenbacher, & Rosen, 2002). These studies clearly support a strong association between ADHD and poor driving; however, given the association between antisociality and problem driving, the extent to which this is at least partly due to the high comorbidity of ADHD and conduct disorder or antisocial personality disorder (Barkley et al., 1993; Nada-Raja et al., 1997; Weiss & Hechtman, 1986) is unclear.

Only a handful of studies have assessed psychiatric problems in drivers specifically identified as aggressive. Fong et al. (2001) used structured telephone interviews to assess drivers recruited through a general medical practice. Drivers who had endorsed experiencing an episode of driving anger and aggression within the past 5 years had more symptoms of psychopathology (diagnoses were not assigned) and higher levels of anger and aggression compared with drivers who denied episodes of anger and aggression. However, this study was limited by potential sample selection and rater bias, in that assessors were aware of respondents' driving behaviors and that the screening measure assessed only a limited number of personality disorders. In a better controlled study, Galovski et al. (2002) conducted in-person structured interviews with treatment-seeking (self-referred and court-mandated) aggressive drivers and matched control participants and found that aggressive drivers had a greater prevalence of intermittent explosive disorder, current and past alcohol and substance abuse, and antisocial and borderline personality disorders. This study was also limited in that raters were aware of driver status (aggressive vs. controls) and because this was a treatment-seeking sample, participants might be expected to have more severe psychiatric problems than general population drivers. However, the findings were similar to those of Malta et al. (in press), who assessed psychiatric disorders in a sample of non-treatment-seeking aggressive and nonaggressive college student drivers in a study in which raters were unaware of driving behaviors.

The hypothesis that psychopathology is associated with increased MVA risk as well as aggressive driving has received empirical support. However, the association appears to be primarily limited to externalizing psychopathology (antisocial personality, borderline personality, ADHD) and alcohol and substance use disorders, with little evidence to suggest that other types of psychiatric problems contribute to MVA risk or aggressive driving.

IMPULSE NONCONTROL THEORY

Impulse noncontrol theory is the least well developed of the theories. It appears to have originated with Suchman, Pelz, Ehrlich, and Selzer's (1967) descriptive study of young male drivers. The authors assessed tension-reduction driving (driving to "blow off steam" after an argument), reckless driving, and anger in response to traffic impediments and summed the results to create an "impulse expression" score. They presented no inferential statistics but found that both traffic violations and MVAs increased linearly with impulse expression and that racing and competitive driving were three times more likely in drivers with high numbers of violations versus low-frequency violators; thus, Suchman et al. suggested that MVA- and violation-prone drivers "use the automobile to express impulses" (p. 102). There does not appear to be any subsequent research that directly tested this hypothesis, but several studies have examined impulsiveness and general aggression in high MVA risk and aggressive drivers.

IMPULSIVENESS

Research has demonstrated an association among impulsiveness or low self-control, increased MVA risk, and reckless driving (Adams, 1970; Hartos et al., 2002; Hilakivi et al., 1989; Mayer & Treat, 1977; Shaw, 1956; Stanford, Greve, Boudreaux, Mathias, & Brumbelow, 1996; Tillman & Hobbs, 1949) as well as aggressive driving (Malta, 2004; Malta & Blanchard,

2004). Lajunen and Parker (2001) did not find a significant relationship between impulsiveness and either driving anger or reactions to provocations while driving. However, DePasquale, Geller, Clarke, and Littleton (2001) proposed that the relationship between aggressive driving and impulsiveness might be moderated by the relationship between impulsiveness and anger. They found a significant correlation between impulsiveness and self-reported aggressive driving but found stronger relationships between impulsiveness and anger, and between anger and aggressive driving, than between impulsiveness and aggressive driving. They suggested that impulsiveness might be problematic for drivers only if it is accompanied by high anger, and this interpretation is consistent with the finding that high-anger drivers are more impulsive and drive more aggressively than low-anger drivers (Deffenbacher, Filetti, Richards, Lynch, & Oetting, 2003). It is also consistent with Barratt's (1991) proposal that impulsive aggression involves an imbalance between anger and impulsiveness and that poor impulse control coupled with high arousal produces aggression. Impulsiveness also correlates with general aggression (Archer, Kilpatrick, & Bramwell, 1995; Buss & Perry, 1992; Stanford & Barratt, 1992; Stanford, Greve, & Dickens, 1995) as well as with sensation seeking (Loo, 1979), and it is possible that the relationship between impulsiveness and aggressive driving is influenced by these behavioral tendencies as well as by anger.

GENERAL AGGRESSION

The early literature supports a reliable relationship between generalized aggression and increased MVA risk (e.g., Conger et al., 1959; McFarland, 1968; McGuire, 1976; Shaw, 1956; Tillmann & Hobbs, 1949). For example, in a prospective study of nearly 3,000 general population drivers, McGuire (1976) found that aggression, hostility, prestige seeking, and competitiveness predicted the number of MVAs over a 2-year follow-up period. More recent studies have demonstrated that general aggression is also associated with self-reported aggressive driving (Dula & Ballard, 2003; Fong et al., 2001; Lajunen & Parker, 2001; Malta, 2004; Malta & Blanchard, 2004) as well as with reckless driving and driving violations (Ulleberg & Rundmo, 2003). However, general aggression is not always associated with reckless driving (Deery & Fildes, 1999), and some drivers with high rates of MVAs and traffic violations do not show elevated levels of aggression (Ulleberg, 2002). These findings suggest that general aggression may be neither necessary nor sufficient for reckless and aggressive driving to occur, and it is possible that, like impulsiveness, aggression is moderated by other variables, such as sensation seeking (Arnett, Offer, & Fine, 1997), to influence driving.

Impulse noncontrol theory has received support from research demonstrating that impulsiveness and general aggression are associated with MVA risk and aggressive driving. However, impulsiveness and general aggression have been observed in drivers characterized as antisocial (Shaw, 1956; Tillmann & Hobbs, 1949) and drivers with chronic externalizing disorders (Galovski et al., 2002; Malta et al., in press). Thus, this theory overlaps with both social maladjustment theory and personal maladjustment theory. To the extent that impulsiveness co-occurs with generalized risk taking, reckless driving might also be better accounted for by risk behavior syndrome theory. Also, because drivers with poor impulse control could be expected to have low frustration tolerance, impulse noncontrol theory overlaps with the frustration–aggression hypothesis of aggressive driving. Thus, the utility of impulse noncontrol theory may be limited to highlighting the role of impulsiveness and general aggression in problem driving.

RISK BEHAVIOR SYNDROME THEORY

The risk behavior syndrome theory of MVA risk (Beirness, 1993; Beirness & Simpson, 1988; Jessor, 1987; Jonah, 1986) began as an extension of Jessor's (1987) problem behavior theory, which posited that behaviors such as delinquency, alcohol and substance abuse, promiscuity, and maladaptive risk taking constituted a generalized response class. Aggressive and reckless driving was purported to be another manifestation of a proclivity toward deviance and risk taking, and this theory has received robust empirical support. Research has shown that individual risky driving behaviors covary with each other (J. E. Donovan, 1992; L. Evans & Wasielewski, 1983; Shope & Bingham, 2002; Wilson & Jonah, 1988), and reckless driving is correlated with other risk-taking behaviors, such as delinquency, drug and alcohol use, and drunk driving (Beirness & Simpson, 1988; Jamison & McGlothlin, 1973; Jessor, 1987; Klepp & Perry, 1990; Wilson & Jonah, 1988). Moreover, alcohol use, peer support of drinking, susceptibility to peer pressure, and deviance tolerance assessed prior to licensure significantly predict non-alcohol-related driving violations and MVAs at 1 and 3 years after licensure (Shope & Patil, 2003). In addition, as discussed, research has demonstrated a consistent association between alcohol and substance abuse and MVA risk (cf. Tsuang et al., 1985) as well as aggressive driving (Galovski et al., 2002; Malta et al., in press).

In further support of risk behavior syndrome theory, numerous studies have found a reliable association among MVA risk, reckless driving, and general sensation seeking (Arnett, 1990, 1994; Arnett et al., 1997; Beirness, 1993; Beirness & Simpson, 1988; Deery & Fildes, 1999; D. M. Donovan, Umlauf, & Salzberg, 1988; Furnham & Saipe, 1993; Hartos et al., 2002;

Hilakivi et al., 1989; Iversen & Rundmo, 2002; Jamison & McGlothlin, 1973; Jonah, 1997; Jonah, Thiessen, & Au-Yeung, 2001; Krahé & Fenske, 2002; Loo, 1979; Malta, 2004; Malta & Blanchard, 2004; Ulleberg, 2002; Ulleberg & Rundmo, 2003; Zuckerman & Neeb, 1980), with a few reports of null findings (Boyce & Geller, 2002; Clement & Jonah, 1984). A few studies have provided evidence of a link between sensation seeking and aggressive driving as well. College students high in sensation seeking also report higher levels of aggressive driving (Jonah et al., 2001; Malta, 2004), and self-reported aggressive driving correlates with sensation seeking (Malta & Blanchard, 2004) and viewing danger as exciting (Krahé & Fenske, 2002).

The research reviewed above suggests that risk-taking behaviors co-occur and that risk-taking proclivity may contribute to reckless and aggressive driving. One limitation of this literature is that only a few studies have specifically examined the association between risk taking and aggressive driving. However, reckless driving and aggressive driving tend to co-occur (Deffenbacher, Deffenbacher, Lynch, & Richards, 2003; Deffenbacher, Lynch, Oetting, & Swaim, 2002; Dula & Ballard, 2003; Malta, 2004; Wells-Parker et al., 2002), and the few studies that have assessed aggressive driving have reported significant findings (Jonah et al., 2001; Krahé & Fenske, 2002; Malta, 2004; Malta & Blanchard, 2004). A second limitation of the research is that many of the studies examined teenagers and young adults, and more research is needed to determine whether the findings generalize to older adults. It should also be noted that because delinquency, deviance acceptance, and alcohol and drug use in part compose the risk-taking behaviors, risk behavior syndrome theory overlaps to some extent with social maladjustment theory.

THE FRUSTRATION–AGGRESSION HYPOTHESIS OF AGGRESSIVE DRIVING

Naatanen and Summala (1976) were among the earliest to suggest that aggressive driving could result from frustration at obstructions such as traffic. Novaco (1991) proposed that driving aggression is produced when environmental triggers interact with a variety predisposing factors, including subjective feelings of stress; physiological arousal; learned cognitive scripts; and disinhibitory cues, such as anonymity and escape potential. He also posited as contributing factors observational learning of roadway aggression and a societal desensitization toward aggression in general. Shinar (1998) also proposed that the frustration–aggression hypothesis was an appropriate model for aggressive driving. He highlighted personal characteristics such as hostility, extroversion, and Type A personality (Rosenman, Swan, & Carmelli, 1988) as increasing the probability of driving aggression, and he emphasized that cultural driving norms and driving conditions can contribute to driving aggression. James and Nahl (2000) also emphasized the role of frustration in driving aggression as well as the influence of cultural norms and peer pressure from other drivers. They suggested that driving is inherently stressful because of its unpredictability, lack of personal control, and extended immobility, and they cited drivers' isolation and sense of territoriality as contributing to aggressive driving. The majority of researchers who have designed aggressive driving interventions also appear to have adopted a frustration–aggression model that emphasizes driving frustration, anger, and stress as key factors in driving aggression (Deffenbacher, Filetti, Lynch, Dahlen, & Oetting, 2002; Deffenbacher, Huff, Lynch, Oetting, & Salvatore, 2000; Galovski & Blanchard, 2002a; James & Nahl, 2000; Larson, 1996b; Larson, Rodriquez, & Galvan-Henkin, 1998; Rimm, DeGroot, Boord, Heiman, & Dillow, 1971). As we review next, a great deal of research has investigated environmental and individual-difference variables that contribute to frustration-evoked driving aggression.

ENVIRONMENTAL FACTORS

Cultural Norms

As we reviewed in chapter 1, prevalence data from U.S. and international studies show cross-cultural similarities as well as disparities, but method variance limits the conclusions that can be drawn from the research. There appears to be only one published survey of drivers in Britain, Finland, and the Netherlands that compared cultural differences in reactions to anger-provoking situations (Parker, Lajunen, & Summala, 2002) and revealed cross-cultural commonalities as well as differences. Reactions to provocations in all three countries were generally mild, and drivers had similar reactions to impeded progress and reckless driving. However, drivers in each country differed in terms of the intensity of driving anger as well as in the type of situations that evoked the most anger and the strongest reactions. There do not appear to be any published cross-cultural comparisons of traits associated with aggressive driving, but research on driver typologies has found that characteristics such as general aggression, hostility, and sensation seeking are associated with reckless and aggressive driving in Australia (Deery & Fildes, 1999), Canada (Beirness & Simpson, 1988), Norway (Ulleberg, 2002), and the United States (D. M. Donovan et al., 1988; Malta, 2004). Moreover, profiles of aggressive drivers in Canada (Tillmann & Hobb, 1949), Great Britain (Parry, 1968), South Africa (Shaw, 1956), and the United States (James & Nahl, 2000; Larson, 1996b; McGuire, 1976) tend to be similar. Thus, although there may be differences in levels of driving anger and reactions to specific provocations, research suggests that the personality characteristics associated with aggressive driving appear to be similar across cultures.

Age and Gender Norms

Research has consistently implicated young drivers as engaging in the most aggressive and high-risk driving (Begg & Langley, 2001; L. Evans, 2002; Hemenway & Solnick, 1993; Jonah, 1986; Lawton, Parker, Stradling, & Manstead, 1997; MacMillan, 1975; Parry, 1968; A. F. Williams, 2003), but individuals of all ages may drive aggressively (James & Nahl, 2000; Mizell, 1997). Male drivers typically exhibit more aggressive and risky driving than female drivers (Begg & Langley, 2001; Beirness & Simpson, 1988; Deffenbacher, Filetti, Richards, Lynch, & Oetting, 2003; L. Evans, 2002; Lajunen & Parker, 2001; M. Miller, Azrael, Hemenway, & Solop, 2002; Parry, 1968). However, Ellison-Potter, Bell, and Deffenbacher (2001) found no gender differences in aggressive driving on a simulator, and Lawton, Parker, Manstead, and Stradling (1997) did not find gender differences in self-reported aggressive driving behaviors after controlling for annual mileage. These findings suggest that observed gender differences may be due in part to driving assessment methods and confounding variables such as annual mileage. Both male and female drivers also endorse similar levels of driving anger (Deffenbacher et al., 2000; Deffenbacher, Filetti, Richards, et. al., 2003; Lajunen, Parker, & Stradling, 1998). Moreover, Ulleberg (2002) found that one high-risk driving group identified by cluster analysis was predominantly female and that high-risk driver trait profiles were similar across genders. These findings suggest that female aggressive drivers share similarities with their male counterparts.

Traffic Congestion and Time Urgency

Some studies have found that traffic congestion contributes to aggressive driving (Gulian, Debney, Glendon, Davies, & Matthews, 1989; Hennessy & Wiesenthal, 1997), but Shinar and Compton (2004) demonstrated that the frequency of aggressive driving behaviors was significantly correlated with the number of vehicles on the road, which suggested that the increase in aggressive driving was due to a greater number of drivers rather than an increase of incidents during times of traffic congestion. However, after controlling for the number of cars on the road, the correlation between time urgency (rush hour driving) and aggressive driving remained significant. Time urgency is not associated with aggressive driving under conditions of low congestion (Hennessy & Wiesenthal, 1999), which suggests that traffic and time pressure jointly influence aggressive driving. Variables such as locale, behaviors of other drivers on the road, and mechanical aspects of traffic lights also appear to interact with congestion and time pressure to increase aggressive driving (Shinar, 1998; Shinar & Compton, 2004).

Additional Situational Factors

Doob and Gross's (1968) classic study of frustration-evoked driver aggression was developed within the framework of the frustration–aggression hypothesis (Dollard et al., 1939; N. E. Miller, 1941). The basic paradigm is that a confederate driver creates a delay at an intersection. Doob and Gross found a greater number of horn honks and a shorter latency to honk when the confederate drove a low-status car (an old vehicle), and they interpreted this as the inhibition of aggression in the presence of a symbol of high status (a newer car). Novaco (1991) and Shinar (1998) have noted the limitations of honking as an outcome variable, because its function can vary from neutral signaling to an expression of annoyance. However, both Novaco and Shinar found that honking correlates with other aggressive driving behaviors and, as described in chapter 1, Hauber (1980) observed a variety of aggressive responses to delays created by a pedestrian. In addition to honking, drivers yelled and gestured, and some failed to stop and nearly ran down the pedestrian.

Subsequent studies of the effects of driver status on driver aggression have produced inconsistent results. Hankes-Drielsma (1974) replicated Doob and Gross's (1968) original finding, but Chase and Mills (1973) found greater honking in the presence of the high-status car. Deaux (1971) found no effect of status but found greater honking in response to female confederates compared with male confederates. More recently, McGarva and Steiner (2000) found that drivers accelerated more quickly away from low-status vehicles, but status had no effect on driver vocalizations, response intensity, or physiological reactivity. The authors suggested that instrumental aggression rather than hostile aggression is affected by status. Noting a participant's comment that "nobody honks their horn here," they also suggested that local driving norms might have influenced the findings.

Variations of Doob and Gross's (1968) paradigm have been used to investigate the effects of driver anonymity and aggression cues on honking in response to delays. The most consistent effects have been found for anonymity, with increased honking in response to delays when either the confederate driver is not visible (Turner, Layton, & Simons, 1975), the participant is not readily identifiable (Ellison, Govern, Petri, & Figler, 1995), or participants are told to imagine that they cannot be identified (Ellison-Potter et al., 2001). The results for the effects of aggression cues have been mixed. Some studies have found that anonymity and aggression cues jointly increase honking (Turner et al., 1975) and aggressive driving in a simulator

(Ellison-Potter et al., 2001). However, Turner et al. (1975) found a complex pattern of results in which aggression cues had no effect on female drivers, and increased honking in males driving new cars, but reduced honking in males driving older cars. Halderman and Jackson (1979) found no significant effect of the presence of a rifle on honking in response to delays but suggested that this might have been because the study was conducted in a rural community in which rifles were fairly common.

Other studies that have used Doob and Gross's (1968) paradigm have found that variables such as ambient temperature (Kenrick & MacFarlane, 1986), urban traffic congestion, perceiving drivers as distracted, and short green light phases (Shinar, 1998) also increased rates of honking in response to delays. Shinar (1998) also found that drivers in low-income neighborhoods were quicker to honk and displayed more impatient gestures when delayed compared with drivers in higher income neighborhoods. These studies suggest that many variables can potentially interact to increase driving aggression.

The collected research on situational variables suggests that anonymity, driver comfort, local driving norms, and congestion all influence responses to frustrating delays, with less consistent findings for perceived driver status and aggression cues. The literature also suggests that multiple influences are at work, and variability in any of these factors across studies might account for some of the disparate findings. Although designing studies that can tease apart a complex array of variables is challenging, our understanding of aggressive driving would benefit from more research examining how environmental factors interact with each other and with individual predispositions to increase driving aggression.

PERSONOLOGICAL FACTORS

Susceptibility to Driving Stress

Driving researchers have hypothesized that subjective feelings of stress contribute to aggressive driving (James & Nahl, 2000; Novaco, 1991), and several studies have examined whether individuals who endorse high levels of stress drive more aggressively. Individuals with Type A personalities typically endorse elevated levels of stress (Rosenman et al., 1988), and Type A behavioral tendencies have been associated with increased traffic violations (Perry, 1986), MVAs (G. W. Evans, Palsane, & Carrere, 1987; Perry & Baldwin, 2000), faster driving speed (Boyce & Geller, 2002; West et al., 1993), and aggressive driving (Blanchard, Barton, & Malta, 2000; Boyce & Geller, 2002; Perry & Baldwin, 2000). However, one problem with the Type A construct is that it comprises stress, impatience, hostility, and competitiveness (Rosenman et al., 1988), and so it is unclear how much of the variability in driving behavior is uniquely accounted for by subjective stress. Because hostility has also been associated with aggressive driving (Deery & Fildes, 1999; Donovan et al., 1988; Malta, 2004; Malta & Blanchard, 2004), it is possible that this component of Type A tendencies is more strongly related to aggressive driving.

Moreover, Matthews et al. (1998) found that the construct of driving stress comprises an aggression factor (irritation and impatience) and a dislike factor (anxiety and tension) and that although the aggression factor positively correlates with aggressive driving on a simulator, speeding, traffic violations, and confrontational coping styles, the dislike factor negatively correlates with these variables. In addition, driving stress is not always associated with aggressive driving behaviors (Gulian, Debney, et al., 1989; Hennessy & Wiesenthal, 1999; Neighbors, Vietor, & Knee, 2002). Taken together, these studies suggest that stress in and of itself does not necessarily produce aggressive driving but likely interacts with other variables (e.g., hostility) to influence driving behaviors.

Susceptibility to Driving Anger

As we discussed in chapter 2, Deffenbacher and his colleagues have provided ample evidence in support of their state–trait model of driving anger, in which trait (general) driving anger predicts situation-specific driving anger and aggressive driving (Deffenbacher, Deffenbacher, et al., 2003; Deffenbacher et al., 2000; Deffenbacher, Filetti, et al., 2003; Deffenbacher, Lynch, Deffenbacher, & Oetting, 2001; Deffenbacher, Lynch, et al., 2002; Deffenbacher, Lynch, Filetti, Dahlen, & Oetting, 2003; Deffenbacher, Lynch, Oetting, & Yingling, 2001; Deffenbacher, Oetting, & Lynch, 1994). Research has also demonstrated that aggressive drivers are high in general anger (Deffenbacher, Deffenbacher, et al., 2003; Deffenbacher et al., 1994, 2000; Deffenbacher, Filetti, et al., 2003; Deffenbacher, Lynch, et al., 2002, 2003; Deffenbacher, White, & Lynch, 2004; DePasquale et al., 2001; Dula & Ballard, 2003; Lawton & Nutter, 2002; Malta, 2004; Malta & Blanchard, 2004; Malta et al., 2001).

However, as we discussed in chapter 2, driving anger does not always lead to an aggressive response (Dukes, Clayton, Jenkins, Miller, & Rodgers, 2001; Parker et al., 2002), and high-anger drivers do not necessarily drive more aggressively than low-anger drivers (Ellison-Potter et al., 2001; Malta, 2004). Moreover, driving anger does not fully mediate the relationship between aggressive driving and characteristics such as aggression, impulsiveness, and sensation seeking (Lajunen & Parker, 2001; Malta, 2004; Malta & Blanchard, 2004), or sensitivity to attacks on self-esteem (Neighbors et al., 2002), and some forms of driving aggression do not appear to be related to driving anger (Deffenbacher, Deffenbacher, et al., 2003; Matthews, Desmond, Joyner, Carcary, & Gilliland, 1997; Ulleberg & Rundmo, 2003). Thus, although trait and driving anger are important contributors to driving aggression, they are neither necessary nor sufficient to fully account for the behavior.

Cognitive Behaviors

Descriptive accounts of aggressive drivers contain many anecdotes of drivers denigrating other road users (James & Nahl, 2000; Parry, 1968), but there do not appear to be any direct empirical comparisons of maladaptive thoughts in aggressive and nonaggressive drivers. However, pejorative labeling, and thoughts of revenge, retaliation, and aggression, correlate with aggressive and reckless driving (Deffenbacher, Petrilli, Lynch, Oetting, & Swaim, 2003; Deffenbacher et al., 2004). Positive attitudes toward committing violations have also been associated with reckless driving (Ulleberg & Rundmo, 2003; West & Hall, 1997) and with less responsiveness to a traffic safety campaign (Ulleberg, 2002). Applying the theory of planned behavior (Ajzen, 1985) to risky driving, Parker and her associates (Parker, Lajunen, & Stradling, 1998; Parker, Manstead, & Stradling, 1995) have also found that beliefs about the reactions of others, anticipated regret, and a sense of personal responsibility significantly correlate with self-reported likelihood of committing driving violations and aggressive driving.

Neighbors and his associates (Knee, Neighbors, & Vietor, 2001; Neighbors et al., 2002) have examined how beliefs about self-determination (i.e., self-determination theory; Deci & Ryan, 1985) contribute to aggressive driving. They found that vulnerability to external pressures and sensitivity to perceived attacks on self-esteem were significantly correlated with self-reported driving violations and aggression. The finding of a relationship between self-esteem and driving aggression is consistent with anecdotal descriptions of aggressive drivers as overrating their driving and denigrating that of others (James & Nahl, 2000; Parry, 1968) as well as with empirical evidence of an association between narcissistic tendencies and aggressive driving (Galovski et al., 2002; Malta, 2004; Malta & Blanchard, 2004; Schreer, 2002) and MVA risk (McGuire, 1976; Shaw, 1956; Tillmann & Hobbs, 1949). It also mirrors Bushman and Baumeister's (1998) finding that individuals who endorse high levels of narcissism respond more aggressively to perceived attacks on their self-esteem compared with individuals who are low in narcissism.

The collected research suggests that a variety of maladaptive thoughts and beliefs can contribute to aggressive and reckless driving, and cognitive–behavioral treatments that target such cognitions have demonstrated effectiveness in reducing driving anger and aggression (Deffenbacher et al., 2000;

Deffenbacher, Filetti, et al., 2002; Galovski & Blanchard, 2002a; Larson et al., 1998). Research that examines how change in cognitions relates to reductions in aggressive and reckless driving could help to further explicate their contribution to aggressive and reckless driving.

SUMMARY OF THE FRUSTRATION–AGGRESSION HYPOTHESIS OF AGGRESSIVE DRIVING

Research has provided support for the frustration–aggression model proposed by Novaco (1991) and Shinar (1998), in which predisposing characteristics and environmental influences jointly contribute to aggressive driving. The challenge for advocates of this theory is to design and execute studies that can more specifically examine the apparently complex interaction of personal and situational variables so as to more fully account for the individual variability in responses to roadway frustrations and provocations. Moreover, although this theory has utility in describing and predicting reactive roadway aggression, it is limited in its ability to account for proactive driving aggression that may be motivated by thrill seeking or competition.

BEHAVIORAL CHARACTERISTICS AND DRIVER TYPOLOGIES

Throughout the latter half of the 20th century, empirical studies (MacMillan, 1975; Malta, 2004; Matthews et al., 1997) and qualitative research (James & Nahl, 2000; Larson, 1996b; Maiuro, 1998) have produced typologies of aggressive drivers. Larson's (1996b) typologies include the "speeder," the "competitor," the "passive–aggressor," the "narcissist," and the "vigilante." Maiuro's (1998) profiles are similar and include the "territorial competitor" and the "hostile competitor," Jekyll and Hyde drivers who are normally unassertive but who become aggressive behind the wheel, and "polite" rule enforcers similar to Larson's vigilante. In addition to "automotive vigilantes," "rushing maniacs," and "competitors," James and Nahl (2000) also highlighted "scofflaw" drivers who feel entitled to break traffic laws and enjoy outsmarting traffic enforcement. Quantitative analyses (MacMillan, 1975; Malta, 2004; Matthews et al., 1997) have revealed two basic maladaptive driving styles that mirror the qualitative profiles: (a) driving that is aggressive, hostile, and antagonistic toward other drivers, driving impediments, or traffic laws, and (b) driving that is competitive, reckless, and thrill seeking in nature.

Several researchers have attempted to characterize drivers in terms of their personality characteristics (Beirness & Simpson, 1988; Deery & Fildes, 1999; Donovan et al., 1988; Hilakivi et al., 1989; Malta, 2004; Shaw, 1956;

Ulleberg, 2002; Wilson, 1991), and two basic problem driver typologies have emerged across the studies. One type drives both aggressively and competitively and tends to be high in general aggression, deviance acceptance, sensation seeking, hostility, irritability, and personal maladjustment (depression, personal problems, resentment). The second type drives in a competitive, reckless fashion and tends to be high in sensation seeking, deviance acceptance, and impulsiveness. This type tends to have variable levels of general aggression, hostility, and irritability but lower levels of personal maladjustment than the first type. These two types of drivers tend to be predominantly male, but the research also identified a third typology that is predominantly female, has an increased risk of MVAs, and exhibits elevated levels of depression, irritability, and feelings of inadequacy (Beirness & Simpson, 1988; Deery & Fildes, 1999). Because these drivers do not appear to drive recklessly or aggressively, their MVA risk may be related to other factors. These typologies contain elements of each of the theories reviewed in this chapter, such as the deviance acceptance associated with social maladjustment, the depression and personal problems associated with personal maladjustment, the general aggressiveness and impulsiveness highlighted by impulse noncontrol theory, the sensation seeking and deviance acceptance associated with risk behavior syndrome, and the hostility and irritability associated with the frustration–aggression hypothesis.

SUMMARY AND CONCLUSIONS

A great deal of research about aggressive and reckless driving accrued during the latter half of the 20th century, and several theories have been proposed to account for it. Each appears to account for samples of aggressive drivers, including those with general antisocial tendencies, problems with general aggression and impulsiveness, or both; young, sensation-seeking, and competitive drivers; and angry, frustrated drivers who sometimes lash out with aggression. Cultural variables, such as age, gender, and regional driving norms, also appear to contribute to driver behavior. Many situational variables, such as frustrating delays, traffic congestion and time urgency, driver comfort, anonymity, and aggression cues in the environment, also appear to affect drivers. Personal predispositions, such as trait anger, hostility, narcissism and sensitivity to perceived attacks, susceptibility to stress and external pressures, perceived behavioral control of driving, anticipated regret, positive attitudes toward aggressive driving, and subjective personal norms, also appear to play a role in aggressive driving. Some aggressive drivers may have serious psychiatric disorders, such as borderline personality disorder and antisocial personality disorder, or ADHD as well as alcohol and substance use disorders.

The collected findings suggest that aggressive driving is a complex behavioral phenomenon and that aggressive drivers are a heterogeneous group. A comprehensive theory is needed to account for the manner in which predisposing characteristics, cultural norms, and multiple situational variables interact to promote aggressive driving. The model should include the various functions that aggressive driving may serve, including saving time, responding to provocations, thrill seeking, and bolstering or maintaining status or self-esteem. The model should also address the possibility that aggressive driving can serve different functions at different times for the same individual and that the same aggressive driving behaviors can have multiple functions for a given individual, depending on the environmental context. The theories that have been developed are a promising beginning and have helped elucidate many of the factors involved in aggressive driving. However, none of the extant theories appears able to fully account for the phenomenon of aggressive driving, and the continued challenge for clinical scientists is to formulate an integrated model with the scope to address the diversity of aggressive drivers as well as the precision to accurately predict and influence individual behaviors. Such a model is germane to the development of effective prevention and intervention programs as well as potential treatment matching.

This book was written primarily for clinicians who treat aggressive drivers and clinical scientists who research aggressive driving. However, the phenomenon of aggressive driving has broader implications for an understanding of the nature of aggression. One interesting question for future research is whether roadway aggression is distinct from other forms of aggression or simply represents an extension of pervasive aggression to a specific context. Anecdotes of normally nonaggressive individuals who "lose it" behind the wheel suggest the former (James & Nahl, 2000; Larson, 1996b; Mizell, 1997), whereas social maladjustment theory, personal maladjustment theory, and risk behavior syndrome theory suggest the latter. It is not surprising that people who are generally aggressive also drive aggressively (Dula & Ballard, 2003; Lajunen & Parker, 2001; Malta, 2004; Malta & Blanchard, 2004), and as with general aggression (Archer et al., 1995; Barratt, 1991; Bushman & Baumeister, 1998; Buss & Perry, 1992; Loo, 1979; Stanford & Barratt, 1992; Zuckerman & Neeb, 1980), traits such as narcissism, impulsiveness, and sensation seeking contribute to driving aggression. Moreover, like general aggression (Berkowitz, 1989; Dollard et al., 1939; N. E. Miller, 1941), roadway aggression can be evoked by frustrations and disinhibited by anonymity and aggression cues (Ellison et al., 1995; Ellison-Potter et al., 2001; Shinar, 1998; Turner et al., 1975). These findings suggest that roadway aggression may merely represent a context-specific form of general aggression. However, some individuals who drive aggressively do not appear to have a history of other types of aggression

(James & Nahl, 2000; Larson, 1996b; Mizell, 1997), and social scientists are still a long way from understanding the confluence of cultural, societal, situational, and personal variables that somehow appear to transform every-day, law-abiding citizens into drivers who become so embroiled in roadway frustrations and provocations that they are willing not only to disregard the law but also to endanger themselves and others in the process. Given that aggressive driving is a relatively common form of aggression, researchers may find, as Doob and Gross (1968) did, that it can provide a useful paradigm with which to test and refine theories of general aggression. Future research investigating similarities and differences between roadway and other forms of aggression could help to further our understanding of both aggressive driving as well as general aggression.

Aggressive driving is an intriguing social phenomenon as well as a serious public health risk. Although it is not new, well-controlled clinical research has emerged only in the past decade. In the meantime, clinicians who treat aggressive drivers are faced with the task of planning and implementing treatments for a diverse population. In the chapters that follow, we present information on the assessment and treatment of aggressive drivers, with the goals of aiding clinicians who treat this population as well providing data for clinical scientists seeking to develop effective prevention programs and treatments for aggressive driving.

II

ASSESSMENT OF
THE ANGRY AND
AGGRESSIVE DRIVER

4

THE ALBANY STUDIES OF AGGRESSIVE DRIVERS: SAMPLE DESCRIPTIONS AND ASSESSMENT PROCEDURES

Altogether, these studies assessed four different samples of aggressive drivers. Two of these samples were undergraduate students at the University at Albany, the majority of whom were participating to satisfy a research requirement for introductory psychology courses. The other two were community samples who were seeking treatment for their aggressive driving. These latter two samples were predominantly court referred because of their conviction for an aggressive driving offense, or else they were self-referred for treatment of their aggressive driving. The latter usually came at the instigation of their families.

Some of the participants in the treatment-seeking samples had incidents of what one might call road rage (see Table 4.1). A detailed description of the group cognitive–behavioral treatment these individuals received is described in the treatment manual provided in chapter 10. The results of these treatments are summarized in chapter 9.

In chapters 5, 6, and 7, we describe assessment information gathered on our various samples. In each chapter, we offer a summary of what is known in each assessment domain from the available English-language

TABLE 4.1
Offenses for Which Court-Referred Participants Were Diverted to Treatment Program: Court-Referred Sample

Offense	Arrest specifics
Assault (3)	1. Driver rammed second car, which was occupied, with his vehicle. 2. Physical assault on second driver after minor motor vehicle accident (MVA). 3. Vehicular assault on fireman (ran over his foot, resulting in hospitalization) who was directing traffic.
Menacing (4)	1. Verbal threats to kill second driver after minor MVA. 2. Threatened second driver with a gun. 3. Threatened fireman who was directing traffic. 4. Threatened second driver with a hammer.
Harassment (6)	1. Threatened to kill elderly driver after minor MVA. 2. Tried to pull second driver from his car to beat him after minor incident. 3. Followed woman off highway to her home to confront her for driving error, yelled at her, pounded on car. 4. Threatened driver who crossed into his lane. 5. Not specified. 6. Damaged other driver's car with his vehicle, then fled.
Reckless endangerment (3)	1. Threw object from his car window at second car after minor incident. 2. Broke windows of car that cut him off. 3. Not specified.
Disorderly conduct (9)	Altercations with police after arrest for aggressive driving offenses.
Reckless driving (8)	No specifics.
Passing on shoulder	Passed on shoulder of crowded 3-lane interstate, driving at speeds in excess of 65 mph.
Failure to comply	Led police on chase after aggressive driving incident.
Failure to keep right (3)	1. Tried to outrun police when they tried to stop him for speeding. 2. No details. 3. No details.
Unsafe lane changes (2)	Weaving in traffic, crossing several lanes at once.
Failure to yield/failure to keep right (3)	No specifics.
Unsafe start (2)	Gunned engine and "peeled out" at traffic light.
Following too closely	Deliberate tailgating.
Crossing a hazard marker	No specifics.
Speeding (11)	20–45 mph over speed limit.
Running a stop sign	No specifics.
Driving while intoxicated (10)	No specifics.

Note. Cohort 1, $N = 20$; Cohort 2, $N = 17$. Numbers in parentheses in left column refer to the frequency with which this offense was a referring charge.

literature. Then we present our results in detail, including norms for some measures for our different samples.

Chapter 5 contains psychiatric diagnostic information and thus could be considered categorical assessment results. It also introduces our work with intermittent explosive disorder (IED), a little-studied disorder that is a fairly common diagnosis among our treatment-seeking aggressive drivers. Chapter 6 contains psychological test results and thus could be considered as comprising dimensional assessment results. Finally, chapter 7 contains psychophysiological assessment results. In order not to repeat the sample descriptions in each chapter, we describe our samples below.

THE TREATMENT-SEEKING SAMPLES

Court-Referred Participants

All of our court-referred participants came from Saratoga County, New York, the county just to the north of Albany. These referrals were made possible by the cooperation of Jim Murphy, the district attorney for Saratoga County. (In chapter 11, we present our ideas about how to approach and negotiate with members of the criminal justice system for referrals to a road rage treatment program.) The cooperating assistant district attorneys and judges offered these drivers, who had been convicted of an aggressive driving offense, either the sentence to which they were entitled or diversion to the Albany Road Rage Treatment Program. Those who accepted the diversion referral were informed by the court, and by us when they first called, that they had to attend the assessment, treatment, and reassessment sessions. Failure to attend would result in the court's being notified and usually the receipt of the original penalty.

This situation raised some human subjects concerns. First, at the initial visit, all of the assessment and treatment attendance requirements were spelled out in detail, in writing.[1] It was made clear that repeated failure to attend sessions would be grounds for dismissal from the program and referral back to the court. We also made clear that at the end of the research involvement (including the 2-month follow-up), a letter would be sent to the court attesting to the driver's attendance and participation in the program. No comments were made to judges about response to treatment, only on attendance. Overall, 3 individuals who were referred to us and who

---

[1] It may be that clinicians dealing with court-referred aggressive drivers might want to have the patient read and sign a full disclosure statement to protect both parties, and the referring officials in the criminal justice system might want to see such a statement. In an effort to help others who want to conduct research on this population, a copy of our consent form is included as Exhibit 11.4.

initially called failed to complete the initial assessment ($n = 1$) or the treatment ($n = 2$). Thus, participation was not completely voluntary in that the driver could not stop participation without potentially suffering consequences (the court's being notified).

To protect the participants' rights as research participants, we also asked them to give consent for the use of their data in the research. Thus, they had to attend and take part in the assessments and treatment as part of the court diversion, but they were free not to participate in the formal research. None of the participants withheld his or her data.

Table 4.1 lists the offenses for which the court-referred drivers were convicted. To protect the identity of the participants, these offenses are not tied to the demographic data. Reading Table 4.1 will give a flavor of the kind of offenses committed in terms of seriousness. (Our own reaction continues to be that we hope not to have to share the road with comparable untreated individuals.)

Self-Referred Participants

As noted above, the small sample of self-referred individuals responded to advertisements and local media coverage of the treatment project that asked for individuals who had a problem with aggressive driving. It was our impression that many of these individuals had been pushed toward treatment by a partner or family member. However, they acknowledged that they had a problem with driving anger and aggressive driving. As we show in chapter 6, they acknowledged more personal psychological distress than did the court-referred drivers. As a group, they had less severe driving records than the court-referred group (see Table 4.2).

Because we had access to relatively unique samples of aggressive drivers (i.e., court-referred drivers and self-identified, self-referred aggressive drivers from the community), in Table 4.2 we have listed, by individual research numbers, the demographic and driving history data for the two cohorts of court-referred aggressive drivers. (Two of the second-cohort drivers were self-referred.) Comparable data on the treatment-seeking self-referred drivers are also given in Table 4.2.

On average, the court-referred aggressive drivers had had between two and three motor vehicle accidents (MVAs), nine convictions of moving violations, and fewer than one conviction of driving while intoxicated. The self-referred aggressive drivers were comparable, except they had about half the number of moving violation convictions. Although women were overrepresented in the self-referred group (5 out of 12) compared with the court-referred group (5 out of 37), it is clear that aggressive driving is not entirely a male problem. We believe the individual participant data in Table 4.2

TABLE 4.2
Demographics and Driving Behaviors of Treatment-Seeking Aggressive Drivers

Participant no.	Years driving	No. MVAs	No. moving violations	DWI conviction(s)	Age (years)	Gender
Court-referred sample, Cohort 1 (N = 20)						
100	4	0	2	0	22	F
101	3	6	4	0	19	M
102[a]	2	2	4	0	18	M
103	2	2	35	0	17	M
104	25	4	7	1	37	M
105	3	2	10	2 (in one night)	21	F
106	10	4	10	4	35	M
107	16	2	4	0	33	F
108[a]	40	2	6	0	55	M
109[a]	24	6	25	0	40	M
110	25	5	5	5	41	M
111[a]	28	3	2	1	40	M
112	4	2	2	1	20	M
113	14	2	1	0	30	M
114	12	0	1	0	28	M
115[a]	14	3	1	0	27	M
116	4	1	2	0	20	M
117[b]						
118[a]	4	1	1	0	20	M
119	17	1	50	1	34	M
120[a]	9	0	4	0	26	F
M	13.8	2.4	8.8	0.65	29.2	
SD	13	1.8	13	1.4	10.1	
Self-referred sample (N = 10)						
200	34	5	1	0	50	F
201	27	1	0	0	43	F
202[a]	33	2	1	1	49	M
203[a]	13	0	9	1	26	M
204	24	5	6	0	40	M
205	11	5	10	0	27	F
206	40	7	6	1	65	M
207	34	5	1	1	50	M
208	6	1	3	0	22	F
209[a]	8	0	2	1	23	F
M	23	3.1	3.9	0.5	39.5	
SD	12.5	2.6	3.6	0.5	14.5	
Court-referred sample, Cohort 2 (N = 19)						
300[a]	7	3	14	1	26	M
301	9	2	8	0	24	M
302[a]	15	4	12	0	31	M
303S[a]	38	4	20	0	56	M
304	5	1	25	1	21	M
305S	17	7	9	1	33	M
306	3	3	25	0	18	M
307	8	2	0	2	21	M

(continued)

TABLE 4.2 *(Continued)*

Participant no.	Years driving	No. MVAs	No. moving violations	DWI conviction(s)	Age (years)	Gender
		Court-referred sample, Cohort 2 (*N* = 19)				
308[a]	10	3	8	1	t25	F
309	8	1	8	1	24	M
310	17	1	2	2	33	M
311	12	1	5	1	29	M
312	2	1	1	1	18	M
313	16	1	5	2	32	M
314	27	2	0	0	43	M
315	16	1	5	0	30	M
316[a]	31	55	100	0	47	M
317	38	2	3	0	56	M
318[a]	4	1	5	9	20	M
M	14.9	5	13.5	0.7	30.9	
SD	11.1	12.2	22.3	0.8	11.7	
M[c]	14.8	2.2	8.7	0.7	30.0	
SD[c]	10.7	1.6	7.8	0.8	11.4	

Note. MVA = motor vehicle accident; DWI = driving while intoxicated; F = female; M = male; S = self-referred.
[a]Met criteria for intermittent explosive disorder. [b]Data for Participant 117 are unavailable. [c]Because Participant 316 claimed (repeatedly) to have been in a very large number of accidents and to have had a great number of moving violations, we present the average of the data for this cohort with his data omitted.

will help readers see the variability present in this population that mere means and standard deviations would obscure.

A topic to which we devote a fair amount of attention in chapter 5 is IED. In chapter 5, we describe, in some detail, the nature of this disorder and how to assess it. As we note there, IED is a very understudied disorder. Because we have found that about one third of treatment-seeking aggressive drivers met criteria for IED (7 out of 20 in court-referred Cohort 1, 4 out of 12 in the self-referred cohort, and 5 out of 17 in court-referred Cohort 2), we have taken advantage of this situation to subdivide our data into those from individuals with IED versus those from a comparable group of aggressive drivers without IED. The first example of this is found in Table 4.3.

The offenses in Table 4.3 are listed in order of decreasing seriousness. As is obvious, there is a preponderance of more serious offenses in the IED column and a preponderance of less serious offenses in the non-IED column. A comparison of the offenses for the two populations yields a highly significant ($p < .001$) difference. Thus, even within the two cohorts of court-referred aggressive drivers there is a significant difference in the seriousness of the offenses for which aggressive drivers with IED were convicted and subsequently referred.

TABLE 4.3
Offenses for Court-Referred Drivers With Intermittent Explosive Disorder (IED) and Without IED

Offense	No. IED cases ($n = 12$)	No. non-IED cases ($n = 25$)
Assault	2	1
Menacing	3	1
Harassment	5	1
Reckless endangerment	1	2
Disorderly conduct	0	9
Reckless driving	1	7
Failure to yield/comply	2	5
Excessive speeding	1	10

Note. The total number of offenses exceeds number of drivers because an individual was often charged with multiple offenses from one incident.

Nonaggressive-Driving Community Sample

We recruited a sample of 30 community volunteers who claimed not to drive aggressively. They participated in the assessment of psychopathology (chap. 5), psychophysiology (chap. 7), and some of the psychological tests (chap. 6) as a comparison group for our initial cohort of treatment-seeking aggressive drivers. They were paid for their participation. The sample comprised 20 men and 10 women whose average age was 34.5 (*SD* = 12.4). They had been driving, on average, for 16 years.

Student Samples

As part of our studies on angry aggressive drivers, Malta (2004) assessed 1,112 undergraduates at the University at Albany using a series of questionnaires, all of which were completed anonymously. Data from 23 (2.1%) were excluded for the following reasons: no current driving license ($n = 3$), age outliers (>34, $n = 3$), excessive missing data ($n = 13$), and unreliable data ($n = 4$). The overall sample was 46.5% female, with an average age of 19.1 years. About one fourth (24.8%) were of minority ethnic status. Among the instruments used was the Driver's Stress Profile (Larson, 1996a), an instrument Blanchard et al. (2000) found to be a reliable and valid self-report measure of the tendency to drive aggressively. Individuals who scored 1 standard deviation or higher above the mean of Blanchard et al.'s (2000) standardization sample (score of 53 or higher) were asked to participate in detailed face-to-face assessments in which a number of structured interviews were used, including the Structured Clinical Interview for *DSM–IV* (First, Spitzer, Gibbon, & Williams, 1996), the Structured Clinical

TABLE 4.4
Demographic and Driving Data on College Students
Who Scored High on an Aggressive Driving Questionnaire

Characteristic	Value
Gender (male/female)	29/24 (54.7% male)
Age (*M*)	19.0 (*SD* = 1.56, range: 18–28)
Years driving (*M*)	3.2 (*SD* = 1.57, range: 1–10)
No. moving violations	1.1 (*SD* = 1.66, range: 0–8)
No. serious MVAs (personal injury)	0.5 (*SD* = 0.78, range: 0–3)
No. minor MVAs (property damage only)	1.0 (*SD* = 1.18, range: 0–4)

Note. MVA = motor vehicle accident.

Interview for *DSM–IV* Axis II Personality Disorders (First, Spitzer, Gibbon, Williams, & Benjamin, 1996), and other measures. Fifty-three of the highest scoring students participated for course credit. The interviewer was unaware of group membership. The psychiatric assessment results from the college student aggressive driving sample are discussed in chapter 5.

Psychological test results from the larger sample are presented as norms in chapter 6, as are the results for the aggressive driving subsample. Driving data from this subsample of students are presented in Table 4.4.

As can be seen in Table 4.4, this student sample of aggressive drivers has a much higher percentage of women (45.3%) than our combined treatment-seeking samples (20.4%). They are also younger and thus have been driving for fewer years. This relative shorter time at risk is probably responsible in part for the lower rate of motor vehicle MVAs (a total average of 1.5 serious and minor accidents) and a noticeably lower lifetime rate of moving violations (1.1 vs. 7.7 across all treatment-seeking participants).

Thus, this sample of college student drivers, who acknowledge a high level of aggressive driving and who have notably poor driving records thus far, are still a relatively benign group compared with the court- and self-referred aggressive drivers who are the central focus of this book. Research on this college population is informative in its own right; however, treatment research on such a population may not be fully relevant to the more serious cases we have investigated.

Mixed Student–Community Sample

Finally, one psychophysiological assessment study (Malta et al., 2001), which we summarize in detail in chapter 7, used a mixed student and community sample. Both the students and the community sample received $20 for undergoing the full assessment. All had self-identified as either aggressive drivers or very nonaggressive drivers during a telephone screen.

The aggressive driver sample consisted of 4 students and 10 community members. There were 5 women and 9 men, with an average age of 34 years (range: 19–55) who had been driving an average of 17.9 years. The nonaggressive driver sample comprised 5 students and 9 community members. This comparison sample also had 5 women and 9 men, with a mean age of 35 years (range: 20–54), who had been driving for an average of 18.1 years.

INITIAL ASSESSMENT OF TREATMENT-SEEKING AGGRESSIVE DRIVERS

Our first step in the treatment program was to develop a structured interview for the initial assessment. This interview schedule has evolved somewhat over our several years of conducting assessment and treatment. The current version is presented at the end of this chapter as Appendix 4.1. We should note that it is set up for computer coding of the information obtained.

The interview schedule, essentially the same for both court-referred and self-referred drivers, contained several parts. After obtaining demographic and locator information, we asked for the participant's description of what offenses led to the court referral. Next, we took a detailed driving history that focused on accidents, moving violations, and instances of being arrested for driving under the influence or driving while intoxicated. We then asked about aggressive driving and specific incidents of it. The next part of the interview obtained detailed information regarding how much driving the participant usually does and his or her typical emotions when driving in various situations. Then it focused on anger or irritation in response to certain situations or factors.

The heart of the interview consisted of questions about aggressive driving. We asked if the participant had ever engaged in the list of 20 behaviors, how many times he or she engages in the behaviors during a typical week, and for ratings of any annoyance or anger the participant feels if confronted with each of 23 behaviors by others or general driving situations.

We then asked for descriptions of driving situations that typically anger or annoy the participant and inquired about details of his or her thoughts, feelings, and behaviors. (These situations provide the basis for the audiotapes used in the psychophysiological assessment; see chap. 7.) The focus then shifted to asking about aggressive driving by family and friends, including possible arrests and MVAs.

The next section obtains a brief psychosocial assessment by having the participant describe the quality of his or her relationships while growing up and currently. There is also a structured inquiry about current life problems. Last are questions about family member psychiatric and anger and aggression problems as well as similar questions about the participant.

From this interview we went directly into the assessment for IED. The interview schedule for this is contained in chapter 5.

Clinical Hint

It has been our experience that court-referred drivers usually start by denying they did anything "really" wrong. We try to take the position at the initial assessment, and again at the beginning of treatment, that we are not going to debate the veracity of the offense with them or whether the police, prosecuting attorney, or judge were wrong or had it in for them. We point out that the court has referred them, they have taken the referral, we know what the court said they did, and now we want to hear their side. One can also expect some denial of any aggressive driving by those who are court referred. We have found that gentle, nonhostile probing usually gains admissions of some aggressive driving.

DRIVING DIARY

At this initial visit we also explained the driving diary to participants and asked them to begin filling it out on a daily basis. In addition to information on time spent in the automobile and approximate miles driven each day, there was room for individuals to record the occurrence of 17 potentially angry and aggressive behaviors (including speech) as well as thoughts. (Development of this measure and its use as a treatment outcome measure are described in chap. 9.) Participants were asked to keep completing the diary for the duration of their involvement in the project. A sample diary page is depicted in Exhibit 4.1.

The remainder of the initial assessment data is described in chapters 5 through 7. We administered several structured psychiatric diagnostic interviews (chap. 5), a number of psychological tests (descriptions of the tests and results are given in chap. 6 [the battery changed from treatment-seeking Cohort 1 to Cohort 2]), and a psychophysiological test (chap. 7).

After treatment, and at the 2-month follow-up, we administered another brief structured interview, which is also available at the end of this chapter, in Appendix 4.2. We also continued to collect driving diary data and repeated part of the psychological test battery at posttreatment and follow-up assessments.

These latter interviews focused on most of the topics covered at the initial assessment specifically for the interval since the initial interview,

EXHIBIT 4.1
Driving Diary

Name: _____

Week of: _____ Pre/Post: _____

Frequency Per Day:

0 ..... Not at all	3 ..... Severely / 5–6 times
1 ..... Slightly / 1–2 times	4 ..... Extremely / more than 6 times
2 ..... Moderately / 3–4 times	5 ..... Consistently throughout the driving day

Date:							
Purposefully slow driving to block others' passage							
Tailgating							
Improper passing							
Failure to yield right of way							
Failure to keep right and blocking others' passage							
Horn honking							
Flashing high beams							
Failing to signal properly							
Obscene gesturing							
Verbal insults							
Throwing objects							
Physical assault							
Giving chase to another driver							
Feeling angry at another driver							
Wishing harm to another driver							
Feeling impatient at intersections, etc.							
Feeling upset at delays, other drivers, etc.							
Other:							
Hours spent in the car:							

and it repeated the questions about aggressive driving behaviors and degree of anger or annoyance at other driver's behaviors or situations. We asked about the most annoying driving situation the participant had encountered over the past week and his or her reactions to it. We then quickly assessed for changes in psychosocial relations and possible psychiatric changes. Last, we reassessed for IED and possible impulsive aggressive acts other than those related to driving that harmed others or property.

We have no reliability or validity data on our structured interviews or diary form other than face validity and possibly construct validity. The interviews gathered the pertinent information on the individual's driving behaviors and formed the beginning basis for the intervention. We believe structured interviews are to be preferred so that all of the same information is gathered on each client. The interview also helps build rapport.

With this systematic clinical information as a starting point, we then moved to assessment of psychiatric comorbidity (chapter 5), to dimensional psychological assessment using reliable and valid measures (chapter 6), and to psychophysiological assessment (chapter 7).

APPENDIX 4.1

Initial Assessment Interview

Subject Name: _____ Date: _____

Subject # ____ ____ ____ * Line ____ ____ ____
      (1)   (2)   (3)   (5)   (6)   (7)

For court-referred subjects only:

Original driving citation: _____

Part I: Driving Interview

Driving History

1. How old were you when you began driving? ____ (9)

2. How long have you been driving? ____ (10)

3. What kind of a car do you usually drive?
   Make: _____ Model: _____
   Year: ____ Sports car? (2 = yes, 1 = no) ____ (11)

4. How many accidents have you been involved in
   as the driver? ____ (12)
   (Describe any serious accidents on back page.)

5. Were there any injuries? (2 = yes, 1 = no)
   Describe the worst one or two. ____ (13)

   _____

   _____

   _____

6. Was there damage to the car? (2 = yes, 1 = no)
   Describe the worst one or two. ____ (14)

   _____

   _____

   _____

7. How many citations have you been issued
   after an accident? ____ (15)

8. What was the nature and dates of those citations?

_____

_____

_____

9. How many moving violations have you received
(e.g., speeding)? _____ (16)

10. What were the nature and dates of those violations?

_____

_____

_____

11. Approximately how many nonmoving violations
have you received? _____ (17)

12. What was the nature of those violations?

_____

_____

_____

13. a) Have you received any DUIs? (#) _____ (18)
b) If so, when? (dates) _____
c) Most recent: Within the past 6 mos. = 1;
Within the past year = 2; Within the past 2 years = 3;
Within the past 3–4 years = 4; (> 4 years ago) = 5;
N/A = 0. _____ (19)

14. a) Have you received any DWIs? (#) _____ (20)
b) If so, when? (dates) _____
c) Most recent: Within the past year 6 mo. = 1;
Within the past year = 2; Within the past 2 years = 3
Within the past 3–4 years = 4; (> 4 years ago) = 5;
N/A = 0. _____ (21)

15. a) Have others called you an aggressive driver?
(2 = yes, 1 = no) _____ (22)
b) Who? Spouse/significant other = 1;
Family = 2; Friends = 3; Other = 4;
N/A = 5
_____ _____ _____ _____
(23) (24) (25) (26)
c) When? Most recent: Within the past 6 mos. = 1;
Within the past year = 2; Within the past 2 years = 3;
Within the past 3–4 years = 4; (> 4 years ago) = 5;
N/A = 0. _____ (27)
d) If yes to 15a, when was the first time you can recall
that someone complained or commented on your
aggressive driving? Year: _____ No. years since: _____ (28)

16. a) Would you describe yourself as an aggressive driver?
(2 = yes, 1 = no)   _____ (29)
b) If yes, since you began driving, how much of your
driving has been aggressive?
N/A = 0
Recently started driving aggressively = 1
Have driven aggressively for some of my life = 2
Have driven aggressively for much of my life = 3
Have driven aggressively for most of my life = 4
Have driven aggressively for all of my life = 5   _____ (30)

17. Please describe your 3 worst incidents of aggressive driving.
(Probe if person denies any).
1) _____
  _____
2) _____
  _____
3) _____
  _____

Driving Information

18. How many hours per week do you drive for:
a) Work/school   _____ (31)
b) Errands/tasks (grocery, dry cleaners, etc.)   _____ (32)
c) Pleasure/recreation   _____ (33)

19. How many days a week do you drive for:
a) Work/school   _____ (34)
b) Errands/tasks   _____ (35)
c) Pleasure/recreation   _____ (36)

20. For nonwork/nonschool related driving, what type of
roads do you generally travel on?
1 = Highways; 2 = Residential roads; 3 = Secondary roads;
4 = N/A

Errands/tasks: Pleasure/recreation:

_____ _____ _____   _____ _____ _____
(37)   (38)   (39)   (40)   (41)   (42)

21. Regarding your commute to work/school:
How many miles are traveled on:
a) Highways: _____ (43)
b) Residential roads: _____ (44)

c) Secondary roads: ___ (45)
d) Total mileage of commute ___ (46)

During your commute:

22. What is your average driving speed? ___ (47)

23. Approximately how many stoplights do you encounter? ___ (48)

24. How many road changes do you have to make? ___ (49)

25. How many times a **week** would you estimate that you experience the following emotions when you are driving:
    Scale 1
    0 = Never
    1 = Once or twice
    2 = 3–4 times
    3 = Every day
    4 = Several times a day

	Work/school	Errands	Pleasure	All combined
A. Irritated/angry	___ (50)	___ (55)	___ (60)	___ (65)
B. Stressed/frustrated	___ (51)	___ (56)	___ (61)	___ (66)
C. Depressed/down	___ (52)	___ (57)	___ (62)	___ (67)
D. Upset/distressed	___ (53)	___ (58)	___ (63)	___ (68)
E. Fine/normal mood	___ (54)	___ (59)	___ (64)	___ (69)

26. Which driving situation (work, errands, pleasure) would you rate as the *least pleasant* for you?
    1 = Work/school; 2 = Errands; 3 = Pleasure ___ (70)

27. Which factors contribute to **anger/irritability** during:
    (2 = yes, 1 = no, 0 = N/A)

	Work/school	Errands	Pleasure	All combined
a. Traffic	___ (9)	___ (21)	___ (33)	___ (45)
b. Other drivers' driving or behavior	___ (10)	___ (22)	___ (34)	___ (46)
c. Other drivers' personal characteristics	___ (11)	___ (23)	___ (35)	___ (47)
d. Weather	___ (12)	___ (24)	___ (36)	___ (48)
e. Stressors at home	___ (13)	___ (25)	___ (37)	___ (49)
f. Interpersonal stress at work	___ (14)	___ (26)	___ (38)	___ (50)

g. Task-related stress at work	____ (15)	____ (27)	____ (39) ____ (51)
h. Feeling ill	____ (16)	____ (28)	____ (40) ____ (52)
i. Major life stressors	____ (17)	____ (29)	____ (41) ____ (53)
j. Running late	____ (18)	____ (30)	____ (42) ____ (54)
k. Time of day	____ (19)	____ (31)	____ (43) ____ (55)
l. Day of the week	____ (20)	____ (32)	____ (44) ____ (56)

28a. If response to Item k in Question 27 ("time of day") was "yes," how?
Scale 2
1 = Worse in the evening, better in the morning
2 = Worse in the morning, better in the evening
3 = Varies/inconsistent
4 = Don't know

Work/school	Errands	Pleasure	All combined
____ (57)	____ (58)	____ (59)	____ (60)

28b. If response to Item l in Question 27 ("day of the week") was "yes," how?
Scale 3
0 = Worse on weekends
1 = Worse on Mondays/early week
2 = Worse on Fridays/late week
3 = Varies
4 = Don't know

Work/school	Errands	Pleasure	All combined
____ (61)	____ (62)	____ (63)	____ (64)

29. Which factors contribute to **poor mood** (not anger)?
(2 = yes, 1 = no, 0 = N/A)

	Work/school	Errands	Pleasure	All combined
a. Traffic	____ (9)	____ (21)	____ (33)	____ (45)
b. Other drivers' driving or behavior	____ (10)	____ (22)	____ (34)	____ (46)
c. Other drivers' personal characteristics	____ (11)	____ (23)	____ (35)	____ (47)
d. Weather	____ (12)	____ (24)	____ (36)	____ (48)
e. Stressors at home	____ (13)	____ (25)	____ (37)	____ (49)
f. Interpersonal stress at work	____ (14)	____ (26)	____ (38)	____ (50)

g. Task-related stress at work	_____ (15)	_____ (27)	_____ (39)	_____ (51)
h. Feeling ill	_____ (16)	_____ (28)	_____ (40)	_____ (52)
i. Major life stressors	_____ (17)	_____ (29)	_____ (41)	_____ (53)
j. Running late	_____ (18)	_____ (30)	_____ (42)	_____ (54)
k. Time of day	_____ (19)	_____ (31)	_____ (43)	_____ (55)
l. Day of the week	_____ (20)	_____ (32)	_____ (44)	_____ (56)

30a. If response to Item k in Question 29 ("time of day") was "yes," how?

> Scale 2
> 1 = Worse in the evening, better in the morning
> 2 = Worse in the morning, better in the evening
> 3 = Varies/inconsistent
> 4 = Don't know

Work/school	Errands	Pleasure	All combined
_____ (57)	_____ (58)	_____ (59)	_____ (60)

30b. If response to Item l in Question 29 ("day of the week") was "yes," how?

> Scale 3
> 0 = Weekends
> 1 = Worse on Mondays/early week
> 2 = Worse on Fridays/late week
> 3 = Varies
> 4 = Don't know

Work/school	Errands	Pleasure	All combined
_____ (61)	_____ (62)	_____ (63)	_____ (64)

Aggressive Driving (2 = yes, 1 = no, 0 = N/A)

31. I'm going to ask you about a number of common aggressive driving behaviors. These behaviors are committed with the intent to express annoyance, compete with or get even with, scare, harm, or "punish" other drivers. We are not talking about lapses in driving skill, errors, or unintentional acts. We want to know if you have **ever** engaged in any of these behaviors:

    a. Purposefully driving slowly with the intent to block another vehicle's passage   _____ (9)

    b. Tailgating   _____ (10)

    c. Improper passing (passing on the shoulder, passing on the right)   _____ (11)

    d. Failure to yield the right of way   _____ (12)

    e. Blocking another driver from merging   _____ (13)

f. Failing to keep right   _____ (14)

g. Horn honking   _____ (15)

h. Flashing high beams   _____ (16)

i. Deliberately using high beams from behind
(keeping them on)   _____ (17)

j. Failing to signal properly   _____ (18)

k. "Racing" or competing with another driver
(toll booths, stop lights)   _____ (19)

l. Obscene gesturing   _____ (20)

m. Verbal insults (covertly)   _____ (21)

n. Verbal insults (overtly)   _____ (22)

o. Throwing objects   _____ (23)

p. Physical assault (on another vehicle or individual)   _____ (24)

q. Giving chase to another driver   _____ (25)

r. Feeling angry at another driver   _____ (26)

s. Wishing harm to another driver   _____ (27)

t. Feeling impatient at intersections   _____ (28)

u. Feeling upset at delays, other drivers, etc.   _____ (29)

v. Other (specify) _____   _____ (30)

32. Now we are going to review the same behaviors. However, this time, I want you to give me a number. How many times **in an average week** do you engage in the following behaviors?

a. Purposefully slow driving with the intent to block another vehicle's passage   _____ (31)

b. Tailgating   _____ (32)

c. Improper passing (passing on the shoulder, passing on the right)   _____ (33)

d. Failing to yield the right of way   _____ (34)

e. Blocking another driver from merging   _____ (35)

f. Failing to keep right   _____ (36)

g. Horn honking   _____ (37)

h. Flashing high beams   _____ (38)

i. Deliberately using high beams from behind (keeping them on)   _____ (39)

j. Failing to signal properly   _____ (40)

k. "Racing" or competing with another driver (toll booth, stop light)   _____ (41)

l. Obscene gesturing   _____ (42)

m. Verbal insults (covertly)   _____ (43)

n. Verbal insults (overtly)   _____ (44)

o. Throwing objects   _____ (45)

p. Physical assault (on another vehicle or individual)   _____ (46)

q. Giving chase to another driver   _____ (47)
r. Feeling angry at another driver   _____ (48)
s. Wishing harm to another driver   _____ (49)
t. Feeling impatient at intersections   _____ (50)
u. Feeling upset at delays, other drivers, etc.   _____ (51)
v. Other (specify) _____   _____ (52)

33. Please rate the following driving situations on the degree of annoyance or anger that they arouse in you. Answers should be based on the following scale:

        Scale 5
        4 = Enraged
        3 = Mad/very angry
        2 = Aggravated/ indignant
        1 = Annoyed/irritated
        0 = Not at all/ no effect

a. Traffic jams/heavy traffic   _____ (53)
b. Stoplights   _____ (54)
c. Being cut off   _____ (55)
d. Women drivers driving poorly   _____ (56)
e. Men drivers driving poorly   _____ (57)
f. Elderly drivers driving poorly   _____ (58)
g. Young drivers driving poorly   _____ (59)
h. Different ethnic groups driving poorly   _____ (60)
i. The driver of an old, rusty "clunker" driving poorly   _____ (61)
j. Toll booth situations   _____ (62)
k. Following a slow driver in the left lane   _____ (63)
l. A slow pedestrian holding you up   _____ (64)
m. People driving slowly in poor weather conditions   _____ (65)
n. Crowded parking lots   _____ (66)
o. Someone taking "your" parking space   _____ (67)
p. Being unable to find a parking spot   _____ (68)
q. Temperature extremes (hot or cold)   _____ (69)
r. Rush hour traffic   _____ (70)
s. Drivers who pass you in excess of the speed limit   _____ (71)
t. People who attempt to merge into your lane of traffic   _____ (72)
u. Being tailgated   _____ (73)
v. Being flashed by high beams   _____ (74)
w. Being honked at   _____ (75)
x. Feeling others aren't obeying the traffic laws   _____ (76)

34. Give a brief account of a typical driving situation that is annoying or frustrating to you. This situation should be one in which you respond with an aggressive driving behavior.

_____

_____

_____

_____

35. During this situation, what do you usually think about:
    a. The other driver? _____
    b. Drivers in general? _____
    c. Road conditions? _____
    d. Your ability to drive effectively? _____
    e. The unfairness of the situation? _____

36. During this situation, how do you feel:
    a. Physically? _____
    b. Emotionally? _____
    c. Mentally? _____

37. For how long would you normally feel this way? _____

38. Name 3 ways in which you might normally handle the situation.
    a. _____
    b. _____
    c. _____

Family Driving History (2 = yes, 1 = no, 0 = N/A)

39. I'm going to list some members of your immediate family. Who would you consider to be an aggressive driver?
    a. Mother _____ (9)
    b. Father _____ (10)
    c. Stepmother _____ (11)
    d. Stepfather _____ (12)
    e. Sister 1 _____ (13)
    f. Sister 2 _____ (14)
    g. Brother 1 _____ (15)
    h. Brother 2 _____ (16)
    i. Maternal grandmother _____ (17)
    j. Maternal grandfather _____ (18)
    k. Paternal grandmother _____ (19)
    l. Paternal grandfather _____ (20)
    m. Others (specify) _____ _____ (21)
        (Can include close friends, significant others, etc.)

40. Have any of these family members been arrested for aggressive driving-type behaviors?
(2 = yes, 1 = no, 0 = N/A) ____ (22)

Please explain. _____

_____

_____

Code # of family members with aggressive driving arrests: ____ (23)

41. Have any of these family members' aggressive driving behaviors ever ended in injury or death to themselves or others?
(2 = yes, 1 = no, 0 = N/A) ____ (24)

Please explain. _____

_____

_____

Code # of family members with injury/death: ____ (25)

Part 2: Psychosocial Assessment

Scale 6
4 = Very good
3 = Good
2 = Fair
1 = Poor
0 = Very poor

1. How would you describe your relationship with your parents while you were growing up? ____ (26)

2. How would you describe your parents' relationship with each other while you were growing up? ____ (27)

3. How would you describe your relationship with your siblings while you were growing up? ____ (28)

4. How would you describe the number and quality of your friendships while you were growing up? ____ (29)

5. How would you describe your school performance while you were growing up? ____ (30)

6. How would you describe your relationship with authority figures while you were growing up? ____ (31)

Currently:

7. How would you describe your relationship with your parents? ____ (32)

8. How would you describe your relationship with your siblings? _____ (33)

9. How would you describe your current number and quality of friendships? _____ (34)

10. How would you describe your current work/school performance? _____ (35)

11. How would you describe your relationship with authority figures? _____ (36)

12. How would you describe your relationship with your children? _____ (37)

13. How would you describe your relationship with your spouse/partner? _____ (38)

Current Life Situation

Scale 6
2 = yes   4 = Very good
1 = no   3 = Good
0 = N/A   2 = Fair
        1 = Poor
        0 = Very poor

14. Are you married? _____ (39)

15. If not, are you in a relationship? _____ (40)

16. How would you describe your marriage/relationship? _____ (41)

17. Are you getting along well? _____ (42)

18. Some people have stress in their marriages/relationships in a number of areas. Are any of the following areas stressful for you and your spouse/partner?
   a. Communication _____ (43)
   b. Finances _____ (44)
   c. Affairs _____ (45)
   d. Situational factors _____ (46)
   e. Illness _____ (47)
   f. Aggressive driving _____ (48)
   g. Other _____ (49)

19. How would you rate your sexual relationship? _____ (50)

20. Do you have problems with your in-laws? _____ (51)

21. Do you have problems with your parents? _____ (52)

22. Are there any difficulties with your children? _____ (53)

23. How would you rate your satisfaction with your job? _____ (54)

24. Are there any problems? _____ (55)

25. How would you rate your relationship with coworkers? _____ (56)

26. How would you rate your relationship with your
supervisor/boss? _____ (57)

27. How would your rate your relationship with supervisees? _____ (58)

28. Do you feel like you're under a lot of pressure at work? _____ (59)

29. How would you rate how well you tolerate work stress
and pressure? _____ (60)

30. Do you feel that work-related stress is related to your
aggressive driving? _____ (61)

Are there any other major life stressors that we haven't talked about? If so,
please elaborate.

_____

_____

_____

Code as presence of other life stressor: (2 = yes, 1 = no) _____ (62)

Part 3: Psychiatric Assessment

Psychiatric Family History

1. To your knowledge, have any of your family members ever been diagnosed
or treated for any kind of mental disorder?

_____

_____

_____

Family history of mood disorder = 1;
Family history of anxiety disorder = 2;
Family history of psychotic disorder = 3;
Family history of substance abuse/dependence disorder = 4;
Family history of impulse control disorder = 5;
Other = 6; None = 0 _____ _____ _____
(63) (64) (65)

2. Has anyone in your family ever had a problem with anger management?
(Probe: Do any family members have "bad tempers"?) If yes, who? _____

Code: # of parents with problem   _____ (66)
Code: # of stepparents with problem   _____ (67)
Code: # of siblings with problem   _____ (68)
Code # of second-degree relatives with problem   _____ (69)

3. Has anyone in your family ever had a problem with aggressive behavior (i.e., getting into fistfights, physical abuse, etc.)? If yes, who? _____

Code: # of parents with problem   _____ (70)
Code: # of stepparents with problem   _____ (71)
Code: # of siblings with problem   _____ (72)
Code # of second-degree relatives with problem   _____ (73)

4. Have any of your family members been in trouble with the law, incarcerated, had restraining orders placed against them? If yes, who? _____

Code: # of parents with problem   _____ (74)
Code: # of stepparents with problem   _____ (75)
Code: # of siblings with problem   _____ (76)
Code # of second-degree relatives with problem   _____ (77)

Personal Psychiatric History

5. Have you ever received any kind of counseling, therapy, psychiatric medication, psychiatric hospitalization? Are you currently in therapy? Please explain the focus of this treatment.

Code: No treatment = 0;
Previous treatment = 1;
Currently in therapy = 2;
Previous treatment and currently in therapy = 4.   _____ (78)

6. Do you think you have a general problem with anger management? (Probe: Has anyone ever told you that you have a "bad temper" or were "hot tempered"?) If yes, describe your problem:

Code: (2 = yes, 1 = no)   _____ (79)

7. Have you ever been in trouble with the law, incarcerated, had restraining orders placed against you?

_____

_____

_____

Code: (2 = yes, 1 = no) _____ (80)

APPENDIX 4.2

Posttreatment Interview

Subject name: _____ Date: _____

Subject # _____ _____ _____ * Line _____ _____ _____
       (1)   (2)   (3)   (5)   (6)   (7)

Referral Source: 1 = Court 2 = Self

Part I: Driving Interview

Since we last talked . . .

1. How many accidents have you been involved in as the driver? _____ (10)
   (Describe any serious accidents on back page)

2. Were there any injuries? (2 = yes, 1 = no, 3 = N/A) Describe the worst one. _____ (11)

   _____
   _____
   _____
   _____

3. Was there damage to the car? (2 = yes, 1 = no, 3 = N/A) Describe worst one. _____ (12)

   _____
   _____
   _____
   _____

4. If the person had any accidents, how many citations have you been issued after an accident? _____ (13)

5. What were the nature and dates of those citations?

   _____
   _____
   _____
   _____

6. How many moving violations have you received (e.g., speeding)? _____ (14–15)

7. What were the nature and dates of those violations?

_____

_____

_____

_____

8. How many nonmoving violations have you received? _____ (16–17)

9. What was the nature of those violations?

_____

_____

_____

_____

10. Have you received any DUIs? (#)   _____ (18)

11. Have you received any DWIs? (#)   _____ (19)

12. a) Has anyone referred to your driving as aggressive?
    (2 = yes, 1 = no)   _____ (20)
    b) Who?
    Spouse/significant other = 1; Family = 2;
    Friends = 3; Other = 4; N/A = 5
    _____ (21)   _____ (22)   _____ (23)   _____ (24)

Driving Information

Since we last talked . . .

13. Has there been any change in the number of hours
    per week that you drive?
    0 = no change; 1 = drives fewer hours;
    2 = drives more hours   _____ (25)

14. Has there been any change in the number of days per
    week that you drive?
    0 = no change; 1 = drives fewer days;
    2 = drives more days   _____ (26)

15. Has there been any change in the type of roads you
    generally travel on?
    0 = no change; 1 = less busy roads; 2 = busier roads   _____ (27)

16. How many times **in the past week** would you estimate that you have experienced the following emotions while driving (if N/A, code = 9):

        Scale 1
        0 = Never
        1 = Once or twice
        2 = 3–4 times
        3 = Every day
        4 = Several times a day

    a. Irritated/angry   ____ (28)
    b. Stressed/frustrated   ____ (29)
    c. Depressed/down   ____ (30)
    d. Upset/distressed   ____ (31)
    e. Fine/normal mood   ____ (32)

Aggressive Driving (2 = yes, 1 = no, 0 = N/A)

17. I'm going to ask you about a number of common aggressive driving behaviors. These behaviors are committed with the intent to express annoyance, compete with or get even with, scare, harm, or "punish" other drivers. We are not talking about lapses in driving skill, errors, or unintentional acts. How many times **in the past week** did you engage in the following behaviors?

    a. Purposefully driving slowly with the intent to block another vehicle's passage   ____ (33–34)
    b. Tailgating   ____ (35–36)
    c. Improper passing (passing on the shoulder, passing on the right)   ____ (37–38)
    d. Failure to yield the right of way   ____ (39–40)
    e. Blocking another driver from merging   ____ (41–42)
    f. Failing to keep right   ____ (43–44)
    g. Horn honking   ____ (45–46)
    h. Flashing high beams   ____ (47–48)
    i. Deliberately using high beams from behind (keeping them on)   ____ (49–50)
    j. Failing to signal properly   ____ (51–52)
    k. "Racing" or competing with another driver (toll booths, stop lights)   ____ (53–54)
    l. Obscene gesturing   ____ (55–56)
    m. Verbal insults (covertly)   ____ (57–58)
    n. Verbal insults (overtly)   ____ (59–60)
    o. throwing objects   ____ (61–62)

p. Physical assault (on another vehicle or individual) ____ (63–64)
q. Giving chase to another driver ____ (65–66)
r. Feeling angry at another driver ____ (67–68)
s. Wishing harm to another driver ____ (69–70)
t. Feeling impatient at intersections ____ (71–72)
u. Feeling upset at delays, other drivers, etc. ____ (73–74)
v. Other (specify) _____ ____ (75–76)

18. **For the past week**, please rate the following driving situations on the degree of annoyance or anger that they aroused in you. Answers should be based on the following scale:

    Scale 4
      4 = Enraged
      3 = Mad/very angry
      2 = Aggravated/ indignant
      1 = Annoyed/irritated
      0 = Not at all/no effect
      9 = N/A

a. Traffic jams/heavy traffic ____ (77)
b. Stoplights ____ (78)
c. Being cut off ____ (79)
d. Women drivers driving poorly ____ (80)
e. Men drivers driving poorly ____ (10)
f. Elderly drivers driving poorly ____ (11)
g. Young drivers driving poorly ____ (12)
h. Different ethnic groups driving poorly ____ (13)
i. The driver of an old, rusty "clunker" driving poorly ____ (14)
j. Toll booth situations ____ (15)
k. Following a slow driver in the left lane ____ (16)
l. A slow pedestrian holding you up ____ (17)
m. People driving slowly in poor weather conditions ____ (18)
n. Crowded parking lots ____ (19)
o. Someone taking "your" parking space ____ (20)
p. Being unable to find a parking spot ____ (21)
q. Temperature extremes (hot or cold) ____ (22)
r. Rush hour traffic ____ (23)
s. Drivers who pass you in excess of the speed limit ____ (24)
t. People who attempt to merge into your lane of traffic ____ (25)
u. Being tailgated ____ (26)
v. Being flashed by high beams ____ (27)
w. Being honked at ____ (28)
x. Feeling others aren't obeying the traffic laws ____ (29)

For the person's most angering/annoying situation . . .

19. During (this situation), what did you think about:
    a. The other driver? _____
    b. Drivers in general? _____
    c. Road conditions? _____
    d. Your ability to drive effectively? _____
    e. The unfairness of the situation? _____

    Clinician rating: N/A = 9
                        Improved in maladaptive cognitions = 2
                        Worsened in maladaptive cognitions = 1
                        No change in maladaptive cognitions = 0
                                                            _____ (30)

20. During (this situation), how did you feel:
    a. Physically? _____
    b. Emotionally? _____
    c. Mentally? _____

21. For how long did you feel this way? _____

    Clinician rating: N/A = 9
                        Physically improved = 2
                        Physically worsened = 1
                        No change = 0   _____ (31)

    Clinician rating: N/A = 9
                        Emotionally improved = 2
                        Emotionally worsened = 1
                        No change = 0   _____ (32)

22. How did you handle the situation?
    a. _____
    _____
    _____

    Clinician rating: N/A = 9
                        Behaviorally improved = 2
                        Behaviorally worsened = 1
                        No change = 0   _____ (33)

Part 2: Psychosocial Assessment

Scale 5
4 = Very good
3 = Good
2 = Fair
1 = Poor
0 = Very poor
9 = N/A

Since we last talked . . .

1. How would you describe your relationship with your parents? _____ (34)

2. How would you describe your relationships with your siblings? _____ (35)

3. How would you describe your relationships with your children? _____ (36)

4. How would you describe your relationship with your spouse/partner? _____ (37)

5. How would you rate your sexual relationship? _____ (38)

6. How would you rate your relationship with your in-laws? _____ (39)

7. How would you describe your current number and quality of friendships? _____ (40)

8. How would you describe your relationships with authority figures? _____ (41)

9. How would you rate your satisfaction with your job/school? _____ (42)

10. How would you describe your current work/school performance? _____ (43)

11. How would you rate your relationships with co-workers? _____ (44)

12. How would you rate your relationship with your supervisor/boss? _____ (45)

13. How would your rate your relationships with supervisees? _____ (46)

14. How would you rate how well you tolerate work stress and pressure? _____ (47)

Since we last talked, are there any new major stressors in your life? If so, please elaborate.

_____

_____

_____

_____

_____

Code presence of new life stressor: (2 = yes, 1 = no)   _____ (48)

Part 3: Psychiatric Assessment

Personal Psychiatric History

15. Since we last talked, have you ever received any kind of counseling, therapy, psychiatric medication, psychiatric hospitalization? [If person was in therapy at initial assessment, ask the following question.] Are you currently in therapy? Please explain the focus of this treatment.

    _____

    _____

    _____

    _____

    Code: No treatment = 0;
    Received treatment since last assessment,
        but not currently in therapy = 1;
    Currently in therapy = 2.   _____ (49)

16. Since we last talked, have you had any general problems with anger management? [Probe with the following if necessary.] Has anyone recently commented that you have a "bad temper" or were "hot tempered"? If yes, describe your problem:

    _____

    _____

    Code: (2 = yes, 1 = no)   _____ (50)

17. Since we last talked, have you been in trouble with the law, incarcerated, or had restraining orders placed against you?

    _____

    _____

    Code: (2 = yes; 1 = no)   _____ (51)

Note: Because it would be not be possible for individuals negative for attention-deficit/hyperactivity disorder (ADHD) at the initial interview to meet criteria for it at posttreatment, ADHD symptoms are not reassessed at posttreatment/wait list or at the 2-month follow-up in individuals who did not meet at least subsyndromal criteria at the initial assessment. Because ADHD, if present at the initial assessment, is highly unlikely to spontaneously remit within a 4- to 8-week period, and treatment does not target problems with attention or hyperactivity, ADHD symptoms are also not reassessed at posttreatment/wait list or at the 2-month follow-up in individuals who met criteria for full or subsyndromal ADHD at the initial assessment. However, if the individual was positive for either full or subsyndromal ADHD at the initial assessment and has since received treatment for it, he or she should be reassessed for the presence of current symptoms using the ADHD interview from the initial assessment.

Since we last talked . . .

1. Have you behaved in an impulsive, aggressive manner that resulted in harm to someone or destruction of objects or other property?

   _____

   _____

   _____

   a. How many times has this occurred? _____
   (Code # of episodes with SCID–I under IED)
   b. Please describe the most recent episode:
   #1) _____

   _____

   _____

   _____

   What provoked this incident? _____

   _____

   _____

   Do you feel as if the incident warranted such behavior?

   _____

   _____

   On a scale of 0–100, where 0 = *no control* and 100 = *total control*, how much control of yourself did you feel during this incident? (Code with SCID–I under IED) _____

   Please describe one other recent incident (since time of last assessment):
   #2) _____

   _____

   _____

What provoked this incident?

_____

_____

Do you feel as if the incident warranted such behavior?

_____

On a scale of 0–100, where 0 = *no control* and 100 = *total control*, how much control of yourself did you feel during this incident? (Code with SCID–I under IED) _____

_____

Note. DUI = driving under the influence; DWI = driving while intoxicated; SCID = Structured Clinical Interview for *DSM–IV*; IED = intermittent explosive disorder.

5

PSYCHIATRIC MORBIDITY AMONG AGGRESSIVE DRIVERS

As we mentioned in chapter 4, we routinely conducted structured psychiatric interviews on the treatment-seeking aggressive driving samples so that we would be able to describe the psychological and psychiatric aspects of these participants from a categorical perspective to complement the dimensional perspective (psychological tests) provided in chapter 6. We used the Structured Clinical Interview for Axis I *DSM–IV* Disorders (SCID; First, Spitzer, Gibbon, & Williams, 1996) to diagnose *Diagnostic and Statistical Manual of Mental Disorders* (4th ed. [*DSM–IV*]; American Psychiatric Association, 1994) Axis I disorders, and the SCID–II (First, Spitzer, Gibbon, Williams, & Benjamin, 1996) to diagnose Axis II personality disorders. In addition, we used a SCID-like interview module, modeled after the work of McElroy, Soutullo, Beckman, Taylor, and Keck (1998), to assess for intermittent explosive disorder (IED) among all participants. We describe this in more detail later in the chapter.

Beginning with the second cohort of court-referred aggressive drivers, and continuing with the student sample of aggressive drivers identified by the Driver's Stress Profile (DSP; Larson, 1996a), we also used structured interviews to assess for attention-deficit/hyperactivity disorder (ADHD), both earlier as a child and currently as an adult, and for possible oppositional defiant disorder, using the structured interview developed by Barkley and

TABLE 5.1
Reliability Coefficients for Current and Lifetime Diagnoses

Diagnosis	n	Current diagnosis		Lifetime diagnosis	
		κ	SE	κ	SE
Attention-deficit/hyperactivity disorder	40	.73	.14	.81	.10
History of conduct disorder	19			.92	.08
Oppositional defiant disorder	40	.82	.10	.86	.08
Intermittent explosive disorder	24	.83	.16	.83	.12
Major depressive disorder	40	.90	.10	.90	.07
Anxiety disorders	94	.91	.04	.90	.04
Alcohol abuse/dependence	33	.81	.13	.92	.08
Substance abuse/dependence	26	1.00	.00	.93	.08
Cluster A personality disorders	27	.86	.12		
Cluster B personality disorders	88	.88	.08		
Cluster C personality disorders	45	.80	.10		

Note. Sample sizes for each diagnostic category differ because (a) diagnoses scored as "absent" because of negative responses to Structured Clinical Interview for DSM–IV Axis I Disorders and Structured Clinical Interview for DSM–IV Axis II Disorders screen questions were not included in the reliability analyses, and (b) composite categories such as personality disorders/anxiety disorders included multiple diagnoses. For all values displayed here, $p = .001$.

Murphy (1998), known as the Attention Deficit Disorder and Oppositional Defiant Disorder Interview.

INTERRATER RELIABILITY

An important part of categorical assessments is interrater reliability. We tape-recorded the interviews for part of the treatment-seeking sample and for the student aggressive drivers. An advanced doctoral student in clinical psychology, with several years of experience in assessing psychiatric populations with the SCID and SCID–II, rescored these tapes while being kept unaware of the initial interviewee's diagnosis or subgroup membership.[1] Kappa values for interrater agreement for disorders commonly found in these populations are listed in Table 5.1.

As can be seen, the kappas for diagnostic agreement were very good to excellent, with all values but one (current ADHD) at .80 or higher. Thus, we believe that our data on reliability of psychiatric diagnoses are of very high quality.

---

[1] We thank Brian Freidenberg for his assistance in this part of our research.

DIAGNOSIS OF INTERMITTENT EXPLOSIVE DISORDER

As we noted earlier, IED is an understudied condition, a point that has been made by several authors who have written about the disorder from a clinical perspective (Lion, 1992; McElroy, 1999) or from the perspective of the clinical researcher (Coccaro, Kavoussi, Berman, & Lish, 1998; Felthous, Bryant, Wingerter, & Barratt, 1991; Mattes & Fink, 1987; McElroy et al., 1998). The reasons for the relative inattention to IED could be its relative rarity (Bryant, Felthous, & Barratt, 1993; Felthous et al., 1991; Monopolis & Lion, 1983) or that individuals with this problem are more likely to be found in the criminal justice system than in the mental health system; that is, they are "bad," not "mad" (Felthous, Bryant, Wingerter, & Barratt, 1991; Lion, 1992; McElroy et al., 1998).

In essence, patients (a) who periodically act very aggressively, resulting in serious assaultive acts or property damage; (b) whose degree of aggression is grossly out of proportion to any provocation or precipitating stressor; and (c) whose behavior cannot be better accounted for by other disorders are diagnosed, according to *DSM–IV* (American Psychiatric Association, 1994, p. 612), with IED. In earlier times, such individuals might have been diagnosed with explosive personality disorder in *Diagnostic and Statistical Manual of Mental Disorders* (2nd. ed.; American Psychiatric Association, 1968), or with "episodic dyscontrol syndrome" (Maletzky, 1973).

Reference to the offenses for which our court-referred aggressive drivers were convicted (see upper portion of Table 4.2) gives one a sense of an aggressive driving response out of proportion to whatever provocation may have been experienced on the roadways. The same can be said of the officials described in our introductory newspaper story or the vignettes in chapter 1. These offenses and others like them across U.S. highways gave birth to the term *road rage*. Because some of our participants seemed to react in an aggressive fashion out of proportion to the provocation, we assessed all treatment-seeking aggressive drivers for IED. We also assessed the student sample that was in the highest 16% on the DSP for IED.

It should be noted that a single aggressive driving offense, no matter how severe, would not be enough to warrant a diagnosis of IED. Instead, we were looking for a pattern of several overaggressive assaultive acts or incidents of property damage out of proportion to any provocation to lead us to diagnose IED.

The *DSM–IV* suggests that one take into account possible exclusionary comorbidity such as borderline personality disorder (BPD), antisocial personality disorder (ASPD), mania, and ADHD. Presence of these comorbid conditions are not, however, absolute exclusions. Instead, the recommendation seeks to determine whether one could better account for the repeated aggressive acts out of proportion to provocation by the other disorders.

Various attempts to deal with comorbidity and exclusion in diagnosing IED have been proposed. For example, Coccaro et al. (1998) proposed research criteria for IED that do not exclude the diagnosis of IED on the basis of any Axis II comorbidity. However, they added two diagnostic criteria: (a) The aggressive behavior is generally not premeditated and is not committed to achieve a tangible objective (money, power, etc.) and (b) aggressive outbursts occur twice a week, on average, for at least 1 month.

Mattes and Fink (1987) took a similar approach by waiving all Axis II exclusionary criteria (but retaining exclusions of individuals with psychotic disorders or bipolar disorder). They did not adopt Coccaro et al.'s (1998) frequency criteria.

Felthous et al. (1991) took the opposite tack in their study of 443 self-referred men with a history of violence. Only 79 (17.8%) showed recurrent aggressive episodes without provocation and were free of any other diagnosable psychopathology. Only 15 of the men (3.4%) met all *Diagnostic and Statistical Manual of Mental Disorders* (3rd ed. [*DSM–III*]; American Psychiatric Association, 1980) criteria for IED.

The middle ground was used by McElroy et al. (1998) in a study of 27 individuals with IED, most of whom were convicted felons or referred by other mental health practitioners. McElroy et al. (1998) used *DSM–IV* criteria and developed a structured interview modeled after the SCID. They took the stance of interviewing in detail, when comorbid exclusionary diagnoses were present, to decide whether the aggressive episodes were best explained by the comorbid disorder or by IED. We have followed this path.

Thus, for example, we saw a female patient with BPD who assaulted her ex-boyfriend's automobile, causing hundreds of dollars of damage, after he had broken off the relationship. This overly aggressive episode without adequate provocation was judged to be part of Criterion 1 of BPD: extreme or frantic efforts to avoid real or potential or imagined abandonment. Thus, this episode would not count toward meeting the criteria for IED.

Our structured interview for IED is quite brief, in line with the *DSM–IV* criteria. It was administered in the context of also administering the SCID and SCID–II to make the interviewer aware of possible comorbid conditions that should be investigated so that appropriate follow-up questions could be asked. It is presented in Exhibit 5.1.

DESCRIPTIVE STUDIES OF INTERMITTENT EXPLOSIVE DISORDER

Because our work with treatment-seeking aggressive drivers has led us to IED, we here include some background on IED research. In one of the best studies of IED diagnosed by *DSM–IV* criteria, McElroy et al. (1998)

EXHIBIT 5.1
Intermittent Explosive Disorder Interview

Subject Name: _____

Subject #: _____

Date: _____

Criterion A. *Several discrete episodes of failure to resist aggressive impulses that result in serious assaultive acts or destruction of property.*

Criterion B. *The degree of aggressiveness expressed during the episode is grossly out of proportion to any precipitating psychosocial stressors.*

Criterion C. *The aggressive episodes are not better accounted for by another mental disorder (ASPD, BPD, psychosis, mania, CD, ADHD)*

A1. Do you feel as if you've ever behaved in an impulsive, aggressive manner that resulted in harm to someone or destruction of property?

_____

_____

_____

  a. How many times has this occurred? _____ (Code # of episodes with SCID–I under IED)

  b. Please describe the worst two:

  Incident #1

  _____

  What provoked this incident?

  _____

  Do you feel as if the incident warranted such behavior?

  _____

  On a scale of 0–100, where 0 = *no control* and 100 = *total control*, how much in control of yourself did you feel during this incident? (Code with SCID–I under IED) _____

  Incident #2

  _____

  What provoked this incident?

  _____

  Do you feel as if the incident warranted such behavior?

  _____

  On a scale of 0–100, where 0 = *no control* and 100 = *total control*, how much in control of yourself did you feel during this incident? (Code with SCID–I under IED) _____

(continued)

EXHIBIT 5.1
Intermittent Explosive Disorder Interview *(Continued)*

c. Please describe the most recent episode:

_____

_____

What provoked this incident?

_____

Do you feel as if the incident(s) warranted such behavior?

_____

On a scale of 0–100, where 0 = *no control* and 100 = *total control*, how much in control of yourself did you feel during this incident? (Code with SCID–I under IED) _____

Diagnostic Summary (Code With SCID–I)

(0 = absent; 1 = evidence of some problems, but does not meet criteria for subsyndromal; 2 = subsyndromal; 3 = present). *Note*: For subsyndromal diagnosis, person must meet full criteria for either A or B and meet full criteria for C.

Current: _____   **Lifetime:** _____

Note. ASPD = antisocial personality disorder; BPD = borderline personality disorder; CD = conduct disorder; ADHD = attention deficit/hyperactivity disorder; SCID–I = Structured Clinical Interview for *DSM–IV* Axis I Disorders.

studied 27 individuals with IED, most of whom were convicted felons or referred by other mental health practitioners. Data on comorbid Axis I disorders showed a high prevalence of current (89%) and lifetime (93%) mood disorders and a relatively high prevalence of current (37%) and lifetime (48%) anxiety disorders and lifetime substance abuse (48%). Detailed data on the phenomenology of the aggressive episodes also were presented, including 88% acknowledging "tension arising with impulses," 75% acknowledging "relief after the aggressive act," 92% acknowledging irritability or rage accompanying impulses to act, and 79% acknowledging these same affective states during the act. Despite the very informative nature of the study (including retrospective reports of which drug treatments had helped), the study suffered from three deficits: (a) No patient control or normal control participants were assessed; (b) Axis II disorders were assessed clinically, rather than with structured diagnostic instruments; and (c) no dimensional assessments with psychological tests were performed.

Some of these problems were corrected in a study by Coccaro et al. (1998) that included 188 individuals, all of whom had personality disorders that had been carefully diagnosed with the Structured Interview for *DSM–III–R* Personality Disorders (Pfohl & Zimmerman, 1989). In this way they circumvented exclusion based on presence of ASPD or BPD. Coccaro et al. compared patients who had personality disorders and who met their revised criteria for IED with patients who had personality disorders who did not meet the criteria on presence of other Axis I disorders (as diagnosed by the Schedule for Affective Disorders and Schizophrenia—Lifetime; Spitzer & Endicott, 1977) and on several psychological dimensions such as impulsiveness and state anxiety aggression. This study thus lacked a nonpatient control population (i.e., persons without personality disorders). Patients with IED had higher prevalence of current mood disorders (39.5% vs. 22.3%) and lifetime mood disorder diagnoses (72.4% vs. 44.6%) as well as drug use disorders (36.8% vs. 18.8%). The groups did not differ on current or lifetime anxiety disorders. It is interesting that 33% of the IED sample, versus only 6% of the non-IED group, met criteria for BPD. Thus, the IED sample is very heavily weighted toward BPD and, by definition, all participants had an Axis II disorder.

In a third descriptive study of patients with "temper outbursts," Mattes and Fink (1987) relaxed two of the *DSM–III* criteria for IED: (a) absence of generalized aggressiveness between episodes and (b) presence of exclusionary diagnoses. They excluded patients with a comorbid diagnosis of psychotic disorder or bipolar disorder. For 33 patients with temper outbursts, 22 met their relaxed criteria for IED, 16 had residual attention-deficit disorder, 15 had alcoholism, and 16 had drug abuse (there were multiple diagnoses).

These patients acknowledged 18.6 verbal outbursts per month over the previous 6 months, 5.8 outbursts per month involving destruction of property, and 1.6 assaults per month. Fourteen had spent some time in jail because of assaultive behavior, but most stays were for only 1 to 2 nights. In the family study portion of the report, Mattes and Fink (1987) stated that 6.9% of first-degree relatives of patients with IED met criteria for IED themselves, and 13.8% of relatives had temper problems.

PSYCHIATRIC MORBIDITY AMONG TREATMENT-SEEKING AGGRESSIVE DRIVERS

To make the data on psychiatric morbidity more understandable and to reduce the number of comparisons, in Table 5.2 we have tabulated the frequencies and percentages of the court-referred and self-referred samples who met criteria for various Axis I disorders; similar data on Axis II disorders are tabulated in Table 5.3.

We have adopted two conventions in assessing Axis II disorders: First, we administered the SCID–II screening questionnaire before the interview. If a participant was positive on the screening questionnaire for the number of symptoms needed to meet criteria for the disorder, or one symptom fewer than the number needed to meet the criteria, then all of the items for

TABLE 5.2
Summary of Psychiatric Morbidity for Treatment-Seeking Aggressive Drivers and Community Control Participants: Axis I Disorders

Disorder	Groups								Analyses (p)	
	Court referred (n = 37)		Self-referred (n = 12)		All tx-seeking (n = 39)		Community controls (n = 30)		Court versus self	Agg. drivers versus controls
	Freq.	%	Freq.	%	Freq.	%	Freq.	%		
Anxiety disorders—current										
Specific phobia	3	8.1	1	8.3	4	8.2			ns	
Social phobia	1	2.7	1	8.3	2	4.1			ns	
Panic disorder	0	0	2	16.6	2	4.1			.01	
OCD	0	0	4	33.3	4	8.2			< .001	
PTSD	0	0	0	0	0	0				
GAD	2	5.4	3	25.0	5	10.2			.05	
Any current anxiety disorders	5	13.5	5	41.7	10	20.4	2	6.7	.04	.099
Anxiety disorders—past										
Social phobia	0	0	1	8.3	1	2.0			.08	
PTSD	1	2.7	4	32.3	5	10.2			.002	
Panic disorder	0	0	1	8.3	1	2.0			.08	
Any past anxiety disorder	3	8.1	5	4.7	8	16.3	3	10.0	.006	ns
Mood disorders—current										
Major depressive disorder	1	2.7	0	0	1	2.0			.57	
Dysthymia	1	2.7	0	0	1	2.0			.57	
Bipolar II	0	0	1	8.3	1	2.0			.08	
Mood disorder NOS	2	5.4	0	0	2	4.1			ns	
Any current mood disorder	4	10.8	1	8.3	5	10.2	0	0	ns	.071
Mood disorders—past										
Major depressive disorder	5	13.5	4	33.3	9	18.4			.12	
Mood disorder NOS	1	2.7	0	0	1	2.0			ns	
Any past mood disorder	5	13.5	5	41.7	10	20.4	6	20	.04	ns

	Freq.	%	Freq.	%	Freq.	%	p	Freq.	%	p
Somatoform disorders										
Somatization disorder	0	0	1	8.3	1	2.0	.08			
Body dysmorphic disorder	1	2.7	0	0	1	2.0	ns			
Eating disorders										
Binge eating disorder	0	0	1	8.3	1	2.0	.08			
Intermittent explosive disorder	12	32.4	4	33.3	16	32.7	ns	0	0	< .001
Alcohol and drug disorders—current										
Alcohol abuse	5	13.5	3	25.0	8	16.3	.19			
Alcohol dependence	2	5.4	0	0	2	4.1	ns			
Substance abuse	3	8.1	0	0	3	6.1	ns			
Substance dependence	2	5.4	0	0	2	4.1	ns			
Any current alcohol or drug disorder	10	27.0	3	25.0	13	26.5	ns	0	0	.002
Alcohol and drug disorders—past										
Alcohol abuse	8	21.6	4	33.3	12	24.5	ns			
Alcohol dependence	4	10.8	2	16.6	6	12.2	ns			
Substance abuse	4	10.8	2	16.6	6	12.2	ns			
Substance dependence	1	2.7	1	8.3	2	4.1	ns			
Any past alcohol or drug disorder	16	48.2	4	33.3	19	38.8	ns	2	6.7	.002
Any Axis I disorder current	20	54.1	8	66.7	28	57.7	.44	2	6.7	< .001
Any Axis I disorder past/current	29	78.4	9	75.0	38	77.6	ns	11	36.7	< .001

Note. tx = treatment; Agg. = aggressive; Freq. = frequency; OCD = obsessive–compulsive disorder; PTSD = posttraumatic stress disorder; GAD = generalized anxiety disorder; NOS = not otherwise specified.

TABLE 5.3
Summary of Psychiatric Morbidity for Treatment-Seeking Aggressive Drivers and Community Controls:
Axis II Personality Disorders

| | Group | | | | | | | | Analyses (p) | |
| Disorder | Court-referred (n = 37) | | Self-referred (n = 12) | | All tx-seeking (n = 49) | | Community controls (n = 30) | | Court versus self | Agg. versus controls |
	Freq.	%	Freq.	%	Freq.	%	Freq.	%		
Antisocial PD	8	20.5	1	8.3	9	18.4	0	0	ns	.013
Antisocial PD[a]	12	32.4	3	25.0	15	28.6	0	0	ns	.001
Borderline PD	2	5.4	3	25.0	5	10.2	0	0	.05	.071
Narcissistic PD	5	13.5	0	0	5	10.2	0	0	.18	.071
Histrionic PD	2	5.4	1	8.3	3	6.1	0	0	ns	ns
OCPD	1	2.7	3	25.0	4	8.2	2	6.7	.01	ns
Avoidant PD	1	2.7	1	8.3	1	2.0	0	0	ns	ns
Paranoid PD	4	10.8	2	16.6	6	8.2	0	0	ns	.046
Any Axis II PD	15	40.5	6	50.0	21	42.9	2	6.7	ns	.001

Note. tx = treatment; Agg. = aggressive; Freq. = frequency; PD = personality disorder; OCPD = obsessive–compulsive personality disorder.
[a]This row includes participants who met criteria for adult antisocial PD criteria but did not meet criteria for conduct disorder.

that personality disorder were asked. If a participant acknowledged fewer symptoms on the screening questionnaire, then that particular personality disorder was omitted from the interview to save time.

Second, in the interest of presenting as much data as possible on the Axis II disorders, we have described a participant as having a subthreshold personality disorder if he or she fully met one fewer than the required minimum number of symptoms (e.g., he or she was positive for four of nine symptoms of BPD instead of the minimum of five). Also, if the participant met the adult symptom criteria for ASPD but did not meet criteria for conduct disorder, we labeled him or her as subthreshold. Following the analytic scheme that Galovski, Blanchard, and Veazey (2002) described in an earlier report on psychiatric disorders found in part of this sample, we compared court-referred and self-referred aggressive drivers on each of the categories and on the summary categories.

We were also able to recruit a group of community volunteers who denied any difficulties with aggressive driving. They were paid to undergo the diagnostic interviews. Their results for the summary diagnostic categories are presented in Tables 5.2 and 5.3. This sample was recruited as part of the Galovski et al. (2002) study and were matched to the Cohort 1 court-referred and self-referred aggressive drivers on age and gender. The comparison sample was 33% female and had an average age of 34.5 years (SD = 12.4). As a second step in the analyses, we compared all treatment-seeking aggressive drivers combined with the community volunteers on summary categories.

Court-Referred Versus Self-Referred Aggressive Drivers

An examination of Table 5.2 reveals that for anxiety disorders, significantly higher percentages of the self-referred aggressive driver group met criteria for current panic disorder, obsessive–compulsive disorder, and generalized anxiety disorder than the court-referred group. The self-referred group (41.7%) also had a significantly (p = .04) higher percentage of any current anxiety disorder than the court-referred group (13.5%). The self-referred group also had a significantly higher percentage of past posttraumatic stress disorder than the court-referred group, as well as a higher percentage (41.7%) of any past anxiety disorder than the court-referred group (8.1%).

In regard to mood disorders, there were no significant differences on any individual current mood disorder or the summary value. In regard to past mood disorders, the self-referred group (33.3%) did acknowledge more past major depression than the court-referred group (13.5%). The summary value for any past mood disorder was significant.

For alcohol and other substance-related problems (abuse or dependence), there were no significant differences between the two treatment-seeking groups on current or past diagnoses or on the summary statistical comparisons. In fact, the samples are quite similar, with 27% of court-referred participants and 25% of self-referred participants having a current diagnosable substance-related condition. It is very important to note that there were no differences between the two groups of treatment-seeking aggressive drivers on IED (32.4% of court-referred drivers vs. 33.3% of self-referred drivers).

Turning now to the data on Axis II personality disorders in Table 5.3, one sees that the self-referred group had significantly greater percentages of participants who met criteria for BPD and obsessive–compulsive personality disorder (OCPD) than the court-referred group. However, the court-referred group had a significantly greater percentage of members who met criteria for narcissistic personality disorder (NPD). Again, the two groups of aggressive drivers were similar in whether they met criteria for any Axis II disorder, with self-referred (50%) drivers slightly more likely to do so than court-referred (40.5%) aggressive drivers.

All Treatment-Seeking Aggressive Drivers Versus the Community Sample

Returning again to Table 5.2, one sees, in regard to Axis I disorders, a trend for aggressive drivers to be more likely to meet criteria for a current anxiety disorder and current mood disorders than the community control participants. There were no differences in past anxiety or mood disorders. The aggressive drivers (26.5%) were significantly more likely to meet criteria for current alcohol or substance disorders than the control participants (0%) but showed only a trend to be more likely to meet criteria for past alcohol or substance disorders. It is not surprising that the aggressive drivers were significantly ($p < .001$) more likely to meet criteria for IED than the community control participants.

An examination of the Axis II data in Table 5.4 reveals that the aggressive drivers, as a group, were significantly more likely than the control participants to meet criteria for ASPD and paranoid personality disorder, with trends for more NPD and paranoid personality disorder. Moreover, the aggressive drivers (42.9%) were also significantly more likely than the controls (6.7%) to meet criteria for any Axis II disorder.

The results described above extend those previously reported by Galovski et al. (2002) in that they include the data from our second cohort of treatment-seeking aggressive drivers (see Table 4.1). In all instances, the differences that Galovski et al. (2002) reported as significant remain significant; in some instances—for example, BPD, OCPD, and NPD—directional differences became significant with the expanded sample.

TABLE 5.4
Axis I Psychiatric Disorders Among College Students Who Reported
High Levels of Aggressive Driving

Diagnosis	Subsyndromal		Full	
	Freq.	%	Freq.	%
Current intermittent explosive disorder	2	3.8	2	3.8
Lifetime intermittent explosive disorder	2	3.8	7	13.2
Current oppositional defiant disorder	8	15.1	6	11.3
Lifetime oppositional defiant disorder	11	20.8	4	22.6
Current attention-deficit/hyperactivity disorder	2	3.8	4	7.5
Childhood attention-deficit/hyperactivity disorder	6	11.3	6	11.3
Mood disorders				
Current major depressive disorder	0		4	7.5
Current dysthymia	0		0	
Current bipolar I and II	0		0	
Current mood disorder NOS	0		0	
Any current mood disorder	0		4	7.5
Lifetime major depressive disorder	3	5.7	13	24.5
Lifetime bipolar	0		0	
Lifetime mood disorder NOS	0		2	3.8
Any lifetime mood disorder	3	5.7	15	28.3
Anxiety disorders				
Current panic disorder	1	1.9	2	3.8
Current social phobia	1	1.9	8	15.1
Current specific phobia	3	5.7	10	18.9
Current obsessive–compulsive disorder	1	1.9	2	3.8
Current generalized anxiety disorder	2	3.8	1	1.9
Current posttraumatic stress disorder	1	1.9	0	
Current anxiety disorder NOS	1	1.9	1	1.9
Any current anxiety disorder	5	9.4	16	30.2
Lifetime panic disorder	2	3.8	3	5.7
Lifetime social phobia	1	1.9	8	15.1
Lifetime specific phobia	3	5.7	13	24.5
Lifetime obsessive–compulsive disorder	1	1.9	5	9.4
Lifetime posttraumatic stress disorder	3	5.7	1	1.9
Lifetime anxiety disorder NOS	0		2	3.8
Any lifetime anxiety disorder	5	9.4	24	45.3
Somatoform disorders	0		2	3.8
Eating disorders	0		2	3.8
Alcohol and substance abuse/dependence				
Current alcohol abuse	0		4	7.5
Current alcohol dependence	0		7	13.2
Current drug abuse	0		2	3.8
Current drug dependence	0		6	11.3
Any current substance disorder	0		16	30.2
Lifetime alcohol abuse	0		4	7.5
Lifetime alcohol dependence	0		11	20.8
Lifetime drug abuse	0		3	5.7
Lifetime drug dependence	0		15	28.3
Any lifetime substance disorder				
Psychotic symptoms	0		0	

Note. N = 53. Freq. = frequency; NOS = not otherwise specified.

Treatment-Seeking Aggressive Drivers With Intermittent Explosive Disorder Versus Treatment-Seeking Aggressive Drivers Without Intermittent Explosive Disorder

As we noted earlier in this chapter, there is a relative scarcity of data, especially data on psychiatric comorbidity, on individuals who meet criteria for IED. We are in the fortunate position of having a set of treatment-seeking aggressive drivers who met criteria for IED ($N = 16$) and what could be considered an excellent comparison group: treatment-seeking aggressive drivers who do not meet criteria for IED ($N = 33$). The two groups are thus equated on critical variables: They are seeking treatment for the same anger–aggression problem, aggressive driving. Also of interest is that our three subsamples contain roughly equivalent percentages of aggressive drivers who meet criteria for IED: court-referred Sample 1 (7/20 = 35%), the self-referred sample (3/10 = 30%), and court-referred Sample 2 (6/19 = 31.6%). Thus, there is not a referral source bias.

Table 5.5 subdivides the treatment-seeking aggressive driver sample into IED positive versus IED negative, and it presents a summary of Axis I groupings as well as Axis II data. Comparisons of the diagnostic results in Table 5.5 reveal a significantly higher likelihood of a current mood disorder among aggressive drivers with IED (23.5%) than among comparable drivers without IED (3.1%). There were no differences in current or past anxiety disorders or current or past alcohol or substance disorders.

Although participants with IED are more likely to meet criteria for several individual personality disorders, only in the category that includes presence of any Axis II disorder do those with IED (64.7%) show a significantly higher likelihood than those without IED (31.3%). There is also a difference on ASPD when the subthreshold cases are included (IED, 52.9% vs. no IED, 18.8%).

Non-Treatment-Seeking College Student Sample With High Aggressive Driving

As described in chapter 4, we identified those college students from Malta's (2004) large survey who scored 1 standard deviation or higher on the DSP (Larson, 1996a), a self-report measure of aggressive driving. Fifty-three of these individuals answered a number of additional questionnaires and took part in the previously described series of structured psychiatric diagnostic interviews. The results from those interviews are summarized in Tables 5.4 and 5.6.

Among these relatively high-functioning young adults, we find very little current mood disorder (7.5%) but a higher level of current anxiety disorders (30.2%). Much of the latter is due to social phobia or specific

TABLE 5.5

Summary of Psychiatric Morbidity (Axis I and Axis II) for
Treatment-Seeking Aggressive Drivers as a Function of Presence of
Intermittent Explosive Disorder (IED)

Disorder	IED present ($n = 17$)		IED absent ($n = 32$)		Analysis	
	Freq.	%	Freq.	%	$\chi^2(1, N = 49)$	p
Any current anxiety disorder	5	29.4	5	15.6	1.30	ns
Any past anxiety disorder	3	17.6	5	15.6	0.03	ns
Any current mood disorder	4	23.5	1	3.1	5.05	.025
Any past mood disorder	3	17.6	7	21.9		
Current alcohol abuse/dependence	2	11.8	8	25.0	1.20	ns
Current substance abuse/dependence	3	17.6	3	9.4	0.71	ns
Any current alcohol or drug abuse	4	23.5	9	28.1	0.12	ns
Past alcohol abuse/dependence	8	47.1	11	34.4	0.75	ns
Past substance abuse/dependence	4	23.5	3	9.4	1.82	ns
Any past alcohol or drug dependence	9	52.9	12	37.5	1.08	ns
Any current Axis I disorder[a]	7	41.2	13	40.6	0.01	ns
Any current/past Axis I	13	76.5	24	66.7	0.01	ns
Antisocial disorder	5	29.4	4	12.5	2.12	.15
Antisocial disorder + sub-antisocial disorder	9	52.9	6	18.8	6.11	.013
Borderline disorder	3	17.6	2	6.3	1.57	ns
Narcissistic disorder	3	17.6	2	6.3	1.57	ns
Histrionic disorder	2	11.8	1	3.1	1.44	ns
Obsessive–compulsive disorder	1	5.9	3	9.4	0.18	ns
Paranoid disorder	3	17.6	3	9.4	0.71	ns
Any Axis II disorder	11	64.7	10	31.3	5.07	.024

Note. Freq. = frequency; PD = personality disorder; sub- = subsyndromal.
[a]Excludes IED.

phobia. Not unexpectedly, there are reasonably high levels of current alcohol and drug problems (30.2%) and noticeable histories of alcohol and substance problems.

When the data from Table 5.4 are compared with the data on treatment-seeking aggressive drivers summarized in Table 5.2, the results are similar for current anxiety disorders (30.2% for students vs. 20.4% for treatment seekers), current mood disorders (7.5% for students vs. 10.2% for treatment seekers), and current alcohol and substance problems (30.2% for students vs. 26.5% for treatment seekers).

The major Axis I difference between the treatment-seeking aggressive drivers and college students who scored high on aggressive driving is the prevalence of IED. For the treatment seekers, 32.7% meet full criteria for IED; in comparison, among the college students only 3.8% meet full criteria for IED, with a total of 13.2% meeting the criteria over their lifetimes. A comparison of these two rates reveals that it is highly significant ($p < .001$)

TABLE 5.6
Axis II Personality Disorders Among College Students Who Reported
High Levels of Aggressive Driving

Diagnosis	Subsyndromal		Full	
	Freq.	%	Freq.	%
Avoidant PD				
Dependent PD			1	1.9
OCPD	5	9.4	4	7.5
Paranoid PD	2	3.8	5	9.4
Schizotypal PD	1	1.9	1	1.9
Schizoid PD				
Histrionic PD				
Narcissistic PD	1	1.9	2	3.8
Borderline PD	3	5.7	4	7.5
Antisocial PD	4	7.5	3	5.7
History of conduct disorder	6	11.3	7	13.2
Any Axis II disorder			14	26.4

Note. Freq. = frequency; PD = personality disorder; OCPD = obsessive–compulsive personality disorder.

in regard to currently meeting IED and continues to be significant ($p = .02$) when the subthreshold IED cases among the student sample are included.

An implication of this finding is that treatment studies that recruit from a college population whose members have scored high on driving anger or aggressive driving (e.g., Deffenbacher, Huff, Lynch, Oetting, & Salvatore, 2000) may not contain many of those drivers who are most likely to commit the noticeably violent, assaultive act, such as those described in Table 4.2. Thus, even highly screened college samples probably have few cases of road rage as it is popularly described.

This is not to say that treatment research on college students who are high in driving anger has no value. Younger drivers, especially young males, have higher rates of motor vehicle accidents and, as Deffenbacher et al. (2000) have shown, college-age drivers who are high in driving anger have higher rates of motor vehicle accidents. Thus, any research that can point the way to helping the angry, aggressive driver operate his or her vehicle in a less angry and aggressive manner is valuable.

Turning to the data in Table 5.6, one can see a relatively low level of personality disorders in this college-age population: Only 26.4% meet criteria for any Axis II disorder, with the most common ones being paranoid personality disorder (9.4%), OCPD (7.5%), and BPD (7.5%). Antisocial personality disorder was diagnosed in only 5.7%, or 13.2% when one includes those who were subthreshold. The comparable data from the treatment-seeking aggressive drivers in Table 5.4 show comparable levels of BPD (10.2%), OCPD (8.2%), and paranoid personality disorder (8.2%). The noticeable differences are in the rate of full ASPD (18.4%) and ASPD including the subsyndromal cases (28.6%). Statistical comparisons of the two groups reveal significantly higher rates of full ASPD among the treatment-seeking population than for the college population of aggressive drivers. Comparisons including subthreshold ASPD cases were also significantly ($p = .03$) different.

CONCLUSIONS

Our earlier comment about differences between our court- and self-referred aggressive drivers and samples recruited from a college population with high scores on aggressive driving or driving anger questionnaires is relevant here when one notices the differences in the prevalence of ASPD between the two groups. Our clinical experience is that drivers with ASPD constitute a particular treatment challenge. This challenge can be answered in part by studying groups who are heterogeneous with regard to age and perhaps referral source.

The last points on which we comment are the noticeable levels of current (11.3%) and lifetime (22.6%) oppositional defiant disorder found among the college student aggressive drivers. Adding the subsyndromal cases brings the lifetime rate to 43.4%. We do not have comparable data on the treatment-seeking aggressive drivers. These values should be contrasted with the *DSM–IV* (American Psychiatric Association, 1994) estimate of 2% to 16%.

There were also 6 cases of adult ADHD and 12 cases (22.6%) of childhood ADHD in the college student sample. The *DSM–IV* (1994) gives a prevalence value of 3% to 5% in school-age children. Again, we do not have comparable data on the treatment-seeking sample. It thus seems clear that this high-functioning sample is coping with a noticeable residue of childhood externalizing and excessive activity problems.

In future treatment research, one might want to take the possible presence of those disorders into account. More important, one should also begin to investigate what role the presence of disorders such as IED, ASPD, ADHD, and oppositional defiant disorder play in treatment outcome when using a standard treatment. We have very preliminary data indicating that aggressive drivers with IED respond less readily to the standard brief four-session group cognitive–behavior therapy treatment we describe in chapter 10 (Galovski & Blanchard, 2002a). As noted earlier, our clinical impression is that the presence of ASPD in group members can make treatment more difficult.

Clinical Hint

We recognize that the detailed level of assessment of Axis I and Axis II disorders is very time consuming and that practicing clinicians might want to omit that portion of the assessment. We believe clinicians need, at a minimum, to assess individuals for IED and ASPD. We believe treatment may need to be altered (primarily lengthened) for individuals who meet the criteria for either of these disorders.

6

PSYCHOLOGICAL CHARACTERISTICS OF ANGRY AND AGGRESSIVE DRIVERS

As we described in chapter 2, although there is considerable overlap among the constructs of anger, aggression, and hostility, there are also differences. Also as noted in chapter 2, some literature exists regarding driving anger and driving aggression and perhaps regarding driver hostility. Chapter 3 contains a review of the literature that seeks to place the angry, aggressive, problematic driver within the broader theoretical ideas in these fields. In part, it summarizes what is known about the characteristics of the angry, aggressive driver from a dimensional or psychological test perspective and is not repeated here.

The present chapter has three parts. Part 1 is a summary of some of the psychological or dimensional assessment literature with special attention to the important work of Jerry Deffenbacher and his colleagues. Part 2 is a summary of the psychological test results on our treatment-seeking samples, with special attention to whether the driver met criteria for intermittent explosive disorder (IED). We also present distributions of the psychological test scores from our 49 treatment-seeking aggressive drivers. Part 3 is a presentation of selected psychological test norms from the more than 1,000 undergraduates on whom we gathered data. These last results are usually presented separately for each gender. In this part, the mean scores of the 53 students from that overall sample who were identified as aggressive drivers, and who received in-depth assessment, are also presented for all of our measures.

The data on the treatment-seeking sample are more limited because of the sample size but are probably of more value to clinicians who are called on to assess or treat an aggressive driver. With these limited distributions, one can have a sense of where one's client falls on several dimensions.

PART 1: RESEARCH ON THE MEASUREMENT OF DRIVING ANGER AND DRIVING AGGRESSION

By far the most systematic program of research on the development and use of measures of *driving anger* has been that of Jerry Deffenbacher and his colleagues at Colorado State University. As we describe below, they have more recently turned their attention to driving aggression and other expressions of driving anger. We have made use of some of their measures and find them to be useful and sensitive to treatment effects.

The Driving Anger Scale

In 1994, Deffenbacher, Oetting, and Lynch published a report on the development of a 33-item scale to measure "frequent and intense anger while operating a motor vehicle" (Deffenbacher et al., 1994, p. 84). A large sample of undergraduates ($N = 1,526$: 724 men and 802 women, average age = 18 years) rated on a scale from 1 (*not at all*) to 3 (*some*) to 5 (*very much*) how much anger they would experience in 53 potentially provocative driving situations. Six somewhat distinct clusters of items were identified that comprised 33 total items. The subscales and number of items are Hostile Gestures (by other drivers; 3 items), Illegal Driving (by other drivers; 4 items), Police Presence (4 items), Slow Driving (by other drivers; 6 items), Discourtesy (9 items), and Traffic Obstructions (7 items). Internal consistency of the whole scale was .90. Mean scores for men (108.8) and women (109.2) did not differ. Norms were also provided.

A short version of the scale, with 14 items, also was described. It had adequate internal consistency (.80) and correlated .95 with the long version. Norms for it were also supplied.

In an important follow-up study, Deffenbacher, Huff, Lynch, Oetting, and Salvatore (2000) screened 1,080 undergraduates in psychology classes with the 14-item Driving Anger Scale (DAS) short form. Respondents were also asked whether they had a problem with driving anger and whether they would like help for it. Fifty-seven (23 men, 34 women) who scored in the upper quartile on the DAS short form and indicated a problem with driving anger and a desire for counseling provided additional data (this is the sample who participated in the treatment study described in chap. 8). These treatment-seekers provided data on the long-form DAS and on sub-scales of Spielberger's (1988) State–Trait Anger Expression Inventory (STAXI). In Table 6.1 we list the mean scores on the long-form (33-item) DAS, as well as the subscales, and on Trait Anger.

An examination of the mean DAS full-scale scores reveals that the first (2000) treatment-seeking sample had a full-scale score of 120, equivalent to the 73rd percentile, or not fully in the upper quartile on the scale. The second (2002) treatment-seeking sample had a full-scale score of 128, which falls at the 86th percentile. Unfortunately, the DAS full-scale value was not available on the high driving anger, non-treatment-seeking group, which was described in the 2003 study.

Deffenbacher's group (Deffenbacher, Lynch, Oetting, & Swaim, 2002) also developed a scale to measure driving aggression. It is called the Driving Anger Expression Inventory and contains 53 items. Analyses revealed a five-factor structure. The most relevant factors in the present context are the following: (a) Verbal Aggressive Expression (12 items, internal consistency α = .88), (b) Personal Physical Aggressive Expression (11 items, internal consistency α = .81), and (c) Use of Vehicle to Express Anger (11 items, internal consistency α = .86). They are combined to form a 34-item scale, Total Aggressive Expression, that has an internal consistency of α = .90.

We have not used this scale in our work, preferring Larson's (1996a) Driver's Stress Profile (DSP), which is described below. However, the Total Aggressive Expression scale certainly provides an alternative measure of aggressive driving that may have more sound psychometric properties. The three subscales intercorrelate from .39 to .48. Mean scores on the Total Aggressive Expression scale for high driving anger participants who had sought treatment were 77.1 (SD = 17.6) for men and 70.7 (SD = 13.7) for women (Deffenbacher, Lynch, Filetti, Dahlen, & Oetting, 2003).

Driver's Stress Profile

The DSP (Larson, 1996a; Blanchard, Barton, & Malta, 2000) is a 40-item scale created by Larson (1996b) to measure changes in reports of aggressive driving in individuals undergoing treatment. It has four 10-item subscales: Anger, Impatience, Competing, and Punishing. Each item is scored on a 4-point frequency scale (0 = *never*, 1 = *sometimes*, 2 = *often*, and 3 = *always*). Blanchard et al. (2000) published some psychometric data on this scale, and we summarize the data here because the scale has not been widely used despite our enthusiasm for it.

One-week test–retest reliability on a sample of 33 individuals (15 male and 18 female; age range: 18–60 years) was .93 for the full scale and ranged

TABLE 6.1

Driving Anger Scale Scores and State–Trait Anger Expression Inventory (STAXI) Scores on Various Samples of College Students With High Driving Anger

| | Sample | | |
Scale or subscale	Treatment-seeking (Deffenbacher et al., 2000)[a]	Treatment-seeking (Deffenbacher, Filetti, et al., 2002)[b]	Non-treatment-seeking (Deffenbacher, Filetti, et al., 2003)[c]
Driving Anger Scale			
Full scale	120.4	128.5	
Hostile Gestures	12.5		
Illegal Driving	11.5		
Police Presence	13.3		
Slow Driving	18.8		
Discourtesy	38.5		
Traffic Obstructions	25.8		
STAXI			
Trait Anger	24.7	24.8	23.2
Anger-In	17.3	17.7	17.9
Anger-Out	17.8	18.7	17.4
Anger Control	20.3	20.7	22.3

[a]Men, n = 23; women, n = 34. [b]Men, n = 238; women, n = 27. [c]Men, n = 21; women, n = 17.

TABLE 6.2
Correlations of Driver's Stress Profile (DSP) Full-Scale Scores With Other Relevant Measures

Measure	Correlation with DSP full-scale score	
Driving Anger Scale	.57	$p < .001$
STAXI		
State Anger	.17	$p <. 05$
Trait Anger	.59	$p < .001$
Anger Expression	−.36	$p < .01$
Anger-In	.16	$p < .05$
Anger-Out	.43	$p < .01$
No. MVAs	.20	$p = .009$
No. MVAs (age) corrected	.28	$p < .001$

Note. MVA = motor vehicle accident.

from .84 (Impatience) to .85 (Anger), to .91 (Punishing) to .96 (Competing). Internal consistency of the full scale on a separate sample of 176 individuals (77 male and 99 female; age range: 17–75 years) was .93.

Separate gender norms on the total score were presented, with 20% of men scoring 25 or lower (compared with 38% of women) and 20% of men scoring 51 or higher (compared with 2% of women). Mean scores for the two genders were significantly different (men: $M = 38.8$, $SD = 16.8$; women: $M = 30.8$, $SD = 30.8$, $p < .001$).

An exploratory factor analysis revealed three factors involving 28 of the items and accounting for 43.4% of the total variance. Factor 1 (29%) was primarily a competition factor, Factor 2 (7.9%) was a mixture of 5 anger and 5 punishment items and thus is characterized by anger and hostility, and Factor 3 (6.3%) was primarily an impatience (7 items) factor with 4 anger items (for a total of 11 items). It reflected impatience and anger at roadway inconvenience.

It is interesting that the total score on the DSP was significantly correlated with self-report of number of motor vehicle accidents ($r = .20$, $p = .009$). When age was covaried, the relation was stronger ($r = .28$, $p < .001$).

Table 6.2 lists the correlations of the full-scale score on the DSP with Deffenbacher et al.'s (2000) full-scale score on the DAS and subscales of Spielberger's (1988) STAXI.

As is obvious, the DSP has considerable overlap with the full-scale DAS (32% shared variance), indicating not only commonality of the measures of driving anger and driving aggression but also that they are measuring somewhat different constructs (see chap. 2 for a review). Likewise, there is considerable overlap (35% shared variance) between the DSP and trait anger as measured by the STAXI.

PART 2: PSYCHOLOGICAL CHARACTERISTICS OF TREATMENT-SEEKING AGGRESSIVE DRIVERS

As we noted in chapter 4, we have assessed 49 treatment-seeking aggressive drivers (37 court referred and 12 self-referred). Several psychological test measures were consistent across the entire 49 and are the primary focus of this portion of this chapter. We present distributional norms of these measures so that readers can compare an aggressive driver for whom he or she is providing assessment or treatment services with a carefully characterized sample.

We will also follow the example of chapter 5, in that (a) we compare all treatment-seeking aggressive drivers with nonaggressive driving controls as well as court-referred with self-referred aggressive drivers, and (b) we compare aggressive drivers who met criteria for IED with aggressive drivers who did not meet IED criteria. In this way, we can add to the very limited available dimensional psychological data on this relatively understudied population.

We changed a number of measures between our assessments on our so-called Cohort 1 (20 court-referred drivers and 10 self-referred drivers) and those on Cohort 2 (17 court-referred drivers and 2 self-referred drivers). The measures available on all 49 treatment-seeking aggressive drivers are briefly described below.

Measures

Driver's Stress Profile and the Driving Anger Scale

The DSP, a 40-item scale that measures aspects of driving aggression, was described in detail in Part 1. The DAS, a 33-item scale that measures aspects of driving anger with six subscales, also was described in detail in Part 1.

State–Trait Anger Expression Scale

The STAXI (Spielberger, 1988) is a 44-item instrument on which participants rate their reactions on a 4-point scale (1 = *almost never*, 4 = *almost always*). It yields scores on six subscales. (a) State Anger (10 items) measures how angry the person feels at the current time. (b) Trait Anger (10 items) measures how the respondent usually feels. (c) Angry Temperament (6 items) reflects the respondent's propensity to experience anger in the absence of specific provocation; a part of Trait Anger is reflected in the Angry Temperament scale. The last three subscales measure how the respondent deals with anger: (d) Anger-In (8 items, measures the tendency to suppress anger and harbor grudges), (e) Anger-Out (8 items, measures typical outward expression of angry feelings), and (f) Anger Control (8 items, measures the degree to which the participant controls outward expression of anger).

Buss–Durkee Hostility Inventory

The Buss–Durkee Hostility Inventory (Buss & Durkee, 1957) is a rationally designed scale of 75 items to measure individual differences in hostility as a personality trait.

Beck Depression Inventory

The Beck Depression Inventory (A. T. Beck, Ward, Mendelson, Mock, & Erbaugh, 1961) is a 21-item measure of depressive symptoms that are answered on a scale that ranges from 0 to 3. It is probably the most widely used measure of depression in the United States, and it has a long history of reliability and validity research (A. T. Beck, Steer, & Garbin, 1988).

State–Trait Anxiety Inventory

The State–Trait Anxiety Inventory (Spielberger, 1983) consists of 20 items, answered on a scale that ranges from 1 to 4, that measure the respondent's current state of anxiety, and 20 other items, also answered on a scale that ranges from 1 to 4, that measure the relatively enduring trait of anxiety. Both scales have good reliabilities and validities.

Comparison of Court-Referred With Self-Referred Aggressive Drivers

Table 6.3 shows the means and standard deviations for the measures of driving aggression (DSP), driving anger (DAS), and general anger (STAXI), for the court-referred and self-referred aggressive drivers. We also tabulated the values for the 28 control participants (see chap. 4) who took part as paid volunteers. Similar tabulations for hostility, depression, and anxiety are also presented in the table.

First, an examination of the comparisons of the two groups of aggressive drivers reveals that the self-referred aggressive drivers scored significantly higher than the court-referred aggressive drivers on the full-scale DSP and its four subscales as well as on the full-scale DAS and each of its six subscales (all $ps < .01$). On the STAXI, the self-referred drivers were higher on the Trait Anger, Anger-Out, and Anger-In subscales (all $ps < .05$). Turning to the measures of psychological distress, there were no significant differences between the two groups of treatment-seeking aggressive drivers; there was, however, a trend ($p = .06$) for the self-referred group to acknowledge more trait anxiety than did the court-referred group.

Turning to the comparisons of all aggressive drivers to the controls, we find a trend for the treatment-seeking aggressive drivers to score higher

TABLE 6.3
Scores for Treatment-Seeking Aggressive Drivers and Control Participants on Measures of Driving Aggression, Driving Anger, General Anger, Hostility, Anxiety, and Depression

Measure	Court (n = 37) M	SD	Self (n = 12) M	SD	All Agg. (n = 39) M	SD	Controls (n = 28) M	SD	Analyses Court vs. self $t(47)$	p	Agg. vs. control $t(65)$	p
Driver's Stress Profile												
Total score	24.16	24.56	60.33	22.98	33.02	28.64	23.18	16.11	4.5	.000	1.93	.057
Anger	7.19	4.89	17.92	5.85	9.82	6.89	9.04	3.60	6.3	.000	0.65	.516
Impatience	6.24	7.08	16.92	7.17	8.86	8.42	6.39	5.27	4.53	.000	1.58	.119
Competing	5.38	8.36	12.67	8.23	7.16	8.83	3.11	4.70	2.64	.011	2.63	.010
Punishing	5.35	6.26	12.83	6.29	7.18	7.00	4.57	4.61	3.59	.001	1.98	.053
Driving Anger Scale												
Total score	72.16	28.96	121.00	20.26	84.12	34.25	80.57	22.73	5.41	.000	0.55	.590
Hostile Gestures	5.92	3.40	11.08	3.29	7.18	4.02	7.43	2.69	4.61	.000	0.32	.750
Illegal Driving	6.84	2.66	13.42	4.36	8.45	4.22	10.18	2.83	4.94	.000	1.93	.057
Police Presence	7.05	3.67	11.25	5.01	8.08	4.38	7.29	4.31	3.14	.003	0.77	.443
Slow Driving	12.54	5.03	22.00	5.27	14.86	6.50	12.93	4.81	5.60	.000	1.49	.142
Discourtesy	22.14	8.27	37.92	5.50	26.00	10.26	27.14	6.57	6.16	.000	0.60	.554
Traffic Obstructions	14.20	5.98	23.83	6.70	16.56	7.39	15.61	6.14	4.71	.000	0.58	.566
State–Trait Anger Expression Scale												
State Anger	14.24	6.03	15.50	9.69	14.55	7.01	10.36	0.83	0.54	.595	4.14	.000
Trait Anger	17.30	6.94	23.92	6.91	18.92	7.44	15.61	4.77	2.87	.006	2.38	.020
Angry Temperament	6.68	3.55	8.58	3.75	7.14	3.52	5.5	1.80	1.67	.103	2.71	.008
Anger-Out	15.95	4.78	19.33	4.77	16.78	4.96	14.14	2.74	2.13	.038	3.00	.004
Anger-In	13.92	4.35	17.50	3.97	14.80	4.50	15.36	4.65	2.53	.015	0.52	.604
Buss–Durkee Hostility:												
Total	25.70	12.70	37.30	17.10	29.60	14.20	21.00	7.70	—	—	2.28	.030
Beck Depression Inventory	6.89	8.19	8.42	6.46	7.27	7.77	3.96	2.99	0.59	.56	2.65	.010
State–Trait Anxiety Inventory												
State Anxiety	45.38	13.39	50.42	21.32	46.61	15.61	27.61	5.96	0.77	.45	7.61	.000
Trait Anxiety	38.05	10.01	44.83	12.45	39.71	39.71	31.39	6.30	1.91	.06	4.23	.000

Note. Court = court referred; Self = self-referred; Agg. = aggressive drivers. Dashes in cells indicate there are no applicable data.

than the control participants on the full-scale DSP. On the Competing subscale, the aggressive drivers were significantly ($p = .05$) higher; they also showed a trend to be higher on the Punishing subscale. On the DAS, the two groups were generally not different with the exception of the Illegal Driving subscale, for which there was a trend for the control participants to score higher than the aggressive drivers.

On the generalized measure of anger (STAXI), the treatment-seeking aggressive drivers were significantly higher than the control participants ($p = .02$ or higher) on State Anger, Trait Anger, Angry Temperament, and Anger-Out. They were also higher than control participants on hostility measured by the Buss–Durkee Hostility Scale. Finally, the aggressive drivers were also significantly ($p < .01$) higher than the control participants on all three measures of psychological distress.

The pattern of the mean scores for the three groups—court-referred, self-referred, and controls—is of interest. For the most part, except for the STAXI subscales and measures of psychological distress, the court-referred aggressive drivers acknowledged the lowest scores, followed by the controls and then by the self-referred group. We suspect that the court-referred participants were deliberately underreporting driving anger and driving aggression and, to a lesser degree, overall anger.

The latter results are somewhat comparable to Galovski and Blanchard's (2002b) earlier report on the first cohort of aggressive drivers, which reported that the treatment-seeking aggressive drivers were significantly ($p < .05$) higher than the controls on the DSP Competing subscale, on DAS Anger (at slow driving and traffic obstructions), on STAXI Trait Anger and Angry Temperament, on the Buss–Durkee Total Hostility scale, and on state anxiety measured on the State–Trait Anxiety Inventory.

Comparison of Aggressive Drivers Who Meet or Do Not Meet Criteria for Intermittent Explosive Disorder

In Table 6.4, the results for the treatment-seeking aggressive drivers are subdivided on the basis of the presence of IED. This presentation is part of our effort, begun in chapter 5, to make available information on IED-positive drivers because of the relative absence of information on individuals with IED.

An examination of Table 6.4 reveals that there are no differences on the driving aggression measure (DSP), only one difference on the driving anger measure (DAS)—namely, greater anger in response to hostile gestures by those with IED—and no differences on the measures of psychological distress. On the measures of generalized anger measured by the STAXI, however, drivers who meet criteria for IED are significantly higher on Trait Anger, Angry Temperament, and Anger-Out. There is also a trend ($p = .09$) for the IED drivers to be higher on hostility. Thus, the major

TABLE 6.4
Scores for Treatment-Seeking Aggressive Drivers on Measures of Driving Aggression, Driving Anger, General Anger, Hostility, Anxiety, and Depression as a Function of Intermittent Explosive Disorder (IED) Status

| Measure | IED present (n = 16) | | IED absent (n = 33) | | | |
	M	SD	M	SD	t(47)	p
Driver's Stress Profile						
Total score	40.44	31.22	29.42	27.07	1.27	.21
Anger	11.06	8.10	9.21	6.27	0.88	.38
Impatience	11.44	9.02	7.61	7.95	1.51	.14
Competing	8.75	9.32	6.39	8.62	0.87	.39
Punishing	9.19	7.03	6.21	6.89	1.41	.17
Driving Anger Scale						
Total score	94.94	36.33	78.88	32.47	1.56	.13
Hostile Gestures	9.06	4.49	6.27	3.49	2.38	.02
Illegal Driving	7.63	4.15	8.85	4.27	0.95	.35
Police Presence	9.81	5.50	7.24	3.51	1.71	.10
Slow Driving	16.00	6.30	14.30	6.61	0.86	.40
Discourtesy	29.94	9.67	24.09	10.13	1.92	.06
Traffic Obstructions	18.84	8.06	15.45	6.90	1.52	.13
State–Trait Anger Expression Inventory						
State Anger	16.31	9.29	13.70	5.56	1.04	.31
Trait Anger	22.69	8.81	17.09	6.01	2.29	.03
Angry Temperament	9.13	4.13	6.18	2.76	2.59	.02
Anger-Out	19.44	4.59	15.48	4.66	2.8	.01
Anger-In	16.25	4.70	14.09	4.29	1.6	.12
Anger Control						
Buss–Durkee Hostility Total	35.80	18.90	25.90	11.60	1.76	.09
Beck Depression Inventory	9.81	9.96	6.03	6.26	1.63	.11
State–Trait Anxiety Inventory						
State Anxiety	49.25	18.95	45.33	13.85	0.82	.42
Trait Anxiety	41.44	11.88	38.88	10.52	0.77	.49

differences are on more core psychological features related to generalized anger and hostility rather than on driving-specific features.

Psychological Test Distributions for Treatment-Seeking Aggressive Drivers

The last information we present on the treatment-seeking aggressive drivers are the distributions of scores from these 49 individuals on the measures described above that were common to the assessment of Cohort 1 and Cohort 2. These data are not norms, because we have mixed the results from the 37 court-referred and 12 self-referred aggressive drivers despite there being mean differences on some measures (see above).

Clinical Hint

This is a limited sample in terms of size; moreover, as we note in chapter 9, many of the court-referred aggressive drivers probably were not completely candid on the measures related to either aggressive driving or driving anger. Nevertheless, this next section does provide the distribution of scores on measures we recommend using for this population if you, as a clinician, are faced with assessing or treating an aggressive driver. After reading the following material, you will know where your driver–client lies relative to a well-characterized sample.

Table 6.5 contains distributions for the DSP full-scale or total score; Table 6.6 contains distributions for each of the subscales. Note that the mean DSP full-scale score for the 49 treatment-seeking aggressive drivers (33) is slightly below the mean (34.3) for the normative adult sample.

TABLE 6.5
Norms for Treatment-Seeking Aggressive Drivers
on the Driver's Stress Profile Total Score

Score	Cumulative %
4	8.2
6	10.2
8	14.3
10	26.5
12	34.7
14	36.7
16	40.8
18	44.9
20	51.0
22	53.1
24	55.1
30	57.1
35	63.3
40	67.3
45	71.4
50	75.5
55	77.6
60	81.6
65	85.7
70	89.8
75	89.8
80	91.8
90	93.9
100	95.9
110	100.0
M	33.0
Mdn	19.0

TABLE 6.6
Norms for Treatment-Seeking Aggressive Drivers on Driver's Stress Profile Subscales: Anger, Impatience, Competing, and Punishing

Anger		Impatience		Competing		Punishing	
Score	Cumulative %	Score	Cumulative %	Score	Cumulative %	Score	Cumulative %
1	6.1	1	14.3	1	40.8	1	14.3
3	20.4	2	20.4	2	51.0	2	32.7
5	32.7	3	32.7	3	53.1	3	42.9
7	51.0	4	46.9	4	59.2	4	53.1
9	55.1	6	53.1	5	61.2	5	55.1
11	61.2	7	61.2	6	63.3	6	59.2
13	71.4	9	63.3	9	67.3	8	67.3
15	77.6	10	67.3	11	73.5	10	73.5
17	83.7	11	73.5	13	77.6	12	79.6
19	93.9	13	79.6	15	81.6	14	87.8
21	95.9	16	81.6	18	87.8	16	91.8
24	98.0	19	85.7	21	89.8	20	95.9
30	100.0	22	89.8	24	93.9	25	95.9
		25	93.9	27	95.9	30	100.0
		30	100.0	30	100.0		
M	9.8		8.9		7.2		7.2
Mdn	7.0		6.0		3.0		4.0

TABLE 6.7
Driving Anger Scale Total Score for Treatment-Seeking Aggressive Drivers

Score	Cumulative %
40	6.1
45	14.3
50	14.3
55	26.5
60	32.7
65	40.8
70	44.9
75	49.0
80	55.1
85	57.1
90	59.2
95	65.3
100	65.3
105	71.4
110	71.4
115	75.5
120	75.5
125	87.8
130	91.8
140	93.9
150	98.0
M	82.0
Mdn	84.1

Table 6.7 shows the distributions for the treatment seekers on the full-scale score of the DAS. Tables 6.8 and 6.9 contain distributions for each of the six DAS subscales.

Like the DSP, the mean full-scale DAS score of 84 is noticeably lower than the mean for Deffenbacher et al.'s (1994) normative sample of college students (109) and well below the means of their treatment-seeking college student samples presented in Table 6.1. This is further evidence of our court-referred treatment-seekers' tendency to minimize, or possibly to "fake good." The self-referred drivers' mean score is comparable to Deffenbacher, Filetti, Richards, Lynch, and Oetting's (2003) treatment samples.

Table 6.10 contains distributions for trait anger as measured by the STAXI (Spielberger, 1988), and Table 6.11 contains distributions for the constructs of Anger-In and Anger-Out. The manuals for the STAXI contain much more comprehensive norms.

Finally, Tables 6.12 and 6.13 contain distributions for our measures of general psychological distress. Table 6.12 has distributions for state and trait anxiety, as measured by the State–Trait Anxiety Inventory (Spielberger, 1983); Table 6.13 has distributions for depressive symptoms as measured by the Beck Depression Inventory (A. T. Beck et al., 1961). It seems clear

TABLE 6.8
Norms for Treatment-Seeking Aggressive Drivers on the Driving Anger Scale Subscales of Slow Driving, Discourtesy, and Traffic Obstructions

Slow Driving		Discourtesy		Traffic Obstruction	
Score	Cumulative %	Score	Cumulative %	Score	Cumulative %
6	6.1	9	4.1	7	10.2
8	16.3	12	8.2	8	14.3
10	26.5	15	18.4	9	22.4
11	36.7	18	28.6	10	26.5
12	46.9	20	34.7	11	28.6
14	61.2	24	51.0	12	32.7
16	63.3	28	53.1	14	44.9
18	75.5	30	67.3	16	55.1
20	79.6	32	69.4	18	59.2
22	83.7	34	75.5	20	72.5
24	87.8	37	83.7	22	81.6
26	91.8	40	87.8	26	87.8
28	95.9	43	95.9	30	93.9
30	100.0	45	100.0	34	98.0
				35	100.0
M	14.9		26.0		16.6
Mdn	13.0		16.0		15.0

TABLE 6.9
Norms for Treatment-Seeking Aggressive Drivers on the Driving Anger Scale Subscales of Hostile Gestures, Illegal Driving, and Police Presence

Hostile Gestures		Illegal Driving		Police Presence	
Score	Cumulative %	Score	Cumulative %	Score	Cumulative %
3	24.5	4	20.4	4	20.4
4	32.7	5	34.7	5	40.8
5	42.9	6	38.8	6	53.1
6	53.1	7	46.9	7	57.1
7	63.3	8	57.1	8	65.3
8	71.4	9	69.4	9	69.4
9	73.5	10	73.5	10	73.5
10	77.6	11	79.6	11	81.6
11	81.6	12	83.7	13	85.7
12	85.7	13	85.7	14	89.8
14	89.8	14	91.8	15	91.8
15	100.0	17	93.9	17	95.9
		18	98.0	19	98.0
		29	100.0	20	100.0
M	7.2		8.5		8.1
Mdn	6.0		7.0		5.0

TABLE 6.10
Norms for Treatment-Seeking Aggressive Drivers on
the State–Trait Anger Expression Inventory: Trait Anger

Score	Cumulative %
10	8.2
11	14.3
12	18.4
13	30.6
14	36.7
15	42.9
16	49.0
17	55.1
18	57.1
19	63.3
20	67.3
25	77.6
30	89.8
35	98.0
40	100.0
M	18.9
Mdn	17.0

TABLE 6.11
Norms for Treatment-Seeking Aggressive Drivers on
the State–Trait Anger Expression Inventory: Anger-In and Anger-Out

Anger-In		Anger-Out	
Score	Cumulative %	Score	Cumulative %
9	10.2	10	8.2
10	20.4	11	18.4
11	32.7	12	22.4
12	36.7	13	32.7
13	42.9	14	40.8
14	53.1	15	44.9
15	59.2	16	55.1
16	63.3	17	59.2
17	71.4	18	63.3
18	83.7	19	67.3
19	87.8	20	75.5
20	87.8	22	83.7
23	95.9	24	85.7
26	100.0	26	95.9
		28	100.0
M	14.8		16.8
Mdn	14.0		16.0

TABLE 6.12
State and Trait Anxiety (State–Trait Anxiety Inventory) Norms
for Treatment-Seeking Aggressive Drivers

State Anxiety		Trait Anxiety	
Score	Cumulative %	Score	Cumulative %
21	4.1	22	4.1
25	8.2	24	12.2
29	12.2	26	18.4
33	20.4	30	26.5
37	28.6	34	32.7
41	34.7	38	42.9
45	46.9	40	49.0
47	51.0	44	57.1
49	67.3	46	73.5
51	73.5	48	81.6
53	79.6	50	87.8
60	89.8	60	95.9
65	89.8	70	100.0
70	91.8		
75	93.9		
80	100.0		
M	46.6		39.7
Mdn	47.0		41.0

TABLE 6.13
Beck Depression Inventory Norms for Treatment-Seeking
Aggressive Drivers

Score	Cumulative %
0	12.2
1	22.4
2	32.7
3	40.8
4	55.1
5	59.2
7	61.2
9	69.4
11	75.5
13	79.6
15	85.7
17	91.8
19	95.9
21+	100.0
M	7.3
Mdn	4.0

that this sample of treatment-seeking aggressive drivers acknowledges very little depression but some moderate levels of anxiety, especially current state anxiety.

PART 3: PSYCHOLOGICAL CHARACTERISTICS OF COLLEGE STUDENTS WHO ACKNOWLEDGE BEING AGGRESSIVE DRIVERS

As we noted in chapter 4, Malta (2004) obtained psychological measures on a large sample of college undergraduates and then interviewed 53 of those who scored 1 standard deviation or higher above the mean of the DSP (Larson, 1996a; Blanchard et al., 2000), our primary measure of aggressive driving. There was some overlap with the measures described in Part 2 of this chapter that were obtained with the treatment-seeking aggressive drivers. However, in some instances newer versions of some measures were used. We now describe the two measures that we used with the college-age sample, for which male and female norms are provided.

Measures

Driver's Stress Profile

The DSP (Larson, 1996a) is a 40-item rationally designed scale that measures the respondent's tendency to drive aggressively. Each item is scored on a scale that ranges from 0 to 3, for a maximum possible score of 120. There are four subscales of 10 items each (see earlier description in Part 1).

Driving Anger Scale

The DAS (Deffenbacher et al., 1994) is a 33-item scale on which items are scored on a scale that ranges from 1 to 5, yielding a maximum total scale score of 165. It measures the degree to which the respondent experiences anger in driving situations. It has six subscales, identified by factor analyses, that range from 3 to 9 items (again see earlier description in Part 1).

The mean and standard deviation scores of the 53 college students who acknowledged being aggressive drivers are listed in Table 6.14. Because there is no comparison group, one has to examine these scores in comparison to either earlier values presented in this chapter or to published norms.

Starting with the driving aggression and driving anger measures, one can see that the mean score on the DSP was in the 90th percentile or higher according to Blanchard et al's. (2000) published norms for the general population. Thus, compared with the general population, this group endorsed very high levels of driving aggression.

TABLE 6.14
Means and Standard Deviations on Measures of Driving Anger, Driving Aggression, and Generalized Anger Among College Students High in Driving Aggression

Measure or subscale	M	SD	Range
Driver's Stress Profile			
Total score	64.7	12.0	53–107
Anger	20.0	3.7	13–30
Impatience	17.1	5.4	0–27
Competing	13.6	6.9	0–30
Punishing	14.0	5.3	4–30
Driving Anger Scale			
Total scale	122.8	18.9	60–161
Hostile Gestures	11.8	3.0	5–15
Illegal Driving	11.5	3.8	5–20
Slow Driving	22.3	4.1	12–30
Discourtesy	37.9	5.7	12–45
Police Presence	14.0	4.2	4–20
Traffic Obstructions	25.3	5.6	14–35
State–Trait Anger Expression Inventory			
Trait Anger	24.0	5.7	14–40
Anger-In	19.0	4.2	11–31
Anger-Out	19.6	4.0	11–30
Anger Control	39.7	8.0	23–63

Looking at the mean score of 123 on the DAS, we find this sample of college students at the 78th percentile according to Deffenbacher et al's. (1994) norms and between the two treatment samples described in Table 6.1. The Trait Anger scores are also very comparable to Deffenbacher, Filetti, Lynch, Dahlen, and Oetting's (2002) samples in Table 6.1. This leads us to conclude that the means and ranges in Table 6.15 are representative of what one should expect from a sample of aggressive-driving college students.

College Student Norms for Selected Measures

To make our material as useful as possible to clinicians faced with young adult aggressive drivers sent for assessment or treatment, we provide norms on the measures of driving anger and driving aggression based on our sample of more than 1,000 college students. Separate tables for men and women are provided because women typically score lower than men on measures of anger and aggression. We also hope this information may be of value to anyone undertaking research with these populations. (Norms are available, of course, on all, or almost all, of these measures, either in the manuals that accompany the tests or in the articles that describe the instrument.)

TABLE 6.15
Male and Female Norms for Full-Scale Driver's Stress Profile Scores
Among College Students

	Cumulative %	
Score range	Men (n = 533)	Women (n = 463)
0–5	1.5	0
6–10	2.4	3.2
11–15	4.3	8.0
16–20	9.6	18.8
21–25	19.1	30.7
26–30	28.1	44.7
31–35	37.9	54.4
36–40	47.3	65.0
41–45	57.0	72.8
46–50	64.5	81.0
51–55	71.9	86.0
56–60	78.2	90.9
61–65	85.0	94.2
66–70	89.9	95.5
71–75	91.7	96.5
76–80	94.9	98.3
81–85	95.9	98.5
86–90	97.6	99.1
91–95	97.9	99.4
96–100	98.3	99.6
101–105	98.5	99.6
106+	100.0	100.0
M	44.5	36.2
Mdn	42.0	33.0

We present normative data on the following measures from the large college student sample: the DSP and its subscales (Blanchard et al., 2000; Larson, 1996a; see Tables 6.15–6.19) and the DAS and its subscales (Deffenbacher et al., 1994; see Table 6.20).

We realize that we have given the reader a great deal of tabular material. We hope it will be useful to clinicians in terms of characterizing an individual client whom one needs to assess before beginning treatment. We have found such clinical norms helpful.

TABLE 6.16
Male and Female Norms for the Driver's Stress Profile Anger Subscale Among College Students

Score range	Cumulative %	
	Men (n = 533)	Women (n = 463)
0	0.8	0
1–2	1.3	0
3–4	2.4	1.5
5–6	4.7	5.4
7–8	11.4	13.2
9–10	20.3	28.1
11–12	34.7	43.0
13–14	49.0	57.2
15–16	63.4	70.2
17–18	75.2	82.3
19–20	85.7	89.8
21–22	93.1	95.2
23–24	96.1	96.1
25–26	98.5	99.6
27–28	99.4	100.0
29–30	100.0	100.0
M	14.8	13.8
Mdn	15.0	13.0

TABLE 6.17
Male and Female Norms for the Driver's Stress Profile Impatience Subscale Among College Students

Score range	Cumulative %	
	Men (n = 533)	Women (n = 463)
0	1.9	0.6
1–2	5.4	5.2
3–4	12.9	12.1
5–6	23.6	24.4
7–8	35.3	37.4
9–10	49.7	54.4
11–12	60.8	66.5
13–14	71.5	75.8
15–16	78.2	84.2
17–18	86.3	88.8
19–20	90.2	92.2
21–22	94.2	95.2
23–24	95.7	97.4
25–26	97.2	98.5
27–28	97.9	99.8
29–30	100.0	100.0
M	11.5	10.8
Mdn	11.0	10.0

TABLE 6.18
Male and Female Norms for the Driver's Stress Profile Competing Subscale Among College Students

Score range	Cumulative %	
	Men (*n* = 533)	Women (*n* = 463)
0	10.3	31.7
1–2	20.6	50.3
3–4	29.3	65.2
5–6	41.8	74.7
7–8	52.3	79.9
9–10	62.1	86.0
11–12	70.4	90.5
13–14	77.3	93.7
15–16	84.8	95.7
17–18	88.4	97.0
19–20	93.1	97.8
21–22	95.1	98.9
23–24	96.6	98.9
25–26	97.6	99.6
27–28	98.5	99.6
29–30	100.0	100.0
M	9.2	4.5
Mdn	8.0	2.0

TABLE 6.19
Male and Female Norms for the Driver's Stress Profile Punishing Subscale Among College Students

Score range	Cumulative %	
	Men (*n* = 533)	Women (*n* = 463)
0	1.3	1.9
1–2	11.6	17.5
3–4	28.7	37.8
5–6	43.3	52.7
7–8	54.6	68.9
9–10	66.2	78.2
11–12	73.9	86.4
13–14	80.5	90.7
15–16	87.2	95.2
17–18	91.2	97.2
19–20	94.6	97.6
21–22	96.1	98.5
23–24	97.9	99.1
25–26	98.7	99.4
27–28	99.1	99.4
29–30	100.0	100.0
M	9.0	7.1
Mdn	8.0	6.0

TABLE 6.20
Male and Female Norms for Driving Anger Scale Full-Scale Scores Among College Students

Score range	Cumulative %	
	Men ($n = 533$)	Women ($n = 463$)
33–55	3.0	2.0
56–65	6.2	6.7
66–75	9.4	12.6
76–80	14.3	19.1
81–85	20.6	24.7
86–90	27.8	30.8
91–95	35.1	36.9
96–100	42.8	44.0
101–103	47.1	48.8
104–106	52.5	54.2
107–109	56.8	57.9
110–112	62.5	64.2
113–115	67.0	69.2
116–118	70.9	73.8
119–121	77.1	77.9
122–124	81.4	81.8
125–127	85.4	85.5
128–130	87.8	88.9
131–133	89.5	91.1
134–136	91.9	93.1
137–140	95.3	95.0
141–145	97.4	97.0
146–150	98.5	98.0
151–155	99.1	99.3
156–165	100.0	100.0
M	104.0	102.9
Mdn	105.0	104.0

7
PSYCHOPHYSIOLOGICAL ASSESSMENT OF AGGRESSIVE DRIVERS

To the best of our knowledge, there have been no psychophysiological studies of aggressive drivers other than the two from our program, which we summarize later in this chapter. Thus, there is no other directly relevant literature. Tangentially related is the work of Stokols and colleagues (Stokols & Novaco, 1981; Stokols, Novaco, Stokols, & Campbell, 1978), who measured participants' blood pressure (BP) and heart rate (HR) at the end of their driving commute in California. Having to deal with higher levels of traffic density (termed by them *impedance*) and longer trips were associated with noticeable increases in BP and HR as well as negative mood.

However, as we established in chapter 2, the three constructs of anger, hostility, and aggression are intimately interrelated. Moreover, as we also noted in chapter 2, there is ample evidence that aggressive drivers may also be angry, hostile, or both (e.g., Arnett, Offer, & Fine, 1997; Deffenbacher, Huff, Lynch, Oetting, & Salvatore, 2000; D. M. Donovan, Umlauf, & Salzberg, 1988). Thus, the general literature on the psychophysiology of anger and hostility is relevant, and we summarize it briefly below.

ANGER AND HOSTILITY

Elevated HR and BP have been associated with the emotion of anger in studies that have used a variety of provocative stimuli, including verbal harassment of participants, imagining personally relevant anger-provoking scenes, and recalling personal memories of anger-provoking situations or even discussing anger-provoking topics (Ax, 1953; Burns, Evon, & Strain-Saloum, 1999; Engerbretson, Matthews, & Scheier, 1989; Foster, Smith, & Webster, 1999; Roberts & Weerts, 1982; Siegman, Anderson, & Berger, 1990; Sinha, Lovallo, & Parsons, 1992). Electrodermal reactivity and muscle tension have been less researched. Foster and colleagues (Foster et al., 1999; Foster, Webster, & Smith, 1997) found that skin resistance decreases during anger provocation as well as during recall or imagining angry events. Ax (1953) found that anger, as compared with fear, was associated with a greater number of electrodermal responses. Several investigators have found that anger produces a pattern of facial muscle activity that is distinct from that associated with other emotions (Dimberg, 1983, 1988; Fillingim, Roth, & Cook, 1992; Fridlund, Kenworthy, & Jaffey, 1992; Slomine & Greene, 1993).

Hostility has been much investigated because of its potential role in Type A behavior and possible cardiovascular disease (R. Williams, 1994). Many investigations have found either elevated levels of systolic BP (SBP) and diastolic BP (DBP) or increased reactivity of BP to provocation in hostile individuals compared with less hostile participants (Davies, Matthews, & McGrath, 2000; Guyll & Contrada, 1998; Houston, Smith, & Cates, 1989; Powch & Houston, 1996; Raikkoenen, Matthews, Flory, & Owens, 1999; T. W. Smith & Alfred, 1989; Suarez, Kuhn, Schanberg, Williams, & Zimmermann, 1998; Suarez & Williams, 1989).

AGGRESSION

A consistent psychophysiological finding has been attenuated electro-dermal reactivity among adult populations with either antisocial personality disorder or antisocial traits. This was initially noted in an early review by Mednick (1977) and in an updated review of that literature since 1977 by Scarpa and Raine (1997). However, not all antisocial individuals are aggressive, and no studies have looked at levels of aggression within antisocial populations participating in psychophysiological research.

In studies of non-antisocial adults, aggressive individuals may exhibit both greater HR reactivity and electrodermal activity. For example, Calvert and Tan (1994) found that playing a violent video game led to increased HR as well as to an increase in number of aggressive thoughts.

Thus, psychophysiological research on aggressive drivers may not only tell us more about this target population but also may shed light on the general topic of aggression and psychophysiology. In the material that follows, we summarize the methodology and results of our two studies of the psychophysiology of aggressive drivers. The first (Malta et al., 2001) involved

TABLE 7.1
Conditions and Instructions for Psychophysiological Assessment of Aggressive Drivers

Condition	Duration (minutes)	Verbal instructions
Adaptation	5–10	Sit quietly with your eyes closed.
Baseline 1	5	Continue to sit quietly with eyes closed.
Mental arithmetic	2–3	Starting at 250, subtract 7 and report results, then subtract 7 from the remainder, and so on.
Baseline 2	5	Relax and sit quietly with eyes closed.
Driving Tape 1	2–3	Now imagine this situation as vividly as you can.
Baseline 3	5	Take the image away and sit quietly with eyes closed.
Driving Tape 2	2–3	Now imagine this situation as vividly as you can.
Baseline 4	5	Take the image away and sit quietly with your eyes closed.
Fear-arousal tape	2–3	Now imagine this situation as vividly as you can.
Baseline 5	5	Take the image away and sit quietly for the next few minutes.

14 volunteers who labeled themselves as aggressive drivers (which was confirmed with testing on the Driver's Stress Profile [Larson, 1996a; see chap. 6]) and who were paid $20 for their participation. The second (Galovski, Blanchard, Malta, & Freidenberg, 2003) involved 30 treatment-seeking aggressive drivers, both court referred and self-referred. They were assessed before treatment and after its completion. The demographic characteristics of these samples are described in chapter 4; their psychological characteristics are described in chapter 6.

Although our previously published reports (Galovski et al., 2003; Malta et al., 2001) contain descriptions of the methodology as well as a detailed description of the results, we repeat this information so that it will be available in one place (this book) for readers. Moreover, we present slightly greater detail on the methodology.

For both studies, we had comparison groups of low-aggressive driving volunteers who also were paid $20 for their participation. Their status as low-aggressive drivers was confirmed by scores on the Driver's Stress Profile.

METHOD

Both of our studies used the same equipment and same procedures. The procedures are outlined in Table 7.1. After an adaptation period of 5 to 10 minutes, the initial resting baseline condition was run. There followed four stressor conditions, each lasting 2 to 3 minutes (M = 2.5 minutes), separated by 5-minute resting baseline phases. The stressors were always presented in the same order: mental arithmetic, Aggressive Driving Tape 1, Aggressive Driving Tape 2, and fear-arousal tape. The specific instructions given to participants are included in Table 7.1.

We used mental arithmetic as a standard cognitive stressor. Most individuals find it mildly stressful. It reliably provokes a pressor response for HR and BP, and it generates electrodermal responses and, usually, facial electromyogram (EMG) responses.

Our primary provocative stimuli were two audiotapes in which participants were asked to imagine driving situations that, by their reports, made them annoyed or angry. Thus, these two narratives were idiosyncratic for each driver. The methodology for creating the audiotape is described below. The last stressor was another idiosyncratic audiotape designed to be fear provoking based on an interview with the participant.

The use of idiosyncratic audiotapes to guide an imaginal experience began with work by Pitman, Orr, Forgue, deJong, and Claiborn (1987) involving Vietnam war veterans with posttraumatic stress disorder. We have used this procedure with motor vehicle accident survivors with possible posttraumatic stress disorder (e.g., Blanchard et al., 1996; Blanchard, Hickling, Taylor, Loos, & Gerardi, 1994) and with pathological gamblers (Blanchard, Wulfert, Freidenberg, & Malta, 2000).

Construction of Idiosyncratic Aggressive Driving Audiotapes

To develop the idiosyncratic aggressive driving audiotapes, we asked each participant, as part of the initial intake interview (chap. 4), to describe a driving situation that would typically annoy or irritate him or her and lead to feelings of anger and a possible aggressive response. Behavior of the other driver was described, and the participant's response to the situation was elicited. Elaboration of the situation was sought, as were descriptions of how the participant might feel and what he or she would probably do, including ideas he or she might have (and even verbalize) and possible aggressive retaliatory behavior. If the participant used particular swear words (the typical situation), these were incorporated into the description. The participant was then asked to try to remember a specific incident when this annoying situation had occurred so as to have more concrete details.

On occasion, a court-referred driver would claim to never become angry or annoyed when driving and thus claim not to be able to generate a situation. This denial was met with mild skepticism; such a mild challenge was usually enough to elicit cooperation.

After the interviewer believed he or she had enough information to describe one scene, the participant was asked for material about another situation that was typically found to be annoying or irritating. The same questions and prompts to elicit details and descriptions of feelings and

Now, I'd like you to try to imagine this scene, try to make it as real and as vivid as you can as though it was happening to you. Try to put yourself in it.

You are driving on the Northway, going at a pretty good clip and up ahead there's a sign "Construction—1000 feet" and you know that the lanes are going to have to merge. You're in the correct lane already, you are slowing down but staying in your lane and cars start to move in as you get closer and closer to the merging point. Now you are coming to a stop; there is a lot of traffic starting to back up. People have to sit and that's pretty aggravating in and of itself.

You are sitting, waiting in your lane and all of a sudden on your left, here comes an idiot, and he is just going to cut in. You are thinking, he couldn't pay attention to the signs, you know, way back saying "Construction, Lanes Merging" . . . No, no, he can't read, just driving along in his own little world, thinks he is just going to come up and cut in. "Yeah, right." So you move your car up because you aren't going to let him cut in front of you, there's no way this asshole is getting in front of you. It's his problem if he can't change lanes in time. He is just going to have to sit there and wait for the traffic to go by. You don't know why these idiots just can't just pay attention and change. They are narcissists, they think they are the only one on the road, cruise up, slip right in, no problem . . . sure, sure, get in front of me, I'll just wait all day for you.

You're getting aggravated. You see these cars a lot. It's aggravating that you have to merge and sit and wait for the traffic that is just inching along. Then, to have one of these idiots try to cut in, you know. You're getting tense, you're gripping the wheel, you can feel your stomach knotting up and getting into a ball. You're just kind of sitting there, and he's still trying, he has his blinker on and he's trying to edge over. So you're thinking "no way, asshole," so you move your car over to the left to totally block him. There is no way he is going to be able to get in the lane. You say out loud, "That will teach you, why don't you learn to read and pay attention to signs. I don't know why this guy thinks he is totally entitled to pass, just to zip through and pass 10 cars because he's the king, he's not going to have to wait. No, no, just cruise up, pass around everybody because the road belongs to you, asshole." You are really getting angrier, you see this all the time and it really bugs you. You're gripping the wheel and you're very, very tense and you are kind of holding your breath and your stomach feels just like a fist, you're so angry. You are just kind of muttering, "What an asshole, I can't believe it." You glance over and he still looks like he wants to try to get in. You're just not going to make eye contact, but you're sort of just gripping the wheel and blocking with your car. There's no way he is going to get past you and you sit there and wait. You find yourself getting angrier and angrier. Then you move forward and go ahead . . .

Now take that scene away.

reactions were followed. A verbatim transcript of the content of one of the aggressive driving audiotapes is contained in Exhibit 7.1.

Fear-Arousal Audiotape

Next, participants were told we were shifting gears and wanted to learn of a hypothetical situation that would make them afraid or fearful, or of a real situation that had made them afraid. The same kinds of probes were used to gather information on the context or situation; what the participant did, said, and felt; and what happened as an outcome. Again, there could be a lack of cooperation from some court-referred participants, particularly young men. If nothing was readily volunteered, they would be asked about potentially observing a threat of harm to someone they cared about, such as a girlfriend, sibling, or parent. The scenes were recorded on audiotapes to be played back to the individual during the psychophysiological assessment as described in Table 7.1.

Self-Report by Participant

In Study 1 (Malta et al., 2001), participants were asked to make a vividness rating ("How vividly were you able to imagine the scene?" on a scale from 0 = *not at all* to 100 = *maximal vividness*) after each imaginal scene.

In Study 2 (Galovski et al., 2003), participants were asked to make the same vividness rating and to rate their emotions on six bipolar adjective scales (*happy – sad, fearful – brave, relaxed – tense, energetic – sluggish, excited – bored,* and *angry – calm*) using ratings of –100 (*as sad as one could possibly feel*) to 100+ (*extremely happy*). A rating of zero indicated that the participant felt neither emotion at that point in time. These ratings were to serve as possible manipulation checks to see if participants differentially reported the emotion of anger, and possibly feelings of being tense or energetic, during the aggressive driving tapes and feelings of being fearful or tense during the fear-arousal tape.

Setting

The participant was comfortably seated in a well-upholstered chair, with a high cushioned back to provide neck support, in the subject room. This room was sound attenuated and had subdued lighting. The psychophysiological recording equipment was housed in an adjacent room. The experimenter could observe the participant through a one-way window and was in continuous voice contact by an intercom.

Apparatus

In Study 1 we used a Grass Instrument Company Model 7 polygraph to measure skin resistance level (SRL; 7P1 preamplifier), forehead EMG (7P3 preamplifier coupled with a 7P10 preamplifier for integration of the signal), and HR (7P4 set in the tachograph mode). We also used a Critikon Dinamapp to measure BP, both SBP and DBP, and HR on a once-per-minute basis.

For SRL, we used silver–silver chloride electrodes filled with Teca Electrode Electrolyte Gel, attached to the ventral surface of the first phalange of the index and fourth fingers of the right hand. The pen of the 7P1 was recentered to zero once per minute so that the value of skin resistance, in ohms, could be read from the potentimeter.

For forehead EMG, we used Grass precious metal electrodes, filled with Grass EC2 Electrode Cream. The skin surface had been cleaned previously with isopropranol wipes. Active electrodes were centered on each eye approximately 2.5 cm above the eye. A ground was midway between them. We recorded the raw EMG with the 7P3, with the settings of 3 Hz as the low band pass and 75 Hz as the upper band pass. The raw EMG signal was fed to the 7P10 integrator calibrated to reset from the ramp function once per 10 s.

HR was recorded from plate electrodes with Parker Redux Cream at the contact medium in a standard Lead II configuration. The 7P4 was set in the tachogram mode to record HR in beats per minute (bpm) for each interbeat interval.

The cuff for BP and HR determinations was placed on the left arm at the level of the heart. Participants sat upright, with their feet on the floor. The Dinamapp produces a digital printout of SBP, DBP, and HR on a once-per-minute basis.

In Study 2, we recorded SBP, DBP, and HR with the Dinamapp. The only other physiological signal recorded was SRL, recorded with a Grass polygraph and 7P1 preamplifier in the same fashion as described above.

Polygraph Data Reduction: Study 1

For the EMG results, we determined the level of pen excursion with a Grass Model SWC10 square wave oscillator with inputs of $20\mu V$ and $50\mu V$ at a frequency of 50 Hz. With this calibration it was possible to record EMG in units of μV s/min. For the 7P4, we set the range at 40 bpm to 120 bpm such that 25 mm of pen excursion equaled 40 bpm. Thus, we could read HR to within 2 bpm on a beat-by-beat basis. This was used to determine peak HR per phase, defined as the highest HR sustained for 2 consecutive beats.

RESULTS

Study 1

We had eight measurement conditions and six different dependent variables (for 48 data cells) but only 14 participants in each of two conditions (total $n = 28$). Thus, an omnibus multivariate analysis of variance was ruled out. Instead, we calculated univariate repeated-measures analyses of variance

TABLE 7.2
Mean Forehead Electromyogram Reactivity Scores for Various Stressors for Aggressive Drivers and Control Participants

Stressor (µV s/min)	Group		Between-groups significance
	Aggressive drivers	Controls	
Mental arithmetic	79.0*	22.8	No
Driving Tape 1	119.1*	–20.5	Yes
Driving Tape 2	172.0**	7.6	Yes
Fear-arousal tape	105.6**	22.8	No
Initial baseline value	286	240.1	No

Note. There was significant within-group reactivity from baseline to stressor. From "Psychophysiological Reactivity of Aggressive Drivers: An Exploratory Study," by L. S. Malta, E. B. Blanchard, B. M. Freidenberg, T. E. Galovski, A. Karl, and S. R. Holzapfel, *Applied Psychophysiology and Biofeedback, Vol. 26*, p. 105. Copyright 2001 by Kluwer Academic Publishers. Adapted with kind permission of Springer Science and Business Media.
*$p < .05$. **$p < .01$.

on each psychophysiological response. We also took the data-reduction step of calculating a change score or reactivity for each stressor by subtracting the value of the immediately preceding baseline (average of last 2 minutes) from the average value found during the stressor. We also did this in Study 2. Thus, we had four values (amount of change due to the stressor) for each psychophysiological variable.

Forehead Electromyogram

The values for change in EMG from baseline to stressor for each stressor for each group of participants are presented in Table 7.2. The primary finding of interest from the analyses was a significant ($p = .001$) Group × Stressor interaction. Follow-up analyses showed that the aggressive driver group showed significantly greater increases in facial EMG than the controls to both aggressive driving audiotapes but no difference to mental arithmetic or the fear-arousal audiotape. Further analyses showed significant within-group changes for each stressor for the aggressive driving group but no significant within-group changes for the controls.

Mean Heart Rate

Table 7.3 shows the values for change in HR from baseline to stressor for each stressor for each group. Again, the Group × Stressor interaction was significant ($p = .040$). However, planned follow-up analyses revealed no instance in which the stressor response for one group was greater than for the other group. Further analyses showed a significant stressor response among the aggressive drivers only for mental arithmetic. The control partici-

TABLE 7.3
Mean Heart Rate Reactivity Scores for Various Stressors for
Aggressive Drivers and Control Participants

	Group		
Stressor (beats/min)	Aggressive drivers	Controls	Between-groups significance
Mental arithmetic	6.1**	12.2***	No
Driving Tape 1	2.5	2.9*	No
Driving Tape 2	2.4	1.4	No
Fear-arousal tape	1.2	3.6*	No
Initial baseline value	69.9	66.5	No

Note. There was significant within-group reactivity from baseline to stressor. From "Psychophysiological Reactivity of Aggressive Drivers: An Exploratory Study," by L. S. Malta, E. B. Blanchard, B. M. Freidenberg, T. E. Galovski, A. Karl, and S. R. Holzapfel, *Applied Psychophysiology and Biofeedback, Vol. 26,* p. 106. Copyright 2001 by Kluwer Academic Publishers. Adapted with kind permission of Springer Science and Business Media.
*$p < .05$. ** $p < .01$. *** $p < .001$.

pants, however, showed significant changes for mental arithmetic, Aggressive Driving Audiotape 1, and the fear-arousal audiotape.

Systolic Blood Pressure

Although the Group × Stressor interaction term was not significant, the planned follow-up analyses did reveal that the aggressive drivers showed significantly greater increases in SBP for both aggressive driving tapes. Like the forehead EMG results, there were no differences in reactivity between the groups to the mental arithmetic or fear-arousal audiotape. The aggressive drivers showed significant within-group SBP responses for all four stressors; by way of contrast, the control participants showed an SBP increase only for mental arithmetic. The SBP results are displayed in Table 7.4.

Diastolic Blood Pressure

As with SBP, the Group × Stressor interaction was not significant for DBP. The planned follow-up analyses revealed that the aggressive drivers were more reactive than control participants only for DBP response to the first aggressive driving audiotape. The aggressive driving group showed significant within-group changes to mental arithmetic, Aggressive Driving Audiotape 1, and the fear-provoking audiotape. The control participants showed significant DBP change only for the mental arithmetic stressor. See Table 7.5 for the numerical values of the DBP responses.

Skin Resistance Level

The interaction of Group × Stressor conditions was significant ($p = .039$) for SRL. Planned follow-up analyses revealed that the degree of de-

TABLE 7.4
Mean Systolic Blood Pressure Reactivity Scores for Various Stressors for Aggressive Drivers and Control Participants

Stressor (mm Hg)	Group		Between-groups significance
	Aggressive drivers	Controls	
Mental arithmetic	7.0***	9.3**	No
Driving Tape 1	6.3***	1.7	Yes
Driving Tape 2	3.9*	−0.5	Yes
Fear-arousal tape	2.9*	1.7	No
Initial baseline value	117.0	111.0	No

Note. There was significant within-group reactivity from baseline to stressor. From "Psychophysiological Reactivity of Aggressive Drivers: An Exploratory Study," by L. S. Malta, E. B. Blanchard, B. M. Freidenberg, T. E. Galovski, A. Karl, and S. R. Holzapfel, *Applied Psychophysiology and Biofeedback, Vol. 26,* p. 108. Copyright 2001 by Kluwer Academic Publishers. Adapted with kind permission of Springer Science and Business Media.
*$p < .05$. **$p < .01$. ***$p < .001$.

TABLE 7.5
Mean Diastolic Blood Pressure Reactivity Scores for Various Stressors for Aggressive Drivers and Control Participants

Stressor (mmHg)	Group		Between-groups significance
	Aggressive drivers	Controls	
Mental arithmetic	5.9***	5.9***	No
Driving Tape 1	2.5**	0.4	Yes
Driving Tape 2	0.6	−0.4	No
Fear-arousal tape	1.9**	0.7	No
Initial baseline value	66.1	63.3	No

Note. There was significant within-group reactivity from baseline to stressor. From "Psychophysiological Reactivity of Aggressive Drivers: An Exploratory Study," by L. S. Malta, E. B. Blanchard, B. M. Freidenberg, T. E. Galovski, A. Karl, and S. R. Holzapfel, *Applied Psychophysiology and Biofeedback, Vol. 26,* p. 105. Copyright 2001 by Kluwer Academic Publishers. Adapted with kind permission of Springer Science and Business Media.
**$p < 01$. ***$p < .001$.

crease in SRL was significantly greater for the aggressive driving group, compared with control participants, only for mental arithmetic. Within-group comparisons revealed a significant decrease in SRL for the aggressive drivers only to Aggressive Driving Audiotape 1. The control participants showed significant decreases for mental arithmetic and the fear-arousal audiotape ($p = .052$). Mean scores for both groups for each of the four stressors are in Table 7.6.

Vividness Ratings of Imagined Scenes

The mean vividness ratings for each group for each of the three imagined stressors are presented in Table 7.7. Analyses revealed no significant

TABLE 7.6
Mean Skin Resistance Level Reactivity Scores for Various Stressors for Aggressive Drivers and Control Participants

Stressor (K ohms)	Group		Between-groups significance
	Aggressive drivers	Controls	
Mental arithmetic	−1.5	−6.8**	Yes
Driving Tape 1	−1.1*	−0.2	No
Driving Tape 2	−0.1	−0.5	No
Fear-arousal tape	−0.7	−2.1*	No
Initial baseline value	16.4	19.7	No

Note. There was significant within-group reactivity from baseline to stressor. From "Psychophysiological Reactivity of Aggressive Drivers: An Exploratory Study," by L. S. Malta, E. B. Blanchard, B. M. Freidenberg, T. E. Galovski, A. Karl, and S. R. Holzapfel, *Applied Psychophysiology and Biofeedback, Vol. 26*, p. 108. Copyright 2001 by Kluwer Academic Publishers. Adapted with kind permission of Springer Science and Business Media.
*$p < .05$. **$p < .01$.

TABLE 7.7
Mean Vividness of Images Ratings for Audiotape Stressors for Aggressive Drivers and Control Participants

Stressor	Aggressive drivers	Controls
Aggressive Driving Tape 1	60.4	60.9
Aggressive Driving Tape 2	64.3	60.7
Fear-arousal tape	67.3	74.6

Note. Table values are participant ratings made on a scale that ranged from 0 (*not at all*) to 100 (*maximal vividness*). No between-groups differences are significant.

between-group differences on any of the imagined stressors and no within-group differences across stressors. In all instances, participants reported that the imagined scenes were moderately vivid.

Summary of Results

The strongest results, in terms of discriminating aggressive drivers from control participants, were obtained for forehead EMG and, to a lesser degree, with BP, especially SBP. Mean HR did not discriminate at all. Electrodermal activity (SRL) discriminated minimally. Very important for our purposes is that the aggressive driving audiotapes, especially the first tape, discriminated between the two groups on forehead EMG, SBP, and DBP, whereas the second aggressive driving tape discriminated between the two groups on forehead EMG and SBP. Mental arithmetic led to a significant between-groups effect on SRL only.

Regarding within-group change, the aggressive drivers showed significant reactivity to all four stressors in forehead EMG and SBP and to three of four stressors for DBP. By way of contrast, the control participants were significantly reactive with HR to three of four stressors (excluding Aggressive Driving Audiotape 2) but to none of the stressors in EMG. Mental arithmetic led to within-group change in both groups to HR, SBP, and DBP, confirming its ability to elicit a pressor response.

The clinical implications of these findings are, first, that aggressive drivers are physiologically responsive to imagining annoying driving situations (and thus probably are physically aroused in real life situations) And, second, that incorporating relaxation strategies into treatment may help counteract some of the arousal and thus could relieve some discomfort. Brief progressive relaxation could be especially important in reducing the EMG response.

Study 2

As noted earlier, we omitted the forehead EMG and peak HR measures in this study.[1] We performed three sets of comparisons on the psychophysiological results in this study. First, we compared the results of the 29 treatment-seeking aggressive drivers (1 court-referred driver refused to participate in the psychophysiological assessment) with those of 14 nonaggressive drivers who participated as paid volunteers.[2] Second, we compared the pretreatment assessment results of the court-referred aggressive drivers with those of the self-referred aggressive drivers. Third, we compared pretreatment psychophysiological reactivity values with posttreatment reactivity values for 24 aggressive drivers who completed treatment and the posttreatment psychophysiological assessment. The posttreatment assessment always followed treatment completion. Thus, the aggressive drivers who were in the wait-list condition (see chap. 9) were retested after the wait list on the aggressive driving and other psychological measures but were not given the psychophysiological testing at that point.

As with Study 1, we omitted the overall omnibus multivariate analysis of variance because of the small sample size ($n = 39$) compared with the 32 experimental conditions. Instead, we calculated change scores or reactivity scores for each stressor by subtracting the average of Minutes 2 through 5 of a preceding baseline phase from the peak value (instead of the average of two or three minute-by-minute values) from the stressor phase. These reactivity scores for each of the four physiological response domains were

---

[1] With hindsight, given the ability of forehead EMG to discriminate between aggressive drivers and control participants, this was probably not a wise decision.
[2] It should be noted that 4 of the aggressive drivers also declined to participate in the fear-arousal segment of the psychophysiological assessment. Thus, samples sizes are reduced by 4 for these comparisons for each physiological response.

then subjected to a Groups (aggressive drivers or control participants) × Stressor Conditions (4 levels) univariate repeated measures analysis of variance. We were, as before, interested in the Group × Condition interaction term. We found significant interactions for SBP and SRL and a trend for HR but no interaction for DBP. We did not conduct omnibus tests in the comparison of pretreatment scores of the two sets of aggressive drivers or the pre–post analysis of treatment effects on the aggressive drivers.

For the remaining comparisons, we conducted either between-groups *t* tests or within-group paired *t* tests. No correction for multiple comparisons has been applied.[3]

Heart Rate

Table 7.8 presents all of the HR reactivity scores for each of the analyses. Thus, we present pretreatment HR reactivity scores for each stressor for (a) initial values for court-referred aggressive drivers versus for self-referred aggressive drivers, (b) initial values for all aggressive drivers combined versus nonaggressive-driving control participants, and (c) pretreatment and posttreatment values for all aggressive drivers for whom data are available. Also included are indications when the *t* test comparisons were significant.

When one examines the values in Table 7.8, one sees first that the self-referred aggressive drivers show a greater HR response to the first aggressive driving audiotape than do their court-referred counterparts. The means are in the same direction for Aggressive Driving Audiotape 2 but are not significantly different. It could be that the self-referred drivers are being more candid and taking part in the imagery procedure more readily. When the aggressive drivers as a group are compared with the control participants, we see that there are no HR differences between these two groups.

Finally, an examination of the HR reactivity of the aggressive drivers before and after treatment reveals two effects of treatment. First, and most important, the HR reactivity to the first aggressive driving tape is significantly reduced, indicating that the ability of this imaginal scene to produce arousal is noticeably abated. There is also a reduction in reactivity to the mental arithmetic stressor.

Systolic Blood Pressure

Comparable values of change scores or reactivity scores for SBP to the various stressors are contained in Table 7.9. Unlike HR, for which 3 of 12

---

[3]Because no correction has been applied, readers may want to use caution in interpreting any of the results.

TABLE 7.8

Study 2: Mean Heart Rate Reactivity Scores for Various Stressors for Different Subgroups of Aggressive Drivers and Control Participants

	Group											
Stressor reactivity score (beats/min)	Court-referred aggressive drivers		Self-referred aggressive drivers		All aggressive drivers		Controls		Pretreatment aggressive drivers		Posttreatment aggressive drivers	
	M	SD	M	SD	M	SD	M	SD	M	SD	M	SD
Mental arithmetic	13.1	7.8	10.3	8.9	12.1	13.6	17.5	13.6	11.8	7.7	8.9	5.8†
Driving Tape 1	2.4	3.6	6.2	6.3*	3.7	4.5	3.9	4.5	3.0	3.4	0.5	2.4**
Driving Tape 2	3.1	5.5	4.9	5.1	3.7	5.4	3.0	4.0	3.3	5.2	2.0	2.6
Fear-arousal tape	1.3	3.3	2.3	4.2	1.7	3.6	2.3	5.5	1.4	3.5	0.5	2.7
Baseline value					69.5	11.0						

†$p < .10$. *$p < .05$. **$p < .01$.

TABLE 7.9
Study 2: Mean Systolic Blood Pressure Reactivity Scores for Various Stressors for Different Subgroups of Aggressive Drivers and Control Participants

| | Group | | | | | | | | | | | |
| Stressor reactivity score (mm Hg) | Court-referred aggressive drivers | | Self-referred aggressive drivers | | All aggressive drivers | | Controls | | Pretreatment aggressive drivers | | Posttreatment aggressive drivers | |
	M	SD	M	SD	M	SD	M	SD	M	SD	M	SD
Mental arithmetic	11.5	6.6	10.3	8.0	11.1	7.0	16.6	10.6†	11.1	7.5	8.5	8.0†
Driving Tape 1	5.7	5.0	11.8	7.0**	7.9	6.4	3.6	5.9*	7.4	5.9	3.1	5.3**
Driving Tape 2	4.4	6.3	7.9	7.4	5.6	6.8	1.3	5.4*	6.0	7.2	2.7	3.6*
Fear-arousal tape	-0.8	3.3	3.6	3.3*	0.8	5.1	0.7	3.8	1.0	3.5	-0.2	2.9
Baseline value					115.1							

†$p < .10$. *$p < .05$. **$p < .01$.

comparisons were significant at the $p < .10$ level, for SBP, 8 of 12 comparisons were significant, with 7 of those at the $p < .05$ level or better.

Again, the self-referred aggressive drivers were significantly more reactive in SBP than the court-referred drivers for the first aggressive driving audiotape (double the response) and for the fear-arousal audiotape. When all aggressive drivers are compared with the control participants, both driving tapes (designed to provoke annoyance or anger) elicited significantly greater SBP responses from the aggressive drivers than found for the control participants (two to four times greater). It is interesting that the control participants show a greater response than the aggressive drivers to mental arithmetic.

There were significant within-group treatment effects on SBP for both of the aggressive driving audiotapes and for the mental arithmetic stressor. The SBP reactivity was reduced by greater than 50% to both aggressive driving tapes.

Diastolic Blood Pressure

The DBP reactivity scores for the various stressors are presented in Table 7.10. The results presented in Table 7.10 indicate that there are few significant differences, and both of these were reactivity to the first aggressive driving audiotape. The self-referred aggressive drivers showed greater increases in DBP than the court-referred drivers; in fact, the value for the self-referred drivers is twice that of the court-referred drivers. It is notable that reactivity to the first aggressive driving tape decreased significantly (by 75%) with treatment.

The changes in DBP reactivity are thus consistent with the changes in SBP reactivity and changes in HR reactivity. However, DBP does not seem nearly as responsive to treatment effects as SBP or HR.

Skin Resistance Level

The values for electrodermal reactivity as indexed by SRL changes from baseline to stressor are listed in Table 7.11. Recall that the indication of arousal in this response is a *decrease* in the signal. Only two differences are significant: The control participants showed a significantly greater decrease in SRL in response to mental arithmetic than did the aggressive drivers. Second, the aggressive drivers who were treated were less reactive to Aggressive Driving Tape 1 after treatment than before.

Self-Report Measures During Psychophysiological Assessment

At the pretreatment assessment, the court-referred and self-referred groups did not differ on any mood ratings during the neutral stressor (mental arithmetic) or during the fear-arousal audiotape. We did not collect mood ratings during the posttreatment psychophysiological assessment.

TABLE 7.10
Mean Diastolic Blood Pressure Reactivity Scores for Various Stressors for Different Subgroups of Aggressive Drivers and Control Participants

Stressor reactivity score (mm Hg)	Group											
	Court-referred aggressive drivers		Self-referred aggressive drivers		All aggressive drivers		Controls		Pretreatment aggressive drivers		Posttreatment aggressive drivers	
	M	SD	M	SD	M	SD	M	SD	M	SD	M	SD
Mental arithmetic	7.1	5.4	6.7	4.0	6.9	4.9	7.5	4.5	6.8	5.3	5.9	5.1
Driving Tape 1	2.7	4.3	5.3	2.3†	3.6	3.9	2.1	1.9	3.6	4.1	0.9	3.5*
Driving Tape 2	1.5	2.5	3.3	3.0	2.1	2.8	1.5	3.5	1.9	2.8	1.0	2.8
Fear-arousal tape	-0.2	3.6	1.5	2.2	0.4	3.2	0.1	2.5	0.3	3.4	-0.3	2.4
Baseline value					64.6							

†$p < .10$. *$p < .05$.

TABLE 7.11
Mean Skin Resistance Level Reactivity Scores for Various Stressors for Different Subgroups of Aggressive Drivers and Control Participants

| | Group | | | | | | | | | | | |
| Stressor reactivity score (K ohms) | Court-referred aggressive drivers | | Self-referred aggressive drivers | | All aggressive drivers | | Controls | | Pretreatment aggressive drivers | | Posttreatment aggressive drivers | |
	M	SD	M	SD	M	SD	M	SD	M	SD	M	SD
Mental arithmetic	-2.2	5.1	-1.5	1.4	-2.0	4.2	-7.7	7.6**	-2.1	4.7	-2.9	4.6
Driving Tape 1	-0.1	1.1	-0.9	1.8	-0.4	1.4	-0.9	4.9	-0.5	1.6	0.2	1.3
Driving Tape 2	0.2	1.6	0.0	2.9	0.1	2.1	0.0	4.4	-0.2	2.0	-0.3	1.4
Fear-arousal tape	-0.3	0.6	-1.0	2.0	-0.6	1.3	-0.5	6.3	-0.4	0.5	0.0	0.8
Baseline value					9.8	11.0						

$**p < .01$.

For the first aggressive driving tape, the self-referred group gave significantly higher ratings on tension (vs. relaxed), anger (vs. calm), and energetic (vs. sluggish) than the court-referred group. The latter group scored higher on excitement (vs. boredom).

For the second aggressive driving tape, the results again showed significantly higher ratings for the self-referred group than for the court-referred group on tension, anger, and excitement. There was a trend ($p < .05$) for the self-referred group to give higher ratings of sadness (vs. happiness) than the court-referred group. There were no differences on any vividness ratings. It thus appears that the self-referred group was either more emotionally affected by the aggressive driving tapes or more willing to acknowledge feeling states than the court-referred group.

Summary of Results

SBP is by far the physiological response that is most responsive to treatment and that shows the greatest between-groups differences. Eight of the 12 comparisons for SBP reactivity were significant, more than were found for the other three response systems combined (a total of seven). It is interesting that four of these seven other significant differences were treatment effects. Moreover, there was a treatment effect in response to the first aggressive driving tape for all four psychophysiological responses. This finding would seem to indicate that treatment was having its intended effect of causing drivers to be significantly less reactive to provocative and annoying driving situations.

Psychophysiological Assessment Results for Aggressive Drivers With and Without Intermittent Explosive Disorder

As with other measures, we subdivided the treatment-seeking sample into those with intermittent explosive disorder (IED; $n = 10$) and those who did not meet the IED criteria ($n = 13$) and compared their initial psychophysiological assessment data. Only significant ($p < .05$) comparisons are described.

Drivers with IED had lower initial baseline HR values (66.0 bpm vs. 74.8 bpm) than the non-IED group. It is interesting that the BP results were in the opposite direction: Drivers with IED were significantly lower than the non-IED participants on all four baseline comparisons of SBP (Baseline 1: IED = 123.6 mm Hg, non-IED = 110.3 mm Hg; Baseline 2: IED = 122.5 mm Hg, non-IED = 111.0 mm Hg; Baseline 3: IED = 123.1 mm Hg, non-IED = 110.8 mm Hg; Baseline 4: IED = 125.7 mm Hg, non-IED – 109.7 mm Hg). In regard to DBP, the IED group had a higher average value (68.1 mm Hg vs. 61.1 mm Hg) than the non-IED group. There were no electrodermal differences between the two groups of participants.

Along with the higher baseline values, the maximum values during some of the stressors were significantly higher for the IED participants than for those who did not meet criteria for IED. Thus, for the mental arithmetic, SBP was higher for those with IED (136.6 mm Hg vs. 121.3 mm Hg) than for those who did not meet IED criteria. Similar significant results were found for DBP: Drivers with IED were higher (76.4 mm Hg vs. 66.3 mm Hg) than those without IED.

For the two audiotapes designed to provoke driving anger, drivers with IED had significantly higher SBP in response to Aggressive Driving Audiotape 1 (132.4 mm Hg vs. 117.7 mm Hg) and in response to Aggressive Driving Audiotape 2 (131.8 mm Hg vs. 114.8 mm Hg) than the non-IED participants. For DBP, the difference was significant only for Aggressive Driving Audiotape 2 (69.2 mm Hg vs. 60.9 mm Hg). For the fear-arousal tape, drivers with IED showed a higher SBP (127.8 mm Hg vs. 108.3 mm Hg) than drivers who did not meet IED criteria.

There were almost no differences in reactivity (stressor value minus preceding baseline value) on any of the four psychophysiological responses for any of the four stressors between individuals who met criteria for IED versus those who did not meet criteria for IED. It would appear that drivers with IED manifested higher values of SBP (and, to some extent, DBP) across the entire assessment, from initial baseline through all stressors and returns to baseline.

These limited psychophysiological assessment data constitute, to the best of our knowledge, the first such report on participants who meet criteria for IED compared with a similar control group matched on age, gender, and reason for participating in the research.

SUMMARY

A comparison of the two sets of results makes it clear that SBP is the one response that replicated across samples: Both community and student aggressive drivers who volunteered for the research (Study 1) and the treatment-seeking aggressive drivers (Study 2) who were more seriously aggressive in their driving showed SBP reactivity to imagery guided by an audiotape. It is important to note that this reactivity is significantly reduced with treatment. HR, DBP, and electrodermal activity are much less reliable at differentiating aggressive drivers from control participants or at revealing treatment effects.

In hindsight, it is unfortunate that we did not include forehead EMG in the second study. Its high level of discrimination between aggressive drivers and control participants in Study 1 leads us to recommend its inclusion in future work in this area.

Future research and treatment work might consider making use of ambulatory BP monitoring equipment that is now readily available in light-weight, unobtrusive modules. We know from Stokols and colleagues' (Stokols et al., 1978; Stokols & Novaco, 1981) studies that routine driving to and from work, at least in southern California, elicits a noticeable BP pressor response. Measuring BP while aggressive drivers are traveling or operating a driver simulator might capture even greater levels of reactivity during provocative driving situations. Measuring it after treatment and finding a reduction in BP reactivity could provide a valuable non-self-report indication of treatment effects.

III

PSYCHOLOGICAL TREATMENT OF THE ANGRY AND AGGRESSIVE DRIVER

8

TREATMENT OF DRIVING ANGER
AND AGGRESSIVE DRIVING:
WORK BY OTHERS

The function, arousal, and reinforcing quality of anger on the roads continue to be investigated in a variety of contexts, as described in previous chapters. Research on aggressive driving has delved into the realm of personality and potential psychopathology in an attempt to investigate profiles and the predisposition of individuals to drive aggressively. Links among anger, hostility, and aggression have been established and researched, and links between aggressive driving and subsequent roadway fatalities, injuries, and property damage have been clearly portrayed. We thus have a fairly clear estimation of the context in which aggressive driving may occur, the specific behaviors involved, and even the type of person who may be performing the majority of the behaviors. We are only beginning to have a clear indication of how to treat the problem. In this chapter, we review the available literature on the treatment of aggressive drivers outside the Albany program.

Drivers can peruse and partake of any number of aggressive driving surveys that are available on various Web sites. Hints and suggestions as to how to control aggressive driving behavior also abound on similar sites, which often are sponsored by driving organizations such as the American Automobile Association. Additionally, one can find self-help manuals such as those by Larson (1996b) and by James and Nahl (2000). However, to the best of our knowledge, there are only two clinician-administered, psychosocial interventions specifically targeting aggressive driving.

In his self-help manual mentioned previously, Larson (1996b) described in full his 1-day intensive treatment program, which was designed for self-referred aggressive drivers. The program encourages drivers to take responsibility for their anger and subsequent aggressive behaviors. Education about anger is provided so that drivers can develop a greater understanding of the properties of the emotion, and they are instructed to rate their personal experience of anger on a provided scale.

Larson's (1996b) intervention then identifies five driver beliefs that can produce anger and aggression. Matching those five beliefs are five specific types of drivers whose attitudes contribute to their specific driving aggression, and aggressive drivers are encouraged to try to identify with one or more of these types of drivers. Once these attitudes or belief systems are identified, drivers can begin the process of making changes in their existing belief systems in order to foster a more positive, less aggressive driving style. These old belief systems are challenged and altered by means of cognitive strategies, and the aggressive driver is not only challenged cognitively but is also offered alternative strategies to better cope with driving stress rather than resorting to aggressive behavior. Larson, Rodriquez, and Galvan-Henkin (1998) reported impressive success of this intervention as measured by pre- and posttreatment changes on the Driver's Stress Profile (Larson, 1996b).

This pioneering work was integral in the construction of our own treatment manual. Although the interventions discussed show promising face value and are intuitively very helpful in addressing aggressive driving, Larson's overall treatment has, to the best of our knowledge, yet to be empirically tested.

As assessed through multiple measures, our Albany study (see chap. 9) offers methodological improvements on Larson's (1996b) pioneering work because of our controlled design and outcome. Furthermore, the Albany project included a court-mandated population whose aggressive driving behavior was considered severe enough to warrant sentencing to the program and thus includes an objectively determined severe and potentially dangerous sample.

Clinical trials in the treatment of aggressive driving are sparse indeed in the psychological literature, much less those adhering to Foa and Meadows's (1997) suggested gold standard criteria for an outcome study. One study conducted by Rimm, DeGroot, Boord, Heiman, and Dillow (1971) randomly assigned 30 research participants to either systematic desensitization, a placebo condition, or a no-treatment control condition. The desensitization technique was described as standard, with deep muscle relaxation as the countercondition. This means that individualized hierarchies of driving situations that provoked increasing degrees of anger were constructed. Scenes from the hierarchy were then presented in imagination for progressively longer intervals while the participant maintained a relaxed state. The placebo condition consisted of an interview that provided educational information on the physiological and psychological aspects of anger. During the systematic desensitization, participants were repeatedly exposed to items on their hierarchy list and provided subjective anger intensity ratings at each exposure. Galvanic skin response (GSR) and heart rate also were measured. The authors reported improvements in subjective ratings of anger and GSR in the systematic desensitization group only. The study is seriously methodologically flawed in its lack of psychometrically sound instruments adequately measuring outcome. The primary outcome measure instead consisted of change recorded on intensity ratings from the hierarchy described above.

Deffenbacher's group at Colorado State University has developed an outstanding driving anger research program, including two controlled treatment outcome trials. In the first treatment study, Deffenbacher, Huff, Lynch, Oetting, and Salvatore (2000) reported a controlled trial in which they compared two active treatment conditions with an assessment-only control condition in a self-identified, high driving anger (aggressive-driving) college population of volunteers who received course credit for participation. The two interventions included eight 1-hour small-group sessions conducted weekly. The groups consisted of approximately 7 to 10 members and were co-led by two female doctoral candidates. The first condition, self-managed relaxation coping skills (RCS), included training in deep relaxation strategies coupled with four relaxation coping skills, with the overarching goal of providing the participant with the skills necessary to relax in a provocative driving situation in an effort to decrease driving anger. The second active condition included a combination of cognitive and relaxation coping skills (CRCS). The CRCS condition included an abbreviated version of the relaxation component from RCS but also included an emphasis on identifying and restructuring faulty cognitions around the driving situation. Specific cognitive distortions (e.g., catastrophization, overgeneralization) and ways to counter them were introduced in Sessions 3 through 8. Rehearsal of alternative statements was coupled with deep relaxation strategies. The overarching goal of the CRCS condition was to reduce driving anger by applying relaxation strategies in stressful or provoking driving situations as well as through reinterpretation of driving stress. Individuals in the no-treatment control condition were not given any treatment and completed the three assessment procedures in return for college credit.

Outcome measures of driving behavior included the Driving Anger Scale (DAS; Deffenbacher, Oetting, & Lynch, 1994), reports of anger to different imaginal driving scenarios that ranged in level of provocation (normal driving conditions, heavy traffic, rush hour traffic, being yelled at by a fellow driver), a daily driving log (number of anger experiences that day, the most angering roadway event, intensity of anger experienced, and engagement in any specified aggressive driving behaviors), and the Driving Survey (a report of accident-related variables and risky and aggressive driving behaviors). Participants were reassessed at posttreatment and again at a 4-week follow-up point. The results indicated greater improvement for both the experimental conditions over the control condition; however, there was very little differential effect between the two active treatment conditions. Specifically, participants in the pure relaxation condition (RCS) improved more on the DAS, whereas participants in the CRCS condition indicated more improvement on variables in the driving diaries. Neither condition indicated improvement on general trait anger as shown on the State–Trait Anger Expression Inventory (Spielberger, 1988).

In speculating as to why participants in the CRCS condition showed less improvement on the DAS, Deffenbacher, Filetti, Lynch, Dahlen, and Oetting (2002) surmised that this poorer outcome might have been due to the manner of implementation of the cognitive component of the intervention. In the aforementioned first controlled trial, the therapists focused on a specific cognitive distortion per session, potentially overlooking additional cognitive distortions that may be more primary in contributing to anger. Thus, in their second treatment study (Deffenbacher, Filetti, et al., 2002) they modified the cognitive component of CRCS such that the participant identified situation-specific inaccurate thoughts and used those as a basis for the remainder of the intervention, as described above. The cognitive intervention became more reminiscent of Beckian therapy in its use of Socratic questions and its exploratory nature. The change was designed to make the cognitive component of therapy more relevant and easier to apply in real-life situations. The RCS treatment condition in this second randomized, controlled clinical trial remained the same as in the original study.

The second treatment study (Deffenbacher, Filetti, et al., 2002) included a research design similar to that of the first treatment study. Fifty-five men and women, who were college students high in driving anger and who received course credit for participation, were randomly assigned to either RCS, CRCS (modified version), or a no-treatment control group. Treatment was conducted in small-group format and co-led by advanced doctoral-level therapists. Similar to the first treatment study, Deffenbacher, Filetti, et al. (2002) measured changes in driving anger and behavior through the use of the DAS, driving scenarios, and driving logs. Additions to these outcome measures included the Personal Driving Anger Situations and the Driving Anger Expression Inventory (DAX; Deffenbacher, Lynch, Oetting, & Swaim, 2002) as measures of aggressive driving (see chap. 6). The former measure asks the participant to describe two driving situations that are most angering to him or her; the DAX measures the expression of driving anger on two general dimensions: (a) hostile–aggressive expression and (b) adaptive–constructive expression.

The results of the second treatment trial indicated that both of the two active treatments, RCS and CRCS, showed reductions of driving anger and poor driving behavior across the various assessment measures. Both treatments also resulted in increases in adaptive driving behaviors as measured by the DAX. These results suggest that the aggressive drivers treated in this program began replacing aggressive behaviors with more appropriate, safer behaviors on the roadways. At the follow-up point 1 month after treatment, only participants in the CRCS condition had maintained the decreases seen in hostile–aggressive expression of driving anger as measured by the DAX. On generalized trait anger (State–Trait Anger Expression Inventory; Spielberger, 1988), the three groups did not differ at posttreatment; however, at the 1-month follow-up the two treated groups had lower scores than the control participants. There were no improvements seen in the no-treatment control group on any of the measures. Overall, the second treatment study provided an excellent replication of the RCS condition's results seen in the first study and an enhancement of the positive results seen in the CRCS condition. Deffenbacher concluded that the addition of the Socratic questions and identification of situation-specific cognitions augmented the original CRCS protocol.

In summary, Rimm et al. (1971) reported reductions of driving anger and GSR during imaginal provoking driving scenes in a systematic desensitization treatment condition. However, the study is methodologically flawed, making the results difficult to interpret. Larson (1996b) reported success in his pioneering, 1-day intensive intervention program specifically targeting aggressive driving among self-referred community volunteers. However, he has yet to test the effectiveness of the program in an empirically controlled fashion consistent with gold standard treatment outcome criteria (Foa & Meadows, 1997). Deffenbacher's group (Deffenbacher, Filetti, et al., 2002; Deffenbacher, Huff, et al., 2000) has developed an elegant program of research treating the college student aggressive driving population. They replicated the success of their primarily behavioral intervention (deep relaxation) and enhanced their cognitive–behavioral intervention within a college sample of angry drivers. The work of these pioneers in the understudied field of aggressive driving provided the stepping stones for the Albany investigators' work with community samples.

9

THE ALBANY AGGRESSIVE DRIVING STUDIES: TREATMENT RESULTS

In this chapter, we describe and summarize the aggressive driving treatment program conducted at the Albany Center for Stress and Anxiety Disorders in 1999–2000 (Galovski & Blanchard, 2002a, 2002b). The treatment manual for this program is presented in chapter 10. In creating the treatment manual for this project, we borrowed heavily from the anger management literature because there existed very little precedent and guidance in the empirical literature on aggressive driving (see chap. 8). Unfortunately, at the time we wrote the Albany manual, neither of Deffenbacher's treatment outcome studies (Deffenbacher, Filetti, Lynch, Dahlen, & Oetting, 2002; Deffenbacher, Huff, Lynch, Oetting, & Salvatore, 2000; Deffenbacher, Lynch, Filetti, Dahlen, & Oetting, 2003) had been published. We were able to use specific aggressive driving interventions provided in Larson's (1996b) self-help text, as is evident in chapter 10. All told, because of the relative paucity of aggressive driving literature to provide guidance in creating the Albany protocol, we turned to the anger management treatment outcome studies to assess the empirical evidence supporting various interventions in parallel angry populations. Relative to research conducted in other areas of human emotion (i.e., depression and anxiety), the information on treating anger is somewhat sparse. However, it offered a starting point from which to begin construction of a treatment targeting aggressive driving.

CONSTRUCTION OF THE TREATMENT MANUAL

Clinical research has yielded a variety of treatment protocols for anger management, stemming from different theoretical perspectives. Each perspective provided valuable guidance and direction in constructing the Albany Aggressive Driving Treatment Manual. *Person-centered* or *humanistic* therapies focus on the intense need for acceptance and the high degree of frustration seen in angry clients (Rogers, 1951). By providing unconditional positive regard, the therapist guides the client toward recognizing his or her own self-worth and empowers the client to discover ways to change maladaptive behavior. Humanistic therapy thus speaks to the importance of the development of rapport and other nonspecific factors included in the course of any successful intervention. As we discuss in more detail in chapter 10, the development of a good working relationship and positive regard for the client is seen as a necessary, although not sufficient, condition for change. Although aggressive driving behavior was never condoned during group sessions, the therapist did not spend what little time was available chastising the drivers. Instead, we attempted to foster a team environment in which the drivers and the therapist were working together toward a common goal. We quickly found that this approach worked best in reducing the defensiveness of the driver and increasing the probability of behavior change.

As important as rapport and a positive, comfortable environment may be, we only had four brief sessions in which to foster change. Anger, perhaps more so than other emotions, often co-occurs with violent, destructive behavior and severe interpersonal crises (in this case, aggressive driving behavior) that require immediate and directive attention. Behavioral interventions focus on these maladaptive behaviors by replacing them with more productive behaviors (Bandura, 1969). Behavioral psychologists have viewed anger as an arousal state precipitating aggression, whereas the clinical and research focus has been on the aggressive behavior itself (Novaco, 1986). Alternatives to aggressive driving behaviors were thus instituted into the driving program (see chap. 10 for specific alternatives to aggressive driving behavior). Many of these alternatives to aggressive driving behavior were borrowed from Larson (1996b) and his program, which we described in chapter 8.

A. T. Beck (1987) hypothesized that three cognitive factors play an integral role in emotion: (a) the negative triad (a negative view of self, the world, and others), (b) schemas (underlying general assumptions about life), and (c) cognitive distortions (ways in which people misinterpret their environment). In essence, one's interpretations of the environment lead one to react emotionally to the environment. For instance, perceiving another person's slow driving as purposeful may lead to an emotional experience of annoyance or anger, which then may trigger an aggressive, punishing type behavior (making a rude gesture, braking intentionally, cutting off the other driver, etc.). Intervention then occurs at the cognitive level rather than at the emotional or behavioral level. Reinterpreting driving situations as less malevolent or other drivers' behavior as less intentional can significantly reduce anger and subsequent aggressive behaviors. As we discuss in chapter 10, the role of cognitive intervention in the treatment of anger was clearly instrumental in the treatment of this aggressive driving population.

Meichenbaum (1986), in his stress inoculation therapy, recognized the importance of the angry emotion underlying aggressive behavior when he postulated that behavior change is achieved at two levels. The first level is the need for the client to become aware of his or her own feelings, thoughts, or behaviors, as well as the impact of his or her behavior on others. Second, the client must be able to interrupt the repetitive or scripted nature of the behavior in order to evaluate responses situationally. In this way, the client recognizes his or her behavior and its impact but does not dwell on these past mistakes. Instead, he or she learns how to reformulate current feelings, thoughts, and behaviors. The client is then challenged to assume responsibility for future behavior and does not flounder in regrets of the past. He or she is thus better able to deal with daily stressors, reduce excessive emotional response, and adopt more appropriate coping behaviors. Education about the experience of anger and related behaviors, acknowledging past engagement in these behaviors, and acceptance of the need to change were critical components of the Albany aggressive driving treatment program.

Novaco (1979) offered a conceptual specification of anger and its therapeutic regulation based on the interrelationship of cognitions, emotions, behaviors, and the environment. His conceptual framework considers anger as an affective stress reaction stemming from cognitive and behavioral determinants. He defined an *affective stress reaction* as "an emotional response to perceived environmental demands that has adverse implications for health and behavior" (Novaco, 1979, p. 243). Given the stress associated with almost any current driving situation in modern times, as we reviewed in chapters 1 through 3, adherence to a model of the relationship between human stress and corresponding anger is appropriate in the treatment of aggressive driving. Thus, the inclusion of several stress reduction and stress inoculation strategies seemed warranted. The goals of such strategies involve not the alleviation or suppression of anger but the prevention of excessive and maladaptive anger, regulation of arousal that does occur, and improvement in skills to cope with or manage provocations. In addition to the behavioral components of the treatment, Novaco (1979) also emphasized (in accordance with research previously cited) the importance of the cognitive components of therapeutic intervention. Thus, we included in this treatment protocol education about anger arousal and personal triggers, identification of particular circumstances precipitating anger, discriminating between adaptive and maladaptive functions and expressions of anger, and introduction of cognitive restructuring.

The different theoretical approaches that inform research result in a variety of interventions targeting different aspects and levels of anger. Success with interventions on individual components of anger has led to the combination of interventions and techniques into multicomponent treatment packages. Novaco (1975) investigated such a treatment package in an elegant, pioneering study after which much subsequent anger management research has been modeled. In that study, three treatments were compared with the combined (cognitive strategies plus relaxation training) treatment package. These three treatments included (a) a purely cognitive treatment, (b) a relaxation training alone treatment, and (c) an elaborate attention control condition. The combined treatment proved to be the most efficacious, with cognitive therapy, relaxation training, and the attention control condition ranking second, third, and fourth, respectively.

Similar results were obtained in a meta-analysis conducted by Tafrate (1995) on anger management treatment studies. Notable effect sizes were shown for a number of treatment strategies, including cognitive interventions, relaxation interventions, systematic desensitization, anxiety management training, and skills training therapies (assertiveness, problem-solving, and social skills training). Similar to Novaco's (1975) results, multicomponent or cognitive–behavioral treatment packages that combine a number of techniques and interventions were found to have a large average effect size (1.00).

More recently, R. Beck and Fernandez (1998) conducted a meta-analysis on cognitive–behavioral anger management treatment packages. This study improved methodologically on Tafrate's (1995) study by comparing 58 relevant studies, including adult and child populations. The grand weighted mean effect size (.70) of cognitive–behavioral therapy for anger management indicates overall moderate treatment gains for the treated participants compared with untreated participants.

On the basis of the empirical evidence for multicomponent treatment packages in the anger management literature and the available aggressive driving literature reviewed in chapter 8, we designed a cognitive–behavioral, multicomponent treatment package designed to specifically target aggressive driving behavior. We also attempted to assess the generalizability of the intervention to overall levels of anger and aggression within this population as measured by standardized psychological instruments. The treatment was administered in group format and conducted once a week for 4 weeks. Each session was approximately 2 hours long. The individual components of the package included the following:

- education about the impact of aggressive driving and anger in general,
- self-identification as an angry driver,
- relaxation training,
- development of alternative coping skills, and
- cognitive restructuring.

It should be noted that although the group process was not systematically measured, we learned anecdotally that the drivers' ability to accept responsibility for their behavior on the roadway appeared to be directly related to treatment progress in a positive, linear fashion. Admission of any driving infraction, much less generally poor driving habits, was very difficult for most drivers. Active participation in the group process and subsequent behavior change appeared to be dependent on the individual's acceptance (even halfhearted) of his or her "aggressive driver" status. Despite the glaring objective evidence that an aggressive driving problem existed (lost drivers' licenses, lost jobs, heavy fines, interpersonal and legal difficulties), most drivers did not realize, or did not care to admit, the extent of their problem.

Clinical Hint

We believe that two of the most critical elements of treatment are encouraging drivers to (a) accept responsibility for their aggressive driving behaviors and (b) focus on changing their own behaviors on the roadway (rather than those of their fellow drivers!). The Albany aggressive driving program can attribute a large part of its success to its attention to these elements.

PARTICIPANTS

Participants in our initial treatment program included adults ages 18 to 70 who acknowledged at least one aggressive driving behavior per day for at least 3 out of 7 days. Exclusion criteria included current diagnosis of bipolar I or II, schizophrenia, schizophreniform psychosis, current alcohol or substance dependence, or current strong suicidal ideation. No potential participants were excluded.

Because aggressive driving is clearly not a diagnosis in the *Diagnostic and Statistical Manual of Mental Disorders* (4th ed.; American Psychiatric Association, 1994), and certainly not a common presenting problem in the average clinician's office, we were doubtful that our clinic would be overwhelmed by requests for aggressive driving treatment from the general public. We also wanted to ensure that we were truly treating significantly aggressive individuals. Toward this end, Tara E. Galovski decided to enlist the cooperation of the criminal justice system (details of this process are described in chap. 11). Because this had never been done in the Albany area, we had no real estimation of the frequency or intensity of aggressive driving behaviors or related arrests on the local roadways. We also did not anticipate the severity of the offenses that would come through our clinic within a 7-month period. The referring arrests ranged from misdemeanors to felonies, and several of the court-referred (CR) drivers chose participation in the program in lieu of heavy fines, imprisonment, or both. In chapter 4 we supplied readers with detailed tables of the driving histories and arrests of the (CR) population. Within a 7-month period, 21 CR drivers were sent to our program (1 of which never appeared, and his information was returned to the courts). These drivers were referred from one county only and reflect only those drivers who were both caught by the police and accepted our program as part of their plea arrangement. We were surprised (and a bit alarmed) at the extent, frequency, and severity of aggressive driving on the roadways that we had driven daily for years.

We also wanted to attempt to gather data from non-CR individuals for comparison purposes. The 10 individuals who responded to our advertisements in local newspapers or who heard about us through the local media coverage of our program were called the *self-referred* (SR) sample. The vast majority of the SR sample reported being cajoled into joining the program by family members or friends who could not tolerate being in the car with them any longer out of fear for their lives! For most of these individuals, the severity of the driving behavior was such that it was probably only a matter of time before an arrest would be made or a serious accident would occur. These 10 individuals' specific driving histories were also described in chapter 4.

In summary, 30 individuals were assessed for treatment (10 SR drivers and 20 CR drivers). Twenty-eight of the 30 entered treatment (2 of the SR drivers could not begin treatment: One fell off a horse and was hospitalized for several months, and the other was fired from his job because of complaints about his driving and had to relocate to secure new employment). All 28 participants completed treatment, but 1 SR individual did not return for a follow-up assessment. Therefore, we have posttreatment data on 27 participants (7 SR and 20 CR). We analyzed the demographic variables to identify any differences between the SR and CR groups. The results indicated that the CR participants were, on average, significantly younger than the SR group participants. The groups were similar in regard to gender, ethnicity, and marital status.

As reference back to chapter 4 will show, the two groups described their driving histories a bit differently. The CR group had statistically significantly more driving-related arrests and arithmetically more instances of being arrested for driving while intoxicated than the SR group. The SR group reported arithmetically more motor vehicle accidents than the CR group. However, when interviewed, the CR group admitted to significantly less aggressive driving behavior and reported feeling significantly less provoked on the roadways. Furthermore, when asked to track aggressive driving behaviors on a daily basis using a driving diary (see chap. 4), the CR group overall endorsed significantly fewer types of driving behavior and less frequency, less intensity, and less severity of aggressive driving. As indicated in chapter 4, the CR drivers' self-report is clearly less than consistent with the driving behaviors for which these individuals were arrested.

Within each referral condition, participants were matched into pairs on the basis of psychopathology, gender, age, and socioeconomic status. One member of each pair was randomly assigned to a 6-week, no-treatment wait list control condition, and the other member of the pair was assigned to immediate treatment. On conclusion of the wait list period, the individual was crossed over into the active treatment condition. The end result was a semi-crossover design with all participants eventually receiving the active treatment.

OUTCOME MEASURES

The primary outcome measure was a locally constructed daily driving monitoring diary (see Exhibit 4.2). The diary lists 13 overt aggressive driving behaviors commonly cited in the literature, as well as 4 covert aggressive driving behaviors, and asks the participant to rate the extent to which he or she has committed or experienced each behavior on a daily basis, using a Likert-type scale. Because the aggressive driving behaviors included in the driving diary ranged in severity, each was weighted independently by 14 doctoral-level students and faculty. These 14 individuals ranked the aggressive driving behaviors according to what each perceived was the level of severity of each driving behavior. These ratings were tabulated, and each driving behavior was weighted accordingly. For instance, "physical assault" was ranked as the highest or most severe behavior on the diary and so was given the highest severity rating of 5. "Feeling angry," "feeling impatient," and "feeling upset" were ranked the lowest and were thus given a severity rating of 1. The other behaviors were weighted accordingly. Participants tracked their driving behavior with these diaries for 2 weeks prior to treatment, 2 weeks posttreatment, and for 1 week at the 2-month follow-up point.

Standardized psychological instruments were also administered at each assessment point (pretreatment, posttreatment, and 2-month follow-up). These included two aggressive driving measures: the Driver Stress Profile

(DSP; Larson, Rodriquez, & Galvan-Henkin, 1998) and the Driving Anger Scale (DAS; Deffenbacher, Oetting, & Lynch, 1994). Changes in psychological distress were also tracked. Depression was assessed with the Beck Depression Inventory (A. T. Beck, Ward, Mendelson, Mock, & Erbaugh, 1961), anxiety was assessed with the State–Trait Anxiety Inventory (STAI; Spielberger, Gorusch, & Lushene, 1970), and generalized anger was assessed with the State–Trait Anger Expression Inventory (Spielberger, 1988).

OVERALL IMPROVEMENT

As noted above, the daily symptom-monitoring diaries were considered the primary outcome measure for assessing change in daily driving behaviors. For purposes of clarity, each driving behavior is considered a "symptom." Using these daily diaries, we calculated a single index, the Composite Primary Symptom Reduction (CPSR) score, following the method of Blanchard and Schwarz (1988). This score is an index of overall change in symptom level and helps reduce potential Type I error that might result from analyzing multiple symptoms. The CPSR score also provides a means for describing clinically significant improvements in symptomatology. Because each driver endorsed particular driving behaviors and did not engage in other driving behaviors, the primary symptoms for each driver included the behaviors endorsed at baseline. For instance, Driver A may endorse honking, tailgating, dangerous passing, and feeling angry. These behaviors, or symptoms, would be considered this individual's primary symptoms for the purposes of analyses. Driver B, on the other hand, may endorse completely different behaviors, such as swearing, feeling impatient, throwing objects, and chasing other drivers. These behaviors would be considered this individual's primary symptoms even though they are entirely different from Driver A's behaviors.

After adjusting for severity using the method described above, we used the following formula to arrive at the CPSR score. The symptoms used in the calculations are examples only. The specific symptoms reported by the participant were included in the formula where appropriate.

$$\text{Assault reduction score} = \frac{\text{Average pretreatment assault ratings} - \text{average posttreatment assault ratings}}{\text{Average pretreatment assault ratings}}$$

This formula provides symptom-reduction scores, which are calculated for each of the symptoms endorsed. These scores are then used to calculate the overall CPSR score as follows:

$$\text{CPSR score} = \frac{\text{Assault reduction score} + \text{improper passing reduction score (etc.)}}{4 \text{ (or 5, or 6, etc., depending on the number of symptoms present)}}$$

Thus, the CPSR score can be considered an average percentage improvement in aggressive driving behavior.

OVERALL TREATMENT RESULTS

The results of the treatment component of the study were published in Galovski and Blanchard (2002a). The overall comparison of the entire treated group ($N = 27$) from pre- to posttreatment is described therein. As mentioned above, the primary outcome measure for reductions in aggressive driving was the daily symptom-monitoring diary from which we derived a CPSR score (which can be conceptualized as a percentage of improvement). The average CPSR score for all 27 participants was .62, indicating that on average, participants decreased aggressive driving behaviors by approximately 62%. Put another way, these participants improved 62% on average. To afford readers a better sense of the clinical meaningfulness of a 62% improvement in driving behaviors, we used categories of clinical improvement established by Blanchard and Schwarz (1988). Using these categories, which were established in different patient populations, we classified the drivers on the basis of their reduction in aggressive driving behavior as reflected by their CPSR score. The "unimproved" category includes all drivers whose CPSR scores worsened or fell within the range of 0% to 24%. "Somewhat improved" drivers were considered to have CPSR scores falling in the range of 25% to 49%. Drivers in the "improved" category realized scores of 50% to >75%. These categorizations are summarized in Table 9.1 so that readers can get a sense of percentages of the entire treated sample that we consider clinically improved.

As seen in Table 9.1, of the 10 participants who were assigned to immediate treatment, 70% indicated clinically significant improvement compared with those in the symptom-monitoring condition, in which none had significant improvement, 50% evidenced no change, and 31% worsened in driving behavior over this wait list period. Once the control participants were crossed over to active treatment, 72% evidenced significant improvement as well. There was little difference between referral source: 70% of the CR participants showed clinically significant improvement compared with 71% of the SR group. Finally, 60% of the entire treated population maintained clinically significant improvement at the 2-month follow-up point.

TABLE 9.1
Distribution of Composite Primary Symptom Reduction Scores by Experimental Condition

Condition	Improved (>75%)		Improved (50%–74%)		Somewhat improved (25%–49%)		Unimproved (0%–24%)		Worsened	
	n	%	n	%	n	%	n	%	n	%
Treatment only (n = 10)	5	50	2	20	1	10	0	0	2	20
Sx. monitoring control (n = 16)	0	0	0	0	3	19	8	50	5	31
Sx. monitoring control after treatment (n = 14)	5	36	5	36	4	28	0	0	0	0
Overall treatment (n = 24)	10	42	7	29	5	21	0	0	2	8
2-month follow-up (n = 20)	7	35	5	25	6	30	0	0	2	10
Court-referred group (n = 17)	7	41	5	29	3	18	0	0	2	12
Self-referred group (n = 7)	3	42	2	29	2	29	0	0	0	0

Note. Table does not include data from 3 participants (108, 109, 114) who did not endorse any aggressive driving behaviors during the course of the self-monitoring. Sx. = symptoms. From "The Effectiveness of a Brief Psychological Intervention on Court-Referred and Self-Referred Aggressive Drivers," by T. E. Galovski and E. B. Blanchard, *Behaviour Research and Therapy*, Vol. 40, p. 1394. Copyright 2001 by Elsevier Science Ltd. Adapted with permission.

Comparison With Wait List Condition

We also compared the immediate-treatment condition with the wait list control condition. The average CPSR score for participants who were randomized into the immediate-treatment condition was .50. We compared this score with the average CPSR score in the wait list condition (.007) and found that the treated sample had improved significantly more than the wait list controls. Table 9.1 summarizes the clinical significance of this improvement following the precedent of Blanchard and Schwarz (1988).

The lack of improvement in the wait list control group was an interesting finding. One might expect to see decreases in driving behavior merely from the punishment of being mandated to a time-consuming program. The lack of improvement within the SR wait list control subset of the population is also curious, because self-monitoring often results in improvement in symptomatology. When crossed over to treatment, this wait list group evidenced an average of 64% improvement. Thus, it may be concluded that the intervention itself (and not necessarily the sentencing or the passage of time) directly influenced the aggressive driving behaviors.

Comparison of Outcome in the Court-Referred Versus Self-Referred Samples

We also wanted to see whether any differences between pre- and posttreatment scores emerged between the CR and SR groups. There were no significant differences in changes in daily driving behaviors as indicated by the CPSR scores, indicating that both groups improved similarly irrespective of their referral source. On average, the CR group indicated a 63% decrease in aggressive driving behaviors compared with the SR group, indicating approximately a 60% decrease. Table 9.1 summarizes the clinical significance of this improvement.

Two months after the treatment took place, each participant was asked to complete the same packet of paper-and-pencil questionnaires along with a week's worth of driving diaries. The results indicated good maintenance of treatment gains. The average CPSR score of the participants was .56, indicating that the drivers had continued to decrease their aggressive driving behaviors by 56% compared with the behaviors in which they had engaged at pretreatment. Practically speaking, the drivers are, for example, feeling half as angry on the roadways, desisting in engaging in half as many aggressive behaviors, or cutting the aggressiveness of any given behavior by half. Theoretically speaking, the chances of a motor vehicle accident, an arrest, and increased stress and resultant psychological distress may be substantially decreased. From a public health and safety perspective, this finding may certainly be considered significant. In addition to the good maintenance of treatment gains in the area of daily driving, many of the self-report measures indicated stable trends and even continued improvement (specifically on measures of psychological distress and DSP subscales).

PSYCHOLOGICAL TEST MEASURES

The paper-and-pencil measures, the DAS and DSP, also were administered before and after treatment. As we noted in chapter 6, the DAS measures the amount of anger a driver experiences on the roadways in response to different events. The test yields a total score of overall driving anger as well as six subscales measuring anger in response to hostile gestures, illegal driving, police presence, slow driving, discourtesy, and traffic obstruction. Our treatment-seeking sample as a whole realized significant reductions in overall driving anger as well as reductions in anger in response to hostile gestures, illegal driving, slow driving, discourtesy, and traffic obstruction.

The DSP results in an overall score of aggressive driving and through its subscales reflects the extent of the driver's anger and impatience while driving as well as the amount of punishing and competing behavior on the roadways. The aggressive drivers realized a significant decrease in competing behavior on the roadways, and downward trends were observed on the overall score as well as each of the remaining subscales. The means, standard deviations, and relevant statistics for all the paper-and-pencil measures are presented in Table 9.2.

As described above, concurrent depression, state and trait anxiety, and general anger were also measured before treatment and 2 weeks after the conclusion of treatment. Significant reductions in state anxiety, trait anger, angry temperament, angry reaction, and anger directed outward emerged on these measures.

Overall, self-report measures indicated significant decreases in state anxiety, trait anger, angry temperament, angry reaction, anger-out, overall driving anger, anger in response to hostile gestures, illegal driving, slow driving, discourtesy, and traffic obstruction, and a reduction in DSP competing behavior. Downward, nonsignificant trends emerged on many of the remaining measures.

Comparison of Treatment With Wait List

To assess differential change on the paper-and-pencil measures between groups, we conducted univariate analyses of variance (ANOVAs) on each measure. It should be noted that these analyses were exploratory in nature,

TABLE 9.2
Pre- to Posttreatment Comparisons of Self-Report Measures, Entire Aggressive Driving Sample

Measure	Pretreatment		Posttreatment		t	p	Modified Bonferroni critical α
	M	SD	M	SD			
DAS			Driving anger and aggression[a]				
Discourtesy	24.67	10.70	19.85	7.48	3.81	.001	.05 / 12 = .004
Total	75.74	33.22	63.85	23.9	3.43	.002	.05 / 11 = .005
Slow Driving	14.07	6.74	11.74	4.9	3.22	.003	.05 / 10 = .005
Illegal Driving	8.30	4.45	7.00	3.42	2.51	.02	.05 / 9 = .006
Hostile Gestures	6.26	3.61	4.89	2.59	2.61	.02	.05 / 8 = .006
Traffic Obstruction	16.00	7.85	14.07	6.24	2.62	.02	.05 / 7 = .007
DSP							
Competing	5.30	6.52	3.59	4.22	2.31	.03	.05 / 6 = .008
Total	27.14	26.56	22.56	17.42	1.84	.08	.05 / 5 = .010
Punishing	5.78	6.62	4.52	3.92	1.73	.095	.05 / 4 = .013
Anger	8.96	7.71	7.89	5.88	1.12	.28	.05 / 3 = .017
Impatience	7.11	7.61	6.22	5.38	1.01	.32	.05 / 2 = .025
Police Presence	6.81	3.72	6.41	2.69	0.72	.47	.05 / 1 = .050
			General psychological distress				
STAI							
State Anxiety	45.41	17.98	31.22	10.54	3.74[a]	.001	.05 / 3 = .017
Trait Anxiety	35.30	12.72	32.70	10.17	1.52[a]	.14	.05 / 2 = .025
BDI	4.69	5.61	3.08	4.35	1.49[b]	.15	.05 / 1 = .050
			General anger[a]				
STAXI							
Angry Temperament	6.74	3.36	5.30	1.60	2.86	.008	.05 / 7 = .007
Trait Anger	17.74	7.79	15.07	5.18	2.58	.02	.05 / 6 = .008
Anger-Out	16.44	4.79	15.04	3.26	2.33	.03	.05 / 5 = .010
Angry Reaction	7.33	3.13	6.52	2.64	2.16	.04	.05 / 4 = .013
State Anger	11.59	5.3	10.37	1.39	1.22	.24	.05 / 3 = .017
Anger Control	23.04	5.87	22.67	6.35	0.39	.70	.05 / 2 = .025
Anger-In	13.44	4.27	13.33	3.17	0.19	.85	.05 / 1 = .050

Note. N = 27. DAS = Driving Anger Scale; DSP = Driver's Stress Profile; STAI = State–Trait Anxiety Inventory; BDI = Beck Depression Inventory; STAXI = State–Trait Anger Expression Inventory. From "The Effectiveness of a Brief Psychological Intervention on Court-Referred and Self-Referred Aggressive Drivers," by T. E. Galovski and E. B. Blanchard, *Behaviour Research and Therapy*, Vol. 40, p. 1396. Copyright 2001 by Elsevier Science Ltd. Adapted with permission.
[a] *df* for *t* values = 26. [b] *df* = 25.

because the overall multivariate analyses of variance conducted on each class of self-report measures (Psychological Distress, General Anger, and Driving Anger) did not yield any significant interactions. These ANOVAs revealed significant Group × Time interactions on Trait Anger, Angry Temperament, and State Anger. These ANOVAs were followed up with analyses of covariance in which the pretreatment test score was used as the covariate. We found that the treated group had changed more than the wait list control group on each measure.

During the wait list period, the control participants also worsened on several self-report measures, including the Beck Depression Inventory, State Anger, and Anger-In. These differences were small and nonsignificant.

In summary, the aggressive drivers who received treatment showed more decreases in State Anger, Trait Anger, and Angry Temperament than did the nontreated sample. However, no differences emerged on the two Driving Anger scales. Possible reasons for this surprising outcome are described in the Limitations in Interpretation of the Data section.

Comparison of Self-Referred Participants With Court-Referred Participants

We also compared the referral sources on the various paper-and-pencil measures using statistical techniques similar to those described earlier in this chapter. We found that the groups did not differ in improvement on measures of psychological distress; However, the groups did differ on their levels of improvements in general anger. The multivariate analysis of variance revealed a significant Group × Time interaction, with follow-up univariate tests indicating that differences between the groups emerged on the Angry Reaction and Anger-In subscales of the State–Trait Anger Expression Inventory and on angry responses to the Hostile Gestures and Discourtesy subscales of the DAS. The SR group showed more improvement in these areas than did the CR group. Other than those subscales' scores, the groups appeared markedly similar at posttreatment.

Both groups showed similar improvements on measures of depression, state anxiety, state anger, trait anger, angry temperament, anger-out, and several driving anger measures. The SR group improved significantly more than the CR group on measures of trait anxiety; anger reactivity; anger-in; overall driving anger; anger in response to hostile gestures, slow driving, and discourtesy; and, on the DSP, impatience and punishing behavior. The CR group evidenced nonsignificant increases in anger directed inward and DSP Anger and Impatience and a decrease in Anger Control. This group showed trends toward improvement on all other subscales. The SR group improved on all self-report measures.

TABLE 9.3

Distribution of Composite Primary Symptom Reduction Scores
of Aggressive Drivers as a Function of Presence or Absence
of Intermittent Explosive Disorder (IED)

Group	Improved (>75%)		Improved (50%–74%)		Somewhat improved (25%–49%)		Unimproved (0%–24%)		Worsened	
	n	%	n	%	n	%	n	%	n	%
Non-IED (n = 17)	9	53	5	29	3	18	0	0	0	0
IED (n = 7)	1	14	2	29	2	29	0	0	2	29

Effects of Presence of Intermittent Explosive Disorder on Outcome

In chapters 5 through 7, we reanalyzed the data on our treatment-seeking sample on the basis of the presence or absence of intermittent explosive disorder (IED). Table 9.3 shows the distribution of pre- to posttreatment CPSR scores, from the daily driving diaries, for Galovski and Blanchard's (2002a) treatment sample. Data are available on only 24 participants, because 2 SR drivers never started treatment, and 3 participants (as noted in Table 9.1) never acknowledged any aggressive driving behaviors during the 2-week pretreatment monitoring period.

As is obvious, aggressive drivers without IED respond more favorably to treatment than do those who meet the diagnosis. Nine of the non-IED drivers (53%), versus 1 (of 7, 14%) of the drivers with IED, were much improved. A comparison of mean CPSR scores revealed values of .72 for the non-IED sample versus .37 for those with IED (p = .06). A comparison of the fraction who were improved (at least a 50% reduction on the CPSR) showed a higher percentage (82%) for the non-IED subsample than for the IED sample (43%), $\chi^2(1, N = 24)$ = 3.74, p = .053.

Clinical Hint

It seems clear that presence of IED is a risk factor for poor response to our treatment. This means that to be forewarned, the treating clinician should assess for it. It probably also means that a longer course of treatment may be required to make a difference with this subpopulation.

LIMITATIONS IN INTERPRETATION OF THE DATA

When one's population involves court-mandated individuals, the likelihood of untruthful or misleading responses is increased. This study was no different from previous work published in related fields with similar populations. As we discussed earlier, the anger and aggressive driving behaviors endorsed by the participants was entirely incongruent with the severity of the behaviors objectively observed by law enforcement officers. In general, the CR group presented as much less forthcoming and more wary in their willingness to disclose information.

There are a number of different hypotheses as to why the validity of some responses may be considered questionable. First, we saw a significant number of people who met full criteria for antisocial personality disorder (see chap. 6). It may hold true that dishonest answers may be part of a larger disregarding or dishonest response style or pattern.

Second, although each individual in the program was assured of the confidentiality of his or her responses, the CR clientele may have been concerned that their answers would incriminate them in their ongoing legal disputes. Over time, the comfort level of most of the CR drivers increased substantially as rapport was built and a positive environment was fostered. However, we cannot rule out the possibility that these individuals may have been faking good for fear of reprisals down the road, particularly at the pretreatment assessment point, given the absence of rapport in the early stages of our relationship. Regardless of the reason behind inconsistent or dishonest responses, when these data were discovered we removed them from the analyses.

Finally, and perhaps most important, the total lack of distress endorsed by some clearly distressed individuals may be attributable to a substantial lack of insight on the part of the participant. The rampant denial of any personal problems with aggressive driving within this population supports this overall-lack-of-insight hypothesis. Almost 100% of the CR population came into the study claiming that the police had gotten the "wrong guy/woman." Some drivers, in fact, felt entirely justified in committing serious and dangerous driving behaviors, especially in response to some perceived misbehavior by some other driver on the roadways. This lack of insight directly informs the administration of treatment within this population. An overriding goal of this program quickly became helping these drivers gain perspective and insight into their behavior and more fully understand the impact of their driving choices on themselves, the passengers in their cars, and the general public. Although not systematically measured, in our opinion the success in reaching this overarching goal directly predicted treatment outcome.

Regardless of why the CR group endorsed low levels of aggressive driving behaviors and psychiatric distress, the fact remains that a less than accurate picture of this group's driving behavior and psychiatric distress may have emerged. This is, of course, problematic for this type of research. As noted above, instances in which a participant's responses were clearly faked resulted in removal of data from analysis. For instance, if a participant circled all "1"s on a measure for which some items are reverse scored (e.g., the STAI), then he or she clearly contradicted him- or herself across the entire measure. When possible, the participants were called and asked to come back into the clinic and complete an entire additional packet of questionnaires. In three cases in our study, the new data were retained and the old data were thrown out.

Another example of faked or incorrect data may include inconsistent data across time on measures for which answers should be consistent. For instance, a response to a question concerning whether one played sports in high school should be consistent at all three points in time. If the answers were not consistent, the data were thrown out. This happened in one instance. For the most part, participants endorsed consistent aggressive driving behaviors across the entire study, particularly on the daily diaries. Answers on measures that should remain consistent across time (e.g., "How many years of education have you received?") remained consistent. Several questionnaires (STAI, etc.) are reverse scored and were answered appropriately across items. One can safely assume that the participants read the questions and answered them systematically rather than randomly.

A second limitation of the study was the small size of the SR sample. Although the program received substantial media coverage and some advertisement, aggressive driving is simply not a common presenting problem for which people seek psychological treatment. In fact, as discussed earlier, aggression and aggressive driving may even be experienced as cathartic or in some sense rewarding. It is not the aggressive driving behavior itself but the precipitant to the behavior that is distressing to the driver. The aggressive driving behavior actually provides the driver with some relief following a stressful or provoking driving situation. Simultaneously, the driving situation affords an individual a safe, anonymous environment from which to express anger and behave aggressively while also providing a means for a quick, easy escape. Thus, people may behave more badly in their automobiles than they would in other areas of life, where they may be recognized and therefore held accountable. Furthermore, the vast majority of individuals in the program (CR and SR) did not believe that they were aggressive drivers; to the contrary, most felt that our efforts would be far better served targeting those "other drivers"! If we could just "take those old people's licenses away, we wouldn't have a problem." Or, if the speaker happened to be a senior citizen, "making those young whippersnappers wait a few more years before they get their licenses" would solve everything. The women felt similarly about the men, and vice versa, and the truckers felt animosity toward the motorcyclists, who felt animosity toward the sport utility vehicle drivers, and so on. As was pointed out in many groups, if all the group members had their wish, there would be no drivers at all!

CONCLUSION

This program contributes to the overall aggressive driving literature and potentially affects the way that mental health professionals and the courts currently deal with aggressive drivers. The Albany research offers methodological improvements over some of the previous outcome studies in this field (which we reviewed in chap. 8). This is the first intervention to use a randomized, controlled design with a CR population. The results of this study provide good evidence for the efficacy of a cognitive–behavioral intervention for aggressive driving behaviors. Rather than ticketing and fining drivers for overt aggression on the roadways, our program offers an intervention that directly targets the problematic behavior and offers alternative driving strategies. We view this program as having potentially the same impact on aggressive driving as defensive driving courses or drunk-driving programs have had on their respective target behaviors in offering the court system a brief, viable alternative. The potential impact on public health and safety is immeasurable. As one participant spontaneously reported, "I think if I hadn't taken this class, I would have eventually become so angry that I would have killed someone on the roads."

The overall effectiveness of a cognitive–behavioral intervention targeting aggressive driving behaviors is demonstrated by the results of this study. Rage, coupled with access to an automobile, can certainly be a lethal combination. As the roadways become more and more congested, and people's lives become more and more hectic, it seems that road rage has become increasingly problematic. *Road rage* is more than just a popular term used by the media to sensationalize a few discrete incidents: We were shocked at the extent and severity of the aggressive driving cases that came through our program in a relatively short period of time. When one considers that these were only the cases that were caught by the police, identified by the assistant district attorney's office, and remanded by the courts, the actual rate of aggressive driving in this fairly rural county is even more worrisome. We hope that these types of brief interventions specifically targeting aggression on the roadways contribute to safer driving and, subsequently, safer roadways.

10

AGGRESSIVE DRIVING
TREATMENT MANUAL

As we summarized in chapter 9, prior to the Albany aggressive driving program, aggressive driving had not been treated in a sample of community drivers in a randomized, controlled fashion (Deffenbacher, Huff, Lynch, Oetting, & Salvatore, 2000; Larson, 1996b). In this chapter we detail the manual we used to modify aggressive driving behaviors in both a court-referred and self-referred aggressive driving population (Galovski & Blanchard, 2002a). Case vignettes and clinical hints are provided to further readers' understanding of both the severity of the population treated and the application of the intervention.

The treatment protocol was typically conducted over four sessions held once a week, with each session lasting approximately 1.5 to 2 hours. We have conducted the treatment in both a group format (2 to 6 participants) and individually. It is, of course, more cost-effective to use the group format. Although we have no data to support this, we have also found that the groups provide a nice forum for the driver to feel a bit more comfortable in admitting to some of his or her aggressive driving behaviors. Often, more information was relayed within sessions than was gathered in the initial assessments as drivers "boasted" to one another about their driving exploits. This information could then be used in both establishing a baseline as well as in gathering examples of poor driving behaviors for use in teaching alternative behaviors and skills over the course of the ensuing 4 weeks of treatment.

Given that this protocol is based on a cognitive–behavioral theoretical orientation, we believe that some level of expertise and experience in cognitive–behavioral therapy is needed by therapists intending to use this intervention. Thus, this treatment protocol is not designed to be a training tool for cognitive–behavioral therapy but a manual to be used by therapists with such a background.

Unlike typical psychotherapy patients, clientele involved in an aggressive driving treatment program may not be doing so voluntarily. Aggressive drivers often are identified either by the court system or by loved ones who cannot tolerate riding in the car with them. We have found that the vast majority of our clients had never been involved in any sort of psychotherapy in the past. Many (especially the court-referred participants) were extremely resistant to the idea that they needed help or that they had a problem at all, despite glaring evidence to the contrary. This resistance, coupled with a relatively brief period of time (4 weeks) in which to accomplish treatment goals, presents a challenge to the therapist. As a result, it may behoove the therapist to designate additional therapy time toward increasing the client's motivation and compliance. Also, we have found it exceedingly helpful to keep revisiting idiosyncratic reasons for not driving aggressively. These may include, but are not limited to, health concerns, such as cardiovascular disease and high blood pressure; legal problems, such as losing one's license or serving jail time; interpersonal relationship problems with loved ones or coworkers; or societal concerns, such as contributing to roadway accident statistics. Regardless of whether the client has chosen to be in the program, a loved one has demanded that he or she attend the program, or he or she has been mandated into treatment by a court, identifying a mutually acceptable reason for changing aggressive driving behavior will increase the probability that the client will use the therapy techniques. Even the most resistant, court-mandated client will have to agree that not having to attend an aggressive driving program is a good reason for changing aggressive driving behaviors!

The following treatment manual is laid out session by session, with the important elements of each session in boldface type. The manual was written for application in a group modality; however, it can be easily adapted for individual administration. The treatment components are included in the text in the order in which they were administered in the sessions. The results of the treatment outcome trial were reported by Galovski and Blanchard (2002a) and in chapter 9.

TREATMENT SESSION 1

Define Aggressive Drivers and Related Behaviors

Because "aggressive driving" is not a psychiatric diagnosis, it is important to make sure that aggressive driving behaviors are clearly defined. Any definition of *aggressive driving* must stress *intent*, meaning that any given behavior must be committed with the intent to scare, annoy, punish, harm, or negatively affect property, another vehicle, or another driver. Making an error in judgment or a lapse in skill does not constitute aggressive driving. For example, forgetting to use your turn signal is not aggressive driving, but intentionally not signaling so as to purposefully not forewarn the other driver of your intent to change lanes in an aggressive or punishing maneuver is indeed consistent with aggressive driving.

Begin Session 1 by outlining the common forms of aggressive driving. Clients can participate in giving examples of what they consider to be aggressive driving behaviors. Such behaviors include, but are not limited to, the following:

- Slow driving with the intent to block other vehicle's passage,
- Tailgating,
- Improper passing (cutting another driver off, passing illegally),
- Failing to yield the right of way,
- Failing to keep right,
- Honking the horn,
- Flashing high beams,
- Failing to signal properly,
- Obscene gesturing,
- Verbal insults,
- Throwing objects,
- Physical assault, and
- Giving chase to another driver.

Ask the group for further examples of aggressive driving. In addition to these actual driving behaviors, there is a list of non-driving-related behaviors that are performed out of anger on the roadways. The following, more subjective, behaviors are often the precursors to aggressive driving incidents. If clients can begin to identify these warning signs, they can prevent most aggressive driving incidents from occurring in the first place. Some of these more subjective behaviors include the following:

- Feeling angry at other drivers,
- Wishing harm to another driver,

- Feeling impatient at intersections, and
- Becoming upset at traffic delays.

Provide a Rationale for Treatment

Once aggressive driving has been defined, a common question is "Why should *I* change my driving behaviors? If everyone else on the roads were as good a driver as me, we wouldn't have this problem." As mentioned above, most aggressive drivers come to the program unwilling to admit that they may have a problem. Furthermore, these drivers may not see any personal benefit in fixing this problem. Providing a treatment rationale gives the therapist the opportunity to point out how treatment directly affects clients' lives. We have identified four major areas in clients' lives that aggressive driving directly influences: (a) overall health and well-being, (b) interpersonal relationships, (c) societal harm, and (d) economics (in terms of finances and time). The treatment rationale emphasizes the impact of aggressive driving on these important areas of functioning.

Possible Script

The research has shown that aggressive driving impacts our lives in a variety of ways. Over long periods of time, the stress experienced in the car can have a negative impact on important areas of your life such as relationships, job performance, and even your health. More immediately, an aggressive act on the road places you and all of the other drivers at a much higher risk for an accident. We've identified four areas in your life that can be negatively affected by your aggressive driving behavior.

First, we've seen that driving aggressively can affect your health over time. People are spending more and more time behind the wheel of a car on a daily basis. The roadways are becoming more and more congested. Thus, we often find ourselves delayed, in traffic jams, or in generally stressful driving situations. The stress of such driving situations can lead to annoyance, leading in turn to anger, and even to rage. High levels of exposure to stress, annoyance, and anger tend to take a physical toll, because our bodies were simply not built to withstand such chronic levels of arousal. Over time, such bodily processes as our immune system, our cardiovascular system, et cetera, begin to break down. As a matter of fact, one of the pioneers in the aggressive driving literature, Dr. John Larson, is a cardiologist from Yale who noticed that many of his young patients were reporting to his office with heart disease. He cites aggressive driving as one of the contributors to their illness (Larson, 1996b).

Second, aggressive driving can have a negative impact on your interpersonal relationships. Feeling stressed and angry in the car does not end when you step out of the vehicle. We tend to carry this stress into the home or the workplace. Aggressive drivers typically report that they enter the home or workplace after their commute feeling angry or easily aggravated. Obviously, feeling this way makes us more prone to snapping at our coworkers, friends, and families. Over time, this behavior can negatively impact even the strongest relationships.

Third, it's clear that aggressive driving can have an enormous impact on society in terms of economic loss, injury, and even death. It's been clearly portrayed in the media over the years how detrimental drunk driving is to society. Recently, experts have realized that aggressive driving takes a similarly high toll in terms of accident statistics. And, similar to drunk driving accidents, most of these accidents due to aggressive driving are preventable.

Finally, aggressive driving has a personal cost to you in terms of money and time. [This is especially true for nonvoluntary participants. The therapist can have them add up any cost in terms of vehicular damage, fines, court, and attorney fees as well as costs in time in attending this program.][1] Think back over your personal history in terms of time and money spent dealing with accidents, insurance companies, police, tickets, and court fees, and even include the time coming here. Now imagine what else you could do with those resources if you could take it all back. . . . Was it worth getting so angry on the roadways?

People often come into this program feeling as if a mistake has been made and they are in the wrong place. However, over time, everyone is usually able to identify at least one area of driving in which they can improve and at least one example of a driving situation in which they feel angry or annoyed. Try to keep your own experiences and examples in mind as we go over this material, because it may be useful some day in the car in a particularly stressful driving situation. Our goal in this program is to reduce any anger and stress that you may be feeling on the roadways in order to make your time in the car safer, more enjoyable, and more tolerable for those around you.

We intend to accomplish this reduction in anger, stress, and aggressive driving in a number of ways. We hope to provide you with some facts and education on aggressive driving and its costs to you and to society. We hope to begin to examine the kinds of thoughts and self-talk that you are currently engaging in on the roadways. We also hope to provide you with a number of alternative behaviors to aggressive driving that you can engage in when you are feeling stressed and angry on the roads. Finally, we hope to teach you some basic relaxation skills that you can use when you sense your body beginning to tense and you are becoming angry. Basically, you can think of this group as building a toolbox. Each skill is a tool that you can learn and place in that

---

[1] Often, a nonvoluntary patient will not admit to any impact of aggressive driving on his or her health or occupational or personal life, but costs in terms of time and money are the least controvertible.

toolbox. Then, when stressful or annoying situations arise while you are driving, you can simply reach into your toolbox and choose a skill to relax yourself and cope with the situation more effectively and safely.

Have Patients Identify Themselves as Aggressive Drivers

After everyone is on the same page as far what aggressive driving is, the negative impact it can have, and what we intend to do about it, the drivers can begin to personally apply these ideas to themselves. This means that everyone must actually verbally acknowledge that at the very least, there is *some* room for improvement. Explain to the group that all the participants are in the program because they themselves, or someone else, has identified them as an aggressive driver. Give results of the group's driving questionnaires. Relate those results to the "normal" population to indicate that there is room for remediation.

Possible Script

> It is not just your family or the court that thinks you have a problem with aggressive driving. According to your answers on the questionnaire, you rank [give results] higher than the general public in aggressive driving behaviors.

At this point in the treatment, it is less important that a driver admit to horribly aggressive driving behaviors. We provide much support for drivers' admitting to anything (even slight infractions) at this stage. The goal is to increase the driver's receptiveness to the idea that changing aggressive driving behaviors is personally applicable and to decrease general resistance to change. It therefore becomes exceedingly important not to pass judgment on the individual for past offenses or to be overly critical if he or she is not forthcoming about roadway transgressions. In our experience, this is one of the most critical junctures of therapy. If the clients' comfort level is increased, and they begin to realize that they will not have to endure being chastised for four sessions, then they are much more likely to become receptive to implementing change.

Case Vignette. Kelly came into the program after being arrested for vehicular assault after he used his car to ram an emergency worker who was directing traffic. He apparently had felt that the fireman had let oncoming traffic through the scene long enough and that it was his turn to proceed. There was a fire at the time, and during the resulting melee and confusion, Kelly thought that he would gun the engine on his sports car; brush past the fireman, maybe scare him a little; and be on his way, undetected and unaccountable. As it turns out, he struck the fireman, who subsequently was hospitalized, and Kelly was very much held accountable. Kelly had a list of previous aggressive driving grievances, and so part of his sentencing was to attend our program. The judge who sentenced Kelly was familiar with the man and concerned enough about his behaviors that he personally called and updated us on the entire case, including Kelly's past history, to give us the opportunity to refuse Kelly entry into the program. Needless to say, Kelly came into the program with very little motivation for change. During the course of the assessment, he was diagnosed with antisocial personality disorder. Not realizing that the therapist was aware not only of the details surrounding the index incident but also his past history, Kelly smoothly denied any culpability in the crime, never mentioned the hospitalization of the fireman, and attributed the whole incident to another example of small-town cops harassing the "richest man in town." Thus it was fairly clear from Day 1 that this client possessed some fairly entrenched characterological features that were not going to remediate in four group sessions targeting aggressive driving. It was also clear that he was not going to admit to any wrongdoing around this incident, and we simply did not have the time to argue with him. Instead, we chose to spend the time encouraging him to identify any personal driving imperfections or at the very least a driving situation that annoyed him:

Therapist: So what brings you to the program, Kelly?

Client: Harassment.

Therapist: Can you be more specific?

Client: Mine is not like these cases that you have here. I was not at fault. In fact, I was the victim, and have been for years. These small-town cops are always jealous of the richest guy in town, my car, etc. . . . They live to harass me.

Therapist: Is there any part of the events that preceded your arrest that you think you could have handled better or, in hindsight, would have done differently?

Client: No.

Therapist: Okay, arrest aside, is there any aspect of your overall driving that you think could benefit from this program and that you'd like to work on?

Client: No. I am president of my own company, and I look at every minute that I spend here as a waste of time and taking me away from being able to accomplish important things at work. I am not an aggressive driver, and so none of this is applicable to me, much less helpful.

Therapist: In all of my experience working with all types of drivers, I have yet to meet a perfect driver. Even my little sweet old grandmother gets at least mildly irritated with the way "kids these days" drive. It sounds like you are a pretty important person with a lot on your plate. Nothing makes me more annoyed than to waste what I consider to be valuable time. It sounds like you are not a time waster, either, but instead a real go-getter. Since you have to be here anyway, try to think of at least one aspect of your driving life that is even mildly annoying or irritating or less than pleasant. Because it sounds like, for you, the bigger crime would be a waste of valuable time.

Client: Well, you mentioned your grandmother. It does irritate me when very old people drive very slowly in the left lane. Not that I have anything against old people, of course. But I do find myself worried and concerned for their safety, so that is a bit irritating.

Therapist: Great, and we just discussed how irritation and stress compounded over the course of the day and multiplied by all the time you spend in the car can add up to an awful lot of annoyance and can have health and behavioral implications for all of us. Hold onto that example as we go through this material over the course of the next 4 weeks and see if there's anything that applies and may be helpful in those situations when you are feeling mildly annoyed.

The goal here is clearly to get the client to the point where he or she can at least hear the information and wisdom that you are attempting to impart over the course of the next few sessions. In our estimation, that is half the battle with this type of resistant client. Refusing to even hear the information presented obviously significantly reduces the probability of actual application of the material. Increasing the palatability of the therapeutic message has the opposite effect.

Pass Out the Aggressive Driving Questionnaire

Ask individuals to give a brief account of an aggressive driving situation they have encountered as per the directions provided on the form entitled "Aggressive Driving Questionnaire." The participants must identify triggers, their appraisals of the driving situation, their appraisals of the other driver, their own reactions, their thoughts, their feelings (physical and emotional), and the duration of their feelings. **Collect and keep these papers for comparison at the end of the program** (see Appendix 10.1). In a group situation, it is helpful to go around the room and ask everyone to share their account out loud. If nonvoluntary drivers deny ever driving aggressively, have them share the incident for which they were mandated to the program. If the person is resistant and has not been mandated by the court, it may be helpful to ask him or her to report what a loved one or family member would typically say about his or her driving, even if the client doesn't agree with the family member.

Begin the Discussion About Anger

Present anger as a continuum. On this continuum, anger ranges from minor annoyance or irritation, to aggravation or indignation, to feeling mad, to fury, to feeling enraged and out of control. Draw this continuum on the chalkboard. Describe goals as being twofold. (See Appendix 10.2.)

Possible Script

> We will try to begin to recognize the signs and signals of anger when it first starts to build in order to address it before it gets out of control. Then we will formulate coping strategies in order to manage sudden onsets of strong anger more efficiently.

Clinical Hint

We have found that clients tend to be very resistant to labeling themselves as "angry." It is unpleasant to think of oneself as an angry person. Some clients find it much more palatable to consider themselves as sometimes "annoyed" or "irritated." Arguing these fine points can be a waste of time. Admitting to annoyance is just as useful for clinical purposes as admitting to anger. It is important, however, to elicit from the client some admittance of anger, at some level. Normalizing the emotion of anger as part of the human experience is often helpful. Many of our clients in this study were not psychologically sophisticated and had always thought of anger as a "bad emotion." Redefining this emotion as normal and useful helped several clients in admitting that they had indeed experienced anger. The intervention, of course, involves changes in the thought processes that precipitate anger as well as the clients' behavior when angered, *not* in their experience of the emotion.

The concept that the therapist wants to get across is the idea that anger escalates quickly and that it is most effective and efficient to deal with anger at the lower levels of the continuum before anger is out of control. A primary treatment goal is to begin to identify anger at its early stages and prevent it from developing into rage and loss of control. The anger continuum can be used throughout therapy in terms of helping a client to track his or her anger through the course of any given incident and to choose treatment strategies appropriate for the level of anger experienced. A second treatment goal is thus to learn to match appropriate treatment interventions to the level of anger experienced. For instance, deep breathing may calm a person when irritated or aggravated but, if a person is enraged, the best strategy is to remove oneself physically from the situation (pull off the road, get out of the car, etc.).

Case Vignette. Joe denied feeling angry in an incident he was describing in a group session. He felt as if a recent arrest was a result of being unfairly targeted by a policeman and that the fault lay entirely with the officer. The therapist asked him to redescribe the incident slowly, piece by piece. He reported that he had parked his truck illegally at a concert, as had a number of other drivers. He was talking to some of his buddies near his truck when an officer pulled up and asked him to move it. At this point, the therapist asked Joe where he would have rated himself on the anger continuum. He labeled himself as a 1 (irritated) because he felt unjustly hassled. Joe then reported that he questioned the officer as to why he should move his vehicle when others were similarly parked. The officer responded by pulling out his ticket book and proceeding to write a parking ticket. Joe reported feeling about a 3 (aggravated) at this point. He and his buddies then began taunting the officer, calling him names, and so on. The officer wrote a second ticket. Joe reported feeling about a 5–6 at this point. Some additional words were exchanged between Joe and the officer. The officer began to leave the scene on his motorcycle when Joe grabbed the back of the bike, dislodging the officer from his seat. At this point, Joe reported feeling about an 8–9. The officer left the scene, but Joe was later picked up at his home by the police and arrested for assaulting an officer. This case example provides a good illustration to clients of how anger can escalate quickly, as can the resulting behaviors. At any point, Joe could have chosen to deal with his anger more effectively (regardless of whether the officer was right or wrong—we chose not to argue these points). More effective coping at any given point in this story could have prevented Joe's subsequent night in jail, legal problems, expenses, and so on. The therapist and group discussed alternatives to Joe's behavior at the different levels of anger in the story and possible outcomes of these alternatives. Most were much more attractive outcomes than the actual arrest and jail time. By breaking down Joe's example and linking it directly to the anger continuum, the clients clearly saw the relationships among anger, behavior, and consequences and the benefit of engaging in the appropriate alternative coping strategy.

Introduce Larson's Five Driver Categories

John Larson developed five categories describing typical aggressive drivers (Larson, 1996b; see Appendix 10.3). They serve as an interesting way for clients to view their "roadway personality." We often found that the drivers in this study would label themselves and others by one or more of these categories in the following sessions. Ask group members to try to place themselves into one or more categories. Pass out the Aggressive Driver sheet for the clients to take home (see Appendix 10.3).

Case Vignette. The group modality is a good venue for discussing Larson's driver categories, because group members often represent each of the five categories. As a result, we almost invariably had passive–aggressors and narcissists sitting across from their worst nightmares, the speeder and the vigilante! Ana was a flamboyant 19-year-old woman in the throes of youth and rebellion who drove a sport utility vehicle. Mike, a 64-year-old traditional gentleman, dismayed at "kids these days," happened to be a participant in the same group. The therapist asked each participant to disclose which categories best described him or her. Ana described herself as a "speeder," saying she was very busy; had a full social calendar; and didn't have time to put up with traffic congestion, much less "the old fogies sitting in the left lane." She reported driving, on average, 15 miles per hour above the speed limit. She also said she had characteristics of the "vigilante," because she and her friends made a game of scaring the "lame ducks" in the left lane by passing on the right, then cutting them off and jamming on the brakes. As she was laughingly describing her driving behaviors and assuming that the rest of the participants were sharing her opinions, Mike was getting redder and redder in the face until he burst out, "You young whippersnappers think you own the road!!! You're going to kill someone!!" The therapist redirected the conversation to him and asked into which driving category he fit. He said he was the passive–aggressor and the vigilante. With "age and wisdom," he had come to realize that he needed to teach these "maniacs" on the roadways a lesson. He said that he purposefully would drive exactly the speed limit in the left lane as the law had intended. He felt perfectly justified in doing so and felt as if he were preventing accidents and providing other drivers with a good role model. He also would "patrol" the highways and called the state police from the road an average of 10 times a week to report errant drivers. It was this behavior that had his wife at her wits' end and had prompted her to insist that he enroll in the program. She was afraid that he would one day get so enraged at the "whippersnappers" that he would have a heart attack while driving. The clear disagreement between these two participants allowed the group members to see, over time, someone else's point of view. They were also able to see how they had jumped to conclusions about other individuals based only on their driving behavior. Finally, Mike and Ana actually grew to like each other and shared some laughs in the course of therapy. Both were able to see how their labeling of each other and their aggressive driving behavior was more harmful than helpful. By the end of therapy, they were laughing at how they had been each other's imagined worst enemy, and now they would call each other friends.

Pass Out Hierarchy List

Ask clients to list the five most typically frustrating or annoying driving situations in which they tend to behave aggressively in the order from the most provoking (at the top of the list) to the least provoking (the bottom item on the list). Give each situation an anger rating describing how much anger the situation generally evokes (i.e., 0–100, with 100 = *extreme anger*; see Appendix 10.4). This sheet can be used as a practice sheet throughout the course of therapy. Clients can begin "practicing" coping skills on the least provoking situations and, as they progress in competence, they can attempt to reduce anger using their skills in the most provoking situations. These sheets also start the client thinking a priori about events in which he or she may become angry and provide the therapist with some good examples to use in later sessions.

Case Vignette. Jan reported that her most provoking driving situation was the tollbooth on the New York State Thruway. She had to pass through it four times every day on her commute to and from work during rush hour traffic. She described the scene as "cars flying all over the place, cutting other drivers off, getting caught in the EZPass Lane without a ticket and holding everyone else up, and traveling on the shoulder to get around cars that had been waiting their turn." She labeled other drivers as "idiots" (and worse) and felt that 95% of drivers were incompetent. She said her stomach would "get in a knot" on approaching the tollbooth and that she would be "steamed" by the time she had exited the plaza. Jan reported that her angry feelings and heightened arousal would last at least another 15 minutes, if not the rest of her commute. Because she was already angry, she knew she was primed for anyone else to make a "dumb" move on the highway. Anger and aggressive driving would just escalate from there. As readers can see, there is room for intervention at any point in this description. Using Jan's and others' examples throughout the course of therapy personalized the interventions and made them more applicable to the client. Jan's frustration with the tollbooth situation was clearly her most provoking driving stressor and was placed at the top of her hierarchy list. She was easily able to come up with four less provoking scenarios on which to practice her new stress reduction skills. When she felt that she had sufficiently reduced her anger in less provoking situations (crowded parking lots, traffic lights, road construction, etc.), she tackled the tollbooth situation. By the end of the program, as Jan approached the tollbooth on her commute, she automatically turned on a fun compilation of music she had prepared on CD and thought of one funny thing that had happened in the last 24 hours. She had a

3-year-old son who was constantly involved in cute antics, so she had plenty of fodder for thought. She discontinued some of her old bad habits (trying to stare down other drivers) and would use deep breathing exercises on an especially crowded highway. Jan reported back to the group that she was amazed at how much more relaxed she was on reaching her destination. She couldn't believe the extent to which the stress from her commute had affected her day even after she left the car. She even remarked that a coworker mentioned to her that he was glad she had stopped regaling her fellow employees every morning with the horrors of her commute.

Introduce Larson's Key Strategies

Begin the discussion of changing driving behaviors. Discuss the need to take old driving beliefs and change them to new, more adaptive beliefs (see Appendix 10.5).

Replace Old Beliefs:	With New Beliefs:
Speeders: Make Good Time	Make Time Good
Competitors: Be Number One	Number One Being
Passive–Aggressors: Try and Make Me	Be My Guest
Narcissists: They Shouldn't Allow Them on the Road	Live and Let Live
Vigilantes: Teach Them a Lesson	Leave Punishment to the Police

Apply Larson's Strategies to Each Item on the List

Pass out five index cards to each individual. On the first side, list old beliefs about a driving situation. On the reverse, list new beliefs. The stressor/event is each of their driving situations on their hierarchy list. See Appendix 10.5 for an example of the application of changing driving beliefs.

Instruct clients to carry the index card with them when they drive. They can review it before starting the car. Instruct clients to keep the new beliefs in mind when driving. Challenge the group to think of more pleasant, healthy, calm ways of getting to work. In particular, focus on applying this technique to the least provoking driving situation on their hierarchy list.

Conduct 16-Muscle Progressive Muscle Relaxation

According to client feedback, the relaxation portion of the intervention was a crowd favorite. To increase adherence to this portion of the protocol, describe some of the overall beneficial effects of relaxation and suggest that it is a good skill to acquire, not only to reduce arousal associated with driving anger but also to reduce muscle tension associated with stress, anxiety, worry, and so on. The relaxation training used in this intervention is based on Bernstein and Borkovec (1973).

Possible Script

Relaxation training is a very old method of therapy that has been shown to effectively help control fear, anxiety, and anger. If you think back to a time when you were angry or upset, you may recall feeling tense and physically aroused. On the other hand, you will not be able to remember a time when you felt completely relaxed and also felt very upset or angry. That's because anger and deep relaxation simply don't occur at the same time. So the goal of this part of the therapy is to teach you to lower your arousal level and become relaxed quickly in order to reduce your anger or annoyance. Relaxation in a therapy situation is a bit different from what most people think of when they consider relaxing. We are referring to a specific, physiological adaptation that is a learned skill. Relaxation training consists of a process of systematically tensing and relaxing the major muscle groups of the body. After learning and practicing the techniques, people are able to learn to feel a subjective feeling of relaxation. With practice, you will be able to learn to relax deeply and completely in a short period of time. Being able to physiologically relax and become calm in situations that are stressful, anxiety provoking, frustrating, or anger provoking allows one to tolerate these situations without high levels of arousal and to cope with them more effectively. The process includes learning to recognize tension in your own body as well as the very different sensations of complete relaxation. This process is one that is very effective, but it can only be acquired through diligent practice. Much like riding a bicycle, however, once the skill is learned, you will own it for the rest of your life.

First, demonstrate tensing and relaxing with each of the 16 muscle groups. Giving the client the opportunity to briefly practice the tensing and releasing of the muscles ensures that he or she will correctly apply the technique both in session and at home. Make sure that the client understands that the goal of the tension/release exercise is to clearly dichotomize between feelings of complete tension and complete relaxation. For a further understanding of progressive muscle relaxation (PMR), the therapist should refer to Bernstein and Borkovec (1973).

Conduct the full 16-muscle relaxation using the following muscle groups:

- Hand and lower arm: right, left, and both together;
- Upper arm: right, left, and both together;
- Lower leg and foot: right, left, and both together;

- Thighs;
- Abdomen;
- Chest and breathing;
- Shoulders and upper back, lower neck;
- Back of neck;
- Lips;
- Eyes;
- Lower forehead; and
- Upper forehead.

Provide the client with a tape of this exercise and instruct him or her to practice once a day.

Possible Script for 16-Muscle Progressive Relaxation

Now, begin to let yourself relax . . . close your eyes and we will go through the relaxation exercises. I want you to begin by tensing muscles in your **right, lower arm** and right hand . . . study the tensions in the back of your hand and your right lower arm . . . study those tensions . . . now relax the muscles. Study the difference between the tension and the relaxation. . . . Just let yourself become more and more relaxed. If you feel yourself becoming drowsy, that will be fine too. As you think of relaxation, of letting go of your muscles, they will become more loose and heavy and relaxed . . . just let your muscles go as you become more and more deeply relaxed.

Next, I want you to tense the muscles in your **left hand and left lower arm** . . . tense those muscles and study the tensions in the back of your left hand and in your left lower arm . . . study those tensions . . . and now relax the muscles . . . Study the difference between the tension and the relaxation . . . .

Now this time I want you to tense both hands and both lower arms by making fists and tensing the muscles in **both hands and both lower arms** . . . Study those tensions . . . and now relax them . . . Study the difference between the tension and the relaxation . . .

You are becoming more and more relaxed . . . calm and relaxed . . . as you become more relaxed, you feel yourself settling deep into the chair . . . all your muscles are becoming more and more comfortably relaxed . . . loose . . . and heavy . . . and relaxed. . . .

This time I want you to tense the muscles in your **right upper arm** by bringing your right hand up towards your shoulder and tensing the biceps muscle . . . Study the tensions here in your right upper arm . . . study those tensions . . . now relax your arm . . . study the difference between the tension and the relaxation . . . .

This time I want you to tense the muscles in your **left upper arm** by bringing the left hand up to your shoulder and tensing the muscles in your left biceps area . . . study those tensions in your left biceps . . .

study those tensions . . . and now relax the arm and study the difference between the tension and the relaxation . . . .

The relaxation is growing deeper and still deeper . . . you are relaxed, drowsy and relaxed . . . your breathing is regular and relaxed . . . with each breath you take in, the relaxation increases . . . each time you exhale you spread the relaxation throughout your body. . .

This time I want you to tense both upper arms together by bringing both hands up to your shoulders, tense the muscles in both upper arms, both biceps areas . . . study those tensions . . . and now relax the muscles . . . study the difference between the tension and the relaxation . . . Just continue to let your muscles relax. . . .

Next, I want you to tense the muscles in your right lower leg . . . tense the muscles in your right lower leg, particularly in your calf . . . study the tensions there in your right lower leg . . . study those tensions . . . and now relax the muscles . . . and study the difference between the tension and the relaxation . . . .

Note the pleasant feelings of warmth and heaviness that are coming into your body as your muscles relax completely. . . . You will always be clearly aware of what you are doing and what I am saying . . . as you become more deeply relaxed . . .

Next, I want you to tense the muscles in your left lower leg, the left calf area . . . study the tensions in your left lower leg . . . study those tensions . . . and now relax the muscles . . . and study the difference between the tension and the relaxation . . . just continue to let your leg relax . . . .

Now, this time I want you to tense both lower legs together . . . tense the muscles in both lower legs . . . both calf muscles . . . study those tensions . . . and now relax your legs . . . study the difference between the tension and the relaxation . . . just continue to let those muscles relax . . . let them relax . . . .

Now the very deep state of relaxation is moving through all the areas of your body . . . you are becoming more and more comfortably relaxed . . . calm and relaxed . . . you can feel the comfortable sensations of relaxation as you go into a deeper . . . deeper . . . state of relaxation . . . .

Next, I want you to tense the muscles in your thighs by pressing your legs together from the knees upward . . . press your upper legs against each other . . . study the tensions throughout your thighs . . . study those tensions . . . now relax the muscles . . . study the difference between the tension and the relaxation . . . just let those muscles continue to relax . . . .

This time I want you to tense the muscles in the abdominal area by drawing your abdominal muscles in tightly . . . draw them in tightly . . . study the tensions across the entire abdominal region . . . study those tensions . . . and now relax the muscles . . . just let them relax . . . and study the difference between the tension and the relaxation . . .

Just let yourself become more and more relaxed . . . as you think of relaxation . . . and of letting go of your muscles . . . they will become more loose . . . and heavy . . . and relaxed . . . just let your muscles go as you become more and more deeply relaxed . . . .

This time I want you to tense the muscles in your chest by taking a deep breath and holding it . . . hold it . . . hold it . . . now relax . . . and study the difference between the tension and the relaxation.

The relaxation is growing deeper . . . and still deeper . . . you are relaxed . . . your breathing is regular and relaxed . . . and with each breath you take in your relaxation increases . . . each time you exhale . . . you spread the relaxation throughout your body . . . .

Next, I want you to tense the muscle in your shoulders and upper back by hunching your shoulders or drawing your shoulders upward towards your ears . . . study those tensions across your upper back . . . study those tensions . . . and now relax your muscles . . . and study the difference . . . between the tension and the relaxation . . . .

Note the pleasant feelings of warmth and heaviness that are coming into your body as your muscles relax completely . . . you will always be clearly aware of what you are doing and what I am saying, as you become more deeply relaxed . . . .

Next, I want you to tense the muscles in the back of your neck by pressing your head backward against the headrest or against the head-board . . . study the tensions in the back of your neck, across your shoulders and the base of your scalp . . . study those tensions . . . and now relax the muscles . . . and study the difference between the tension and the relaxation . . . .

Next, I want you to tense your muscles in the region around your mouth by pressing your lips together tightly . . . press your lips together tightly without biting down and study the tensions in the region around your mouth . . . study those tensions . . . and now relax the muscles . . . and study the difference between the tension and the relaxation . . . .

You are becoming more and more relaxed . . . drowsy and relaxed . . . as you become more relaxed . . . you can feel yourself settling deep into the chair . . . all your muscles are becoming more and more comfortably relaxed . . . loose and heavy . . . and relaxed . . . .

This time I want you to tense the muscles in the region around your eyes by closing your eyes tightly . . . just close your eyes tightly . . . and study the tensions . . . . all around your eyes and upper face . . . study those tensions . . . and now relax the muscles . . . just continue to let them relax . . . and study the difference between the tension and the relaxation.

The very deep state of relaxation is moving through all the areas of your body . . . you are becoming more and more comfortably relaxed . . . drowsy and relaxed . . . you can feel the comfortable sensations of relaxation as you go into a deeper and deeper state of relaxation . . . .

This time I want you to tense the muscles in your lower forehead by frowning and lowering your eyebrows downward . . . study the tensions there in your lower forehead, the region between your eyes . . . study those tensions . . . and now relax the muscles . . . and study the difference between the tension and the relaxation. . . .

This time I want you to tense the muscles in your upper forehead by raising your eyebrows upward and wrinkling your forehead . . . raise them up and wrinkle your forehead and study the tensions in the upper part of your forehead . . . study those tensions . . . and now relax the muscles . . . and study the difference between the tension and the relaxation . . . .

Now I want you to relax all the muscles of your body . . . just let them become more and more relaxed . . . I am going to help you to achieve a deeper state of relaxation by counting from 1 to 5 . . . and as I count you will feel yourself becoming more and more deeply relaxed . . . farther and farther down into a deep restful state . . . of deep relaxation . . . 1 . . . you are going to become more deeply relaxed . . . .2 . . . down . . . down into a very relaxed state . . . 3 . . . 4 . . . more and more relaxed . . . 5 . . . deeply relaxed . . .

Now I want you to remain in your very relaxed state . . . and I want you to begin to attend just to your breathing . . . breathe through your nose . . . notice the cool air as you breathe in . . . and the warm moist air as you exhale . . . just continue to attend to your breathing . . . and each time you exhale mentally repeat the word RELAX . . . inhale . . . exhale . . . RELAX . . .

[A pleasant imagery scene can be inserted here if time allows. If not, allow the clients to experience the pleasant feelings of relaxation while focusing on their breathing techniques for 5 minutes.]

Now I'm going to help you return to your normal state of alertness . . . In a little while I will begin counting backwards from 5 to 1 . . . you will gradually become more alert . . . . When I reach 2, I want you to open your eyes . . . when I get to 1 you will be entirely aroused up in your normal state of alertness . . . READY? . . . 5 . . . 4 . . . you are becoming more and more alert . . . you feel very refreshed . . . 3 . . . 2 . . . now your eyes are open and you are beginning to feel very alert, returning to your normal state of alertness.

Homework Assignments

- Practice 16-muscle PMR once a day with tape.
- Practice old–new beliefs in the car during your least provoking driving situation (from the hierarchy list) once during the week.

TREATMENT SESSION 2

Each session begins with a review of the last week's key points and a review of the completed homework assignment. As is often the case in psychotherapy, the client may not have completed his or her homework assignment. Given that the aggressive driving clients are often resistant to change at worst and dubious about a pressing need for change at best, it is impractical to imagine that every client will satisfactorily complete his or her assignments. We strongly encourage and praise even the slightest effort at applying the therapeutic skills in the actual driving situation. That being said, we certainly do not like the client to have the take-home message that it is somehow okay to not engage in therapy and not complete homework assignments. So although it may not be realistic to reassign the homework for the next session, as one would normally do in psychotherapy, we do require that the client make some effort to complete some aspect of the homework in the session. Clients cannot obviously begin practicing PMR in session, but they can certainly think of some aggressive driving incident over the course of the last week and apply last week's material in the current session. This requires that the client recall some of last week's material and its application. Experiencing a "pop quiz" in this manner can cause a bit of discomfort for the client. Such discomfort may be productive insofar as it increases the probability of the client's attending to material presented a bit more closely in the future. That bit of information may be all that is required to prevent a dangerous aggressive driving incident in the future.

Review Last Week's Key Points

- Negative impact of aggressive driving on health, work, and relationships
- Anger continuum
- Larson's five driver categories
- The need to change old beliefs to new beliefs
- 16-muscle PMR

Review Homework

- Each person was supposed to apply driving coping strategies to the least provoking item on their hierarchy list. Ask each group member, in turn, how successful he or she was in this endeavor. Ask about the particular driving situation, the level of anger, and the resultant behavior. Record progress in the client's chart (see Appendix 10.6).

Ask about each person's relaxation practice. Inquire as to a relaxation rating based on a scale of 1 to 10 (with 10 indicating the most relaxed), asking how relaxed the client was able to get on average over the week.

Clinical Hint

Many clients do not adequately complete the homework assigned, and many (still denying that they are less-than-perfect drivers) say they cannot apply driving coping strategies because they were not annoyed on the roadways over the course of the last week. We choose not to argue these points with the drivers. Instead, we ask them to then apply the strategies to an incident in the past while normalizing feeling angry on the roads (i.e., "Everyone feels angry sometimes on the roads. Even my sweet 85-year-old grandmother sometimes feels angry when riding in the car and she doesn't even drive!") Our goal as therapists is to teach the skills and concepts and not get into battles over whether clients should or should not be classified as aggressive drivers. If nothing else, the nonvoluntary drivers (usually the more resistant clients) could at least apply the coping skills to their arrest situation. The important point is that everyone provide a personal example and demonstrate a working knowledge of how to apply a given coping strategy.

ABCs: Antecedents, Behaviors, and Consequences

This section addresses the need to be **prepared** for driving situations that may trigger anger and aggressive driving behavior. Begin to discuss particular driving situations that increase the probability of aggressive driving behavior. We want to be able to identify the antecedents, the behaviors, and the consequences of the behaviors (see Appendix 10.7)

Possible Script

> Last week, we discussed the anger continuum. We talked about the fact that it's easier to cope with more mild degrees of anger than it is to handle anger when it reaches the point of rage. Therefore, we want to begin to identify driving situations that seem to be triggers for frustration, anger, and aggressive driving behaviors and that typically result in strong feelings of anger. We will call these *trigger situations*. If we can identify our individual trigger situations, we can plan coping strategies to deal with anger before the client loses control or reaches the point of rage.

Example:

Antecedent or trigger situation:	The morning, rush hour commute to work
Behavior:	Pass on the right, speed, cut off other driver
Consequence:	Muscle tension, headache, bad mood, arrive late to work

Discuss Alternative Coping Strategies

Use Larson's (1996b) strategies as examples and ask group members for additional ideas. Every group came up with an idea that others had not thought of before, so this section is a work in progress.

Larson's strategies include the following: "Be my Guest," leave yourself an extra 15 minutes for the morning commute, refuse to allow yourself to go over the speed limit, listen to enjoyable music in the car, enjoy your companion, and enjoy the scenery.

Case Vignette. Doug reported that he often engaged in a "beat-the-clock" game on his commute. He had established a contest with himself to see how much time he could "save" on his daily commute and other trips in his vehicle. He reported that it added a sense of excitement to an otherwise boring trip. However, in leaving too little time for his commute, Doug was habitually late to work. His boss had become increasingly less tolerant of his tardiness over the course of the last month and had recently warned him that his job was in jeopardy if he were late one more time. As Doug tells it, Monday morning dawned too bright and too early. He knew that it took him approximately 15 minutes to travel to work, and he left the house with only 14 minutes until punch-in time. As usual, Doug figured he could make up the extra time on his commute and, as usual, Monday morning traffic was in a jam. His 14 minutes were quickly ticking away, and little progress was being made. Doug swerved in and out of the three lanes of highway, cutting off vehicles right and left only to "get stuck behind yet another slow, &*$#@* driver." The highway was packed; there was no place to go. Doug's tension mounted, as did his anger. He began to yell and scream at the other drivers on the highway and engaged in more and more risky, fruitless maneuvers to advance in traffic. With horns blaring all around (at him!), he made one final attempt to reach work on time—he floored the accelerator and sped off on the shoulder of the highway at a rate of 72 mph. He knows it was 72 mph because that was the exact speed at which the arresting police officer clocked him. Needless to say, Doug received several tickets and was incredibly late to work. Although intervention was appropriate at several levels for this client, he responded best to a very simple behavioral intervention. The group suggested that he leave 15 minutes early for work for 1 week. This strategy would ensure that he would arrive to work in a timely manner, because he was never more than 5 or 10 minutes late. Second, the group suggested that Doug cover the clock on his car's dashboard and refrain from wearing a watch on his commute. Thus, he would not be able to have a "race against the clock." The group suggested that, instead of watching the clock, he take the time to notice five stimuli that were pleasurable to him (scenery, attractive passing cars, particular song on the radio, etc.). Doug complied with the suggestions and was a new man in the next session. Not only was he able to save his job, but he also attested to the pleasure of driving to work in a relatively stress-free environment and an improved mood on arriving to work.

Cognitive Distortions, Coping Self-Statements, and Challenging Faulty Assumptions

Although cognitive therapy can be complex, and there is certainly not enough time to fully administer the intervention (a full course of cognitive therapy typically takes substantially longer to administer—i.e., 12 sessions), the goal of this section of the protocol is to point out to the client that his or her thoughts contribute to his or her anger. Often, the thoughts that cause the most anger are illogical or distorted. By identifying which thoughts are illogical and then modifying these distorted thoughts, one can make the resultant anger diminish or disappear. The goal here is for the client to begin to take some ownership of the anger and realize that his or her thoughts contribute to the resultant aggressive driving situation. If the client can begin to *think* about driving and his or her fellow drivers differently, then he or she may begin to *feel* and *behave* differently on the roadways. To help explain some of these premises, hand out the Cognitive Distortions sheet (see Appendixes 10.8 and 10.9). Discuss the distortions and generate examples.

Possible Script

> The anger you feel while driving is a part of you and is harmful to you and those who surround you on the roads. Begin to identify the thought processes that you engage in on the roads. For instance, when you are frustrated with another driver, what thoughts go through your head? Begin to challenge these thoughts. If we think differently about situations, we behave differently. [We often provide the following example:] For instance, I am driving in the car with my very sweet mother. We stop at a four-way stop sign, and a driver traveling in the perpendicular street fails to make the stop. I immediately call the driver names, my heart races, and I clench the steering wheel lamenting the lack of consideration of drivers these days. I feel quite self-righteous in my anger. My sweet mother, on the other hand, is wringing her hands worrying that there is an emergency and hoping against hope that

everything works out for the best. Both of us experienced the exact same situation. Both of us reacted very differently depending on our interpretation of that situation. Thus, we can see how our thoughts can certainly lead to our anger and our angry behavior. It is our goal, then, to start to challenge these illogical thoughts and reduce our subsequent anger.

Example: "The other crazy drivers on the road"

"Things *should* be a certain way"

Challenge: Where is your evidence for that?

Says who? Why does it have to be that way?

What's another way of looking at that?

Do you know of anyone who may do that differently or look at that differently?

And why shouldn't this happen to you?

Clinical Hint

Cognitive distortions seen in aggressive driving often involve some stereotypes. Examples of black-and-white thinking and labeling include "old drivers should have their licenses taken away," "women drivers are awful," and "kids these days tear up the road and care for no one but themselves." These types of stereotypes can be challenged at the most basic level. The truth is that any driver on any given day can drive well or poorly, can make a mistake or drive perfectly. This includes the drivers in the treatment group. The therapist can begin by asking each driver to recall a time when he or she made an error on the roadways (everyone has!). Explain that no driver is perfect. Point out how thinking that all elderly people are poor drivers primes the client to be angry or irritated when he or she comes into contact with an elderly driver on the road. Then, when that driver makes the least mistake or drives too slowly, and so on, the angry driver feels justified in his or her anger (self-fulfilling prophecy). Point out the irrationality of that thought process. Ask the client to try to recall any older driver who drives well (mother, father, grandfather, etc.). Challenge the client to actively make an effort to identify three elderly drivers (for instance) every day who are driving satisfactorily or even well. The idea is to expose the clients to evidence to contradict his or her faulty thought patterns.

Case Vignette. Sam was convinced to come through the program by friends who were tired of his behavior in the car. At the slightest infraction or perceived disrespect on the roadways, Sam would scream and curse and drive more and more dangerously. His aggressive driving behavior had escalated to the point that he had hopped out of the car at an intersection and put a tire iron through another driver's rear window. The discussion ensued as follows:

> *Sam:* I hate all of these @#$%^ drivers on the @#$%*& roads. They are all a bunch of *$#@^!! I can't even leave my house to drive to the store without facing possible death at the hands of these idiots. They should all stay off the roads and get the #$@*# out of my way. Then, God forbid you should defend yourself. They look at you like you are the bad guy. Lady, you got the wrong person in here! You should go get some of them in here.

Even in this one statement one can see samples of several cognitive distortions and inaccurate interpretations that are clearly contributing to escalations in the client's anger. Particularly noteworthy are labeling ("@#$%^ drivers"), some mind-reading ("they look at you like you are the bad guy"), magnification ("I can't leave my house . . . without facing possible death"), and inappropriate "should" statements ("they should all stay off the roads"; "you should go get some of them in here"). Basically, this client's inaccurate self-talk is fueling his rage. These statements can be challenged using typical cognitive strategies. The following is a sample of challenging the inaccuracy of his labeling and his magnification of events.

> *Therapist:* OK, let's take this one step at a time. You are clearly quite upset. What number would you give your anger on the anger continuum?
>
> *Sam:* You're #@$%* right I'm upset. I'm a 10 on your scale.
>
> *Therapist:* How much time do you spend on average in the car on a daily basis?
>
> *Sam:* Three hours
>
> *Therapist:* And how many bad driving situations do you encounter on a daily basis?
>
> *Sam:* Separate incidents? At least four a day.
>
> *Therapist:* And how long does each driving incident typically last?
>
> *Sam:* Well depending on the situation, sometimes I am stuck behind an idiot at a light or behind slow drivers in the left lane forever until I can get around them and blow by them.
>
> *Therapist:* So a traffic light situation may last for 3 minutes, all told? And you might be behind someone for maybe 5 minutes in the left lane until you get around him or her?
>
> *Sam:* [*boasting*] If that! I'll find a way to get around them or get up real close behind them and get them back in the slow lane where they belong.

Therapist: So let's use the maximum numbers here and estimate that four incidents at 5 minutes an incident equals 20 minutes. Now how many drivers would you say you come in contact with on average during those 3 hours of travel time?

Sam: I have no idea. In the city, they are all around and the highway can be packed, so at least 100 an hour, maybe more.

Therapist: So using this estimate, 100 drivers an hour times 3 hours equals 300 drivers, and you've already said that you encounter approximately four bad drivers during the day. Are you telling us that you experience 4 out of 300 drivers as problematic and 20 out of 180 total driving minutes as being stressful?

Sam: I guess that's about right.

Therapist: That's a little different than "all these @#$*# drivers" being idiots and thinking that you are not able to leave your house due to possible death. But let's look at the four problematic drivers and those 20 stressful minutes. Out of that total time, how often have you been faced with an actual life-threatening situation?

Sam: Well, I was exaggerating about that one. I've never been in a wreck, but it's always a possibility.

Therapist: That is absolutely true. But it really doesn't sound like a high probability given that you've spent all of this time in the car over the course of your life and have never even been in an accident. Now, in terms of possibilities and probabilities, do you think you are increasing your risk of being injured or killed when you drive dangerously or approach someone's car and smash their rear window?

Sam: [grinning] Naw, that lady was so scared. She just took off.

Therapist: What if the lady had had a gun? What if the driver had not been scared and had in fact been Joe [gestures to another group member who had, in fact, beaten another driver with a hammer]? Do you think Joe would have been scared and taken off? Fact of the matter is, looks like you are increasing your risk on the roadways, as opposed to other drivers increasing your risk.

Sam: [laughs a little nervously] No, I wouldn't want to mess with Joe!

Therapist: Finally, in terms of other drivers being idiots and out to get you, what's your evidence to support those assertions? Do you actually know if those people are idiots or whether they are rocket scientists? It might help to consider different possibilities, including that the person is having a really bad day and distracted (someone's mom just died, kid is sick, just got fired, stuff we all deal with in life), that the person may have just made a mistake (missed a turn, forgotten to put on a blinker, gave too quick a look in the rearview mirror and didn't see you), or that the person is just a bad driver but really good at other things and actually a reasonable person. As soon as we put a label on someone, that person becomes that label in your mind. The label takes on the form of gospel truth. It's easy to get angry and behave badly toward a "no-good idiot." It doesn't feel so self-righteous and justified to do so toward a "reasonable person who is already having a bad day." Depending on our thought process, we experience very different emotions and levels of emotions. As in the example provided earlier, my very sweet mother and I could be driving in the car and come to a four-way stop sign. Another driver blows through the intersection. My mother and I both witnessed the incident. I have steam coming out of my ears and curse the day the driver was born! My mother, on the other hand, is wringing her hands and hoping that there's not an emergency, imagining that the driver is a heart surgeon and will be saving someone's life soon if only she can get to the hospital on time. As you can see, we both had very different interpretations of the same incident and very different resultant emotions based on those interpretations. So the next time you experience an unpleasant driving situation and a lot of unpleasant emotion and stress stemming from it, consider your thoughts and how they are contributing to the stress. The good news is, you can change your thoughts and in making them more accurate, reduce unnecessary unpleasant affect. You might as well, because the one thing you cannot control is other people's driving behavior.

Four-Muscle Relaxation Training

Conduct the four-muscle relaxation portion of the PMR training. Given the brevity of this particular treatment program, we chose to deviate from Bernstein and Borkovec's (1973) suggested administration of this training. Thus, we skip the eight-muscle-group training (which typically follows the 16-muscle-group training) and reduce the length of relaxation in Session 2 to the following muscle groups. We do, however, provide the eight-muscle-group relaxation tape as well as the four-muscle-group and relaxation-by-recall tape. Clients can opt to use the eight-muscle tension–release cycle if they so desire.

Four-muscle-group relaxation training focuses on the following areas:

- Arms (both together, closed fists, arms flexed slightly at elbow);
- Chest (hold breath);
- Neck (hunch shoulders, draw in back of neck); and
- Face (close eyes tightly while drawing up the rest of face).

Next, move right into the four-muscle relaxation-by-recall training portion. The client can remain comfortably seated with the lights dimmed while the therapist provides the next instruction.

Possible Script

> One goal of the training is for you to be able to become completely relaxed readily and quickly in most situations. This requires you to practice these skills on a daily basis. To help achieve this goal, we are going to try something different: to see if you can become relaxed without going through the tension–release cycle. I will be asking you to recall or remember what the relaxed state felt like in your mind and body and to try to achieve that state without tensing the muscle.

Before starting, arrange for the client to signal you by raising a forefinger if he or she has not been able to relax a particular muscle group. Begin the relaxation-by-recall by asking the client to (a) focus his or her attention on the muscles in his or her hands and arms and (b) very carefully identify any feelings or sensations of tension or tightness that may be present, especially focusing on any feelings of tension.

Then ask the client to relax and recall what it was like when he or she released the tension from that particular muscle group and then re-emphasize having the client relax, letting go of those particular muscles and allowing them to become more and more deeply relaxed. Allow 30 to 40 seconds to elapse with the interjection of the usual suggestions.

Then ask the client to signal if he or she is not deeply relaxed. If he or she indicates that the muscles are not relaxed, try the suggestions again. If he or she indicates that the muscles are still not relaxed, then go through the actual tension-release cycle. If he or she indicates that the muscles are relaxed, go to the next muscle group. At the end of the four-muscle group, again go through the deepening by counting and attention to breathing and subvocalizing the word *relax* with exhalation for about 2 minutes. If the client was completely successful with recall, tell him or her to switch to this procedure for home practice. Instruct the client to return to the tension–release cycle during home practice if he or she is not able to achieve relaxation through the recall process.

Assign Homework

- Practice the strategies that were learned in Session 2 on the three least provoking items on the hierarchy list. These strategies include challenging faulty assumptions, changing old beliefs, and using some of the alternative coping strategies for trigger situations.
- Practice the four-muscle-group recall-relaxation tape daily. Give client the eight-muscle-group tape to practice as a shorter version of full relaxation. Instruct client to practice the eight-muscle-group tape if more relaxation is required.

TREATMENT SESSION 3

Review the Last 2 Weeks' Key Points

- Negative impact of aggressive driving on health, work, and relationships
- The anger continuum
- Larson's five driver categories
- Changing old beliefs
- ABCs and trigger situations
- Alternative coping strategies
- Coping self-statements, cognitive distortions, and challenging faulty assumptions
- Relaxation-by-recall

Review Homework

- Relaxation-by-recall: Record number of practice sessions per individual and the level of relaxation on a scale of 1–10 (10 = *most relaxed*).
- Application of one or more of the coping strategies to the three least provoking driving situations on the hierarchy list. Was client successful? Record this in the progress note.

Discuss Reinforcements for Aggressive Driving Behavior

As noted earlier, aggressive driving is not a psychiatric diagnosis. In fact, the actual behavior of aggressive driving can be very reinforcing. The therapist's job then becomes working to remove these reinforcers by pointing out that the negatives and risks outweigh the positives and benefits.

Example:	Speeding
Reinforcement:	Beating other drivers, making good time
Challenge:	How much time do you actually save?
	What are the risks to other drivers?
	What are the risks to yourself?
	Do the risks outweigh the benefits?

Practice Role Plays

Using the strategies presented, each group member offers one of his or her items on the hierarchy list, and the group will offer some coping strategies. For example, one person explains a trigger situation and the subsequent driving behavior engaged in when faced with that situation.

The individual does the following:

- Identify old beliefs involved in that situation,
- Identify faulty assumptions and thoughts behind that situation,
- Identify the driver category into which the situation falls, and
- Identify where the situation falls on the anger continuum.

The group does the following:

- Offer new beliefs,
- Offer alternative coping strategies, and
- Offer coping self-statements and challenges to faulty assumptions.

Case Vignette. Bob (a 35-year-old man) described himself as a very caring and solicitous person. He lived with an elderly parent and would run errands on a daily basis for this parent. Running these errands required that Bob cross a busy intersection controlled by a traffic light. Bob reported that time and again other drivers would run the red light, thus impeding his progression across the intersection in what he described as an "unjust, unsafe, and illegal" maneuver. Recently, Bob had approached the intersection and, sure enough, a female driver ran the red light. Infuriated, Bob followed the woman some distance to her home and into her driveway. The woman happened to be pregnant and also had a toddler strapped into a car seat in the back seat of her vehicle. Bob angrily verbally confronted this woman, who fled into the house with her child and called the police. Bob was arrested for harassment. As he explained it, the arrest was ridiculous and unreasonable because he was actually promoting safe driving by "correcting the woman's unsafe driving behavior." (According to the policeman's report, the woman felt more threatened than corrected.) Bob and another group member role played the scenario, and the group worked together to challenge

Bob's thoughts and behaviors. The group challenged Bob's belief that he was police, judge, and jury of the roadways (Larson's [1996b] vigilante). The idea that drivers always ran the red light at that intersection was challenged as an all-or-nothing statement, as was the faulty assumption that these driving infractions were intentional and not just errors in judgment or lapses in driving skill. Bob was able to approximately calculate the number of times he passed through that intersection in a given month and estimate the number of times a driver ran that light. The figure ended up somewhere less than 10%, or about once per month. Bob figured that it was highly unlikely (except in the case of a true sociopath) that anyone was trying to hurt or harm him and that the driving infraction was much less likely to be intentional than attributable to poor judgment. Bob had been feeling very self-righteous in his anger and had felt justified in his behavior because he had believed that running this particular red light could eventually result in his harm or death. The group argued that instead of becoming angry, following a driver home (because who knows if the driver has a gun, etc.), and engaging in a confrontation, it may be more fruitful for Bob to merely take a few extra seconds before crossing the intersection to ensure that no one was running the red light and that he was in no imminent danger. Bob realized that if he had merely interpreted the situation differently, his anger would have been much lower on the anger continuum, and his resultant behaviors and their consequences would have been much different.

Review Relaxation-by-Recall

It is hoped that the clients have practiced this skill over the course of the last week. The rationale and technique of relaxation-by-recall are quickly reviewed, and then the concept of cue-controlled relaxation is presented.

Introduce Cue-Controlled Relaxation

Conduct four-muscle relaxation-by-recall. Use the deepening procedure by counting to three and suggesting that the client is becoming more completely relaxed with each count. Pay particular attention to breathing and subvocalizing the word *relax*.

Have the client take a deep diaphragmatic breath, exhale, and subvocalize the word *relax*. Repeat this several times. Now, check to see if he or she is becoming relaxed using the deep breathing technique in conjunction with the subvocalization of the word *relax*. Label this procedure *cue-controlled relaxation*.

Assign Homework

- Instruct the client to practice cue-controlled relaxation several times a day, especially during driving activities. Ask the client to notice if the deep breathing helps him or her to relax the tension and stress.
- Instruct the client to practice one of the longer tapes, if necessary, during the week.
- Instruct the client to practice the coping strategies learned during the trigger situations listed on the hierarchy list. Ask the client to challenge him- or herself by practicing on all five items on the list, especially the two most provoking ones.

TREATMENT SESSION 4

Session 4 is primarily a wrap-up session. Each of the previous sessions involved a lot of material. Some time is spent reviewing the material and making sure that the clients get at least one take-home message from each lesson or skill. The idea of the toolbox is revisited, and clients are asked to indicate which particular "tool" was most helpful. Invariably, clients have come up with new and interesting alternatives to aggressive driving in each session. These are typically shared during this session.

Review All Strategies Learned

- Changing old beliefs
- Identifying ABCs
- Cue-controlled relaxation
- Alternative coping strategies
- Coping self-statements and challenging faulty assumptions
- Challenging reinforcers

Review Homework

- Identify the most effective strategies per individual.
- Discuss hierarchy items and troubleshoot any difficulties dealing with driving situations.
- Discuss relaxation and record how often the technique was practiced and the extent to which the individual felt relaxed (on a scale of 1–10).

Reintroduce Aggressive Driving Questionnaires

- Ask the individual to rewrite the original aggressive driving situation in accordance with how he or she would cope with the frustration and anger now (see Appendix 10.10).
- Compare this account with their description of their behavior in the same situation in the first week of treatment.
- Point out areas of improvement and areas for future work.

Clinical Hint

Throughout the entire four-session intervention, we try to instill as much humor into the program as possible. Although we do not take aggressive driving lightly, we do see humor as a panacea for anger. The experiences of humor and anger are often incompatible, and thus humor may serve as a deterrent to aggressive driving in and of itself. Perhaps more important, however, we have found that humor makes the group a bit more tolerable for everyone. Clients often begin therapy feeling as if they are beginning a punishment. (One court-mandated client told me his choices were community service involving shoveling excrement out of cages in a local animal shelter and our program. According to him, we barely made the cut.) It has been fairly well documented in the psychotherapy literature that rapport is an important nonspecific factor and increases the probability of behavior change, as does patient engagement in the actual intervention. Thus, we approached therapy with this group of clients in a humorous and lighthearted way whenever possible. A fine line does exist between engaging the client and minimizing the need for behavior change, but it has worked for us. Several clients returned at the 2-month follow-up and spontaneously reported that our remarks and our escapades in group occasionally came to mind when they were feeling provoked on the roadways. Often, laughing at us is enough to cause the client to pause and engage in an alternative, less risky behavior. As aggressive driving therapists, perhaps that is the most we can ask.

Encourage Continued Usage of Coping Strategies and Reinforce Good Learning

We try to end the final group by finding at least one example of change and improvement in each client. For the most part, this is not difficult.

CONCLUSION

Working with this clientele has been rewarding in many ways. Small changes in driving behavior can greatly affect the lives of the drivers and the lives of the rest of us who share the roadways with them. In many cases, this change was perpetuated by merely gaining insight into the level of anger experienced in driving situations. Minor tweaks in behavior such as leaving 10 minutes early for work, focusing on the scenery, or recalling a humorous event significantly reduced roadway frustration. Using deep-breathing techniques such as cue-controlled relaxation, or even just counting to 10, often gave the drivers enough pause to prevent an impulsive, risky driving maneuver. Understanding that one's own thoughts contribute to one's anger allowed the drivers to begin to challenge some of their more distorted thoughts. Many drivers began to take more ownership of their anger and, subsequently, more responsibility for their driving behavior. Although four sessions will not markedly influence the levels of Axis I and II psychopathology found in this population, we hope that the lessons learned will contribute to change in the more discrete area of driving behavior. As one client spontaneously reported at the 2-month follow-up session:

> When I got sent to this program, I thought there had been a mistake. I didn't consider myself an aggressive driver. I didn't realize the extent of the anger inside of me. I think if I hadn't taken this class, I would've eventually become so angry I would've killed somebody.

APPENDIX 10.1
Aggressive Driving Questionnaire

1. **Give a brief account of a typical driving situation that is annoying or frustrating to you. This situation should be one in which you respond with an aggressive driving behavior.**

   _____

   _____

   _____

   _____

   _____

2. **During this situation, what do you usually think about:**

   a. The other driver? _____

   b. Drivers in general? _____

   c. Road conditions? _____

   d. Your ability to drive effectively? _____

   e. The unfairness of the situation? _____

3. **During this situation, how do you feel:**

   a. Physically? _____

   b. Emotionally? _____

   c. Mentally? _____

4. **For how long would you normally feel this way?** _____

5. **Name 3 ways in which you might normally handle the situation.**

   a. _____

   b. _____

   c. _____

APPENDIX 10.2

Anger Continuum

```
/   /   /   /   /   /   /   /   /   /   /
0       1       2       3       4       5       6       7       8       9       10
(not        (minor          (aggravation/          (mad/               (furious)          (rage/out of
at          annoyance/      indignation)          very angry)                             control)
all)        irritation)
```

Scale:

0 = Not at all
1 = Minor annoyance/ irritation
3 = Aggravation/ indignation
5 = Mad/ very angry
7 = Furious
10 = In a rage/out of control

APPENDIX 10.3

The Aggressive Driver (based on Larson, 1996b)

The Speeder. This driver races against the clock. This person's goal is to reach a given destination as quickly as possible and "make good time." When these efforts are thwarted or obstructed, this driver quickly becomes angry.

The Competitor. This driver attempts to bolster self-esteem by creating contests out of driving situations and attempting to "beat" other drivers in given situations (i.e., will attempt to race another driver at a neighboring toll booth to get through first). Losing these battles increases the Competitor's anger and aggressive driving behavior.

The Passive–Aggressor. This driver thwarts other drivers' attempts to pass, drive faster, merge, and so on. This type of driver feels that giving in to another driver results in loss of status or self-esteem. Although this driver may not speed or tailgate, preventing others from achieving their goals increases anger and hazard on the road just as effectively.

The Narcissist. This driver sets rigid standards regarding proper driving behavior and feels angry when infractions of these standards are observed. These infractions may include actual driving behavior or characteristics of a given driver: sex, age, type of car, and so on.

The Vigilante. This driver considers him- or herself a self-appointed enforcer, judge, and jury of fellow drivers. This driver feels justified in punishing infractions of traffic laws and will engage in a spectrum of punishing behaviors, from shouting, swearing, and obscene gesturing to cutting off drivers and even to killing other drivers.

APPENDIX 10.4

Driving Situation Hierarchy List

Directions: Create a list of situations that prompt you to drive aggressively. Rank them in order from the most provoking to the least provoking. The top situation should be the most provoking to you and the bottom situation should be the least upsetting, annoying, or frustrating out of all the situations that bother you. Give each item on the list an anger rating based on the scale below.

Anger Ratings:

/	/	/
1	**5**	**10**
(totally calm)	(moderately upset/ moderately aggressive)	(enraged/loss of control)

Anger Rating   **Situation**

_____

_____

_____

_____

_____

Name: _____ Date: _____

APPENDIX 10.5

Larson's Key Strategies (based on Larson, 1996b)

It's important to recognize old belief systems that contribute to aggressive driving behavior. These old beliefs cause your driving experience to be frustrating, stressful, and even hazardous. Old beliefs can be hazardous to your safety, your passenger's safety, and other drivers' safety on the roads. These old beliefs can also be hazardous in much less noticeable ways. They can damage your mood, your health, your relationships with other people, and your work performance. Identifying these old belief systems is the first big step in improving your driving experience.

Some examples of old belief systems are provided below for each type of aggressive driver. These old belief systems have been replaced with newer, healthier, and more adaptive beliefs.

Replace Old Beliefs:

Speeders: Make Good Time
Competitors: Be Number One
Passive–Aggressors: Try and Make Me
Narcissists: They Shouldn't Allow Them on the Road
Vigilantes: Teach Them a Lesson

With New Beliefs:

Speeders: Make Time Good
Competitors: Number One Being
Passive–Aggressors: Be My Guest
Narcissists: Live and Let Live
Vigilantes: Leave Punishment to the Police

APPENDIX 10.6

Progress Notes

Name: _____

Date: _____ Session # _____

Homework review:

    Driving Situation:

    _____

    _____

    Response Behavior:

    _____

    _____

    _____

    Anger Rating (based on scale in Anger Continuum): _____

    Coping Strategy Used:

    _____

    _____

    How Successful:

    _____

    _____

    Relaxation:

    # of practices: _____ Average level of relaxation (1–10): _____

Other:

APPENDIX 10.7

ABCs of Driving Behavior: Antecedents, Behaviors, and Consequences

Many people experience common driving situations that frequently seem to frustrate and annoy them. These driving situations are known as **trigger situations** or **antecedents** because they seem to always trigger one's anger. If we can identify these trigger situations and the aggressive driving **behaviors** involved with them, we can try to find ways to deal with these situations more effectively. Thus, we can better prepare ourselves for our trigger situations. Being prepared for a stressful driving situation *before* it occurs, allows us to cope with it more effectively. Coping with situations more effectively avoids the negative **consequences** that result from aggressive driving behaviors.

Here's an example:

Trigger situation or *Antecedent*:	Slow driver in the left lane
Common aggressive *Behavior*:	Flash high beams, tailgate
Result or *Consequence*:	Rear-end the driver when he or she brakes quickly, bad mood, muscle tension, anxiety, get a ticket, etc.

Identify one of your own trigger situations or antecedents, one behavior, and one resulting consequence:

Antecedent: _____

Behavior: _____

Consequence: _____

APPENDIX 10.8

Cognitive Distortions

Anger and frustration result from the meaning that you give to an event, not from the event alone. If you modify your cognitions, the anger and frustration will lessen.

Cognitive Distortions Responsible for Anger

- *Labeling:* Anger is directed at someone personally, rather than at his or her behavior. Moral superiority while blaming others results in a self-fulfilling prophecy for continued warfare.
- *Mind reading:* One invents motives to explain why the other person did what he did. The explanation is usually inaccurate.
- *Magnification:* As the importance of a negative event is exaggerated, the intensity of one's reaction grows stronger.
- *Inappropriate "should" and "should not" statements:* Imposing your sense of justice and fairness on others may result in anger on your part and on the part of the other person.

Distinguishing Adaptive From Maladaptive Anger

- Is anger directed towards someone who knowingly, intentionally, and unnecessarily acted in a hurtful manner?
- Is the anger useful? Does it help to achieve a desired goal?

Techniques Useful in Relieving Anger

- Develop a desire to get rid of the anger. List the advantages and disadvantages of feeling angry and retaliating and the advantages and disadvantages of eliminating anger.
- Use imagining techniques: Anger and concomitant thoughts often seem like a script in a movie played out with increasing anger. Anger can be reduced through modifying the script. Change the scenario so that it is humorous or thought stopping.
- Rewrite the rules: Unrealistic rules on the road lead to frustration and anger, for example, "If I let someone into traffic, then someone should do the same for me."
- Learn to expect some craziness and stupidity on the roads.

APPENDIX 10.9

Important Considerations in Modifying Anger

- The events of the world don't make you angry. Your thoughts make you angry.
- Most of the time, your anger will not help you out.
- Thoughts that generate anger tend to contain distortions. Correcting distortions will reduce anger.
- Anger is caused by your belief that someone is acting unfairly or that an event is unjust. The intensity of your anger will increase with your perception of the level of intent or injustice.
- If you can understand others' point of view, you may be surprised to learn that actions are not unjust from their viewpoint.
- Usually other people do not feel that they deserve your rage. This may cause further deterioration and function as a self-serving prophecy.
- A great deal of anger involves defense against loss of self-esteem when people criticize you, disagree with you, or fail to behave as you wish.
- Frustration results from unmet, often unrealistic expectations.
- A crucial question is whether it is to your advantage to get angry.

Aggressive Driving Questionnaire (Post)

1. **Give a brief account of a driving situation that was annoying or frustrating to you, which occurred in the last week.**

_____

_____

_____

_____

_____

2. **During this situation, what did you think about:**

   a. The other driver? _____

   b. Drivers in general? _____

   c. Road conditions? _____

   d. Your ability to drive effectively? _____

   e. The unfairness of the situation? _____

3. **During this situation, how did you feel:**

   a. Physically? _____

   b. Emotionally? _____

   c. Mentally? _____

4. **For how long did you feel this way?** _____

How did you handle the situation?

_____

_____

_____

11

INVOLVING THE CRIMINAL JUSTICE SYSTEM IN THE RECRUITMENT AND TREATMENT OF AGGRESSIVE DRIVERS

Accessing the aggressive driving population is perhaps one of the largest obstacles in treating this group of individuals. Aggressive driving is not a common presenting problem in the typical mental health professional's office. To the contrary, drivers behaving aggressively on the roadways often experience reinforcement of the aggressive driving behavior insofar as it tends to decrease in a cathartic fashion the distress, anxiety, or anger caused by roadway provocations. Many aggressive drivers do not consider their driving behavior and style to be aggressive at all. In fact, many drivers in our program were incredulous as to why they had been remanded to such a program. Many of our drivers viewed the problematic driving as entirely the fault of other drivers in obstructing their goal-directed activity. We also saw a significant subset of individuals who met criteria for antisocial personality disorder or intermittent explosive disorder. For these individuals, aggressive driving may be just one example of a larger repertoire of hostility, aggression, or impulsivity commonly demonstrated across a variety of domains of functioning. Even the individuals who did appear voluntarily in our program were often present at the strict request (if not orders) of family members and friends who feared for their lives as passengers in the car.

In our research program, treatment was conducted free of charge in exchange for participation in the lengthy assessment processes. Because insurance typically does not cover mental health services for aggressive driving, it may be prohibitive for families to pay out of pocket for such an intervention in a general practitioner's office. Because of these rather unique barriers to entering therapy, clinicians may not often find themselves treating a voluntary aggressive driver.

Tara E. Galovski (the principal investigator), who at the time of our study was a doctoral candidate trying to finish her dissertation in a timely manner, was concerned about the anticipated lack of voluntary participation. She decided to establish a collaborative relationship with the local district attorney's (DA's) office, justices, and other law enforcement agencies. In this chapter we describe this endeavor.

We realized that most of the individuals (DAs, judges, etc.) who would be integral in establishing this program are busy people; thus, the development of any successful referral system between our program and their various offices would have to involve the bare minimum effort on their part. In other words, our program could not be onerous to the extent that it added more layers of effort and paperwork to the already-overburdened offices of the justice system. Involvement in our program also needed to be mutually beneficial to all parties in order to offset whatever effort was required. Thus, we suggest that before approaching potential collaborators, clinicians should have a proposed referral system drafted but also be willing to accommodate any necessary changes for the convenience of potential collaborators.

THE ALBANY REFERRAL SYSTEM

As noted above, we wanted to expedite the flow of participants between the courts and our program. Toward this end, we created a 1-page referral form that clearly outlined the information needed to contact the defendant and commence his or her participation in the program. All that was required from the collaborator was to fill in the blanks and fax the form to us. The principal investigator's name and all corresponding information were also clearly denoted on the document in the event that the referring party wished to speak to her directly with any questions or concerns. A sample copy of this form is included in Exhibit 11.1.

We also created a flyer outlining the study, including the requirements of participation with all contact information provided once again. This flyer, a copy of which was attached to each referral form, was intended to answer any questions that the defendant or referring party may have had about the specifics of the program at the time of the defendant's sentencing.

EXHIBIT 11.1
Aggressive Driving Program Referral Form

Date: _____

Mr./Ms. _____
(Name of the Defendant)

has been sentenced to participation in the SUNY Albany Aggressive Driving

Modification Program as of _____
(Date of Sentencing)

Defendant's Phone Number: _____

Defendant's Address: _____

_____

Nature of Citation/Offense:

_____

_____

Referring Judge: _____

Contact:
Tara Galovski
Center for Stress and Anxiety Disorders
1535 Western Avenue
Albany, NY 12203
(518) 442-4025
Fax: 442-4027

Note. SUNY = State University of New York.

Once the defendant agreed to participate (as a diversion from his or her sentence), the flyer could be detached from the referral sheet and sent home with the defendant. In this way, the defendant had our information and instructions to contact us in a timely manner. As soon as the court or attorney faxed the referral sheet, every effort was made to contact the defendant immediately. However, on a number of occasions it was exceedingly difficult to contact the remanded individual. After all, these participants were not exactly overjoyed about participating in the program! The system using the flyers put responsibility on the defendant to contact us and enroll in the program. Thus, there was no excuse for nonparticipation in the event we were not able to get in touch with the defendant.

We also created a simple 1-page form entitled "Completion Letter." A sample copy of this letter is shown in Exhibit 11.2. For reasons of confidentiality, described below, this was the extent of the documentation returned to the courts as proof of the defendant's completion of the program. The requirements for completion were clearly outlined in the informed consent

EXHIBIT 11.2

July 24, 2000

The Honorable Joseph Smith
Saratoga Springs City Court
36 Main Street
Saratoga Springs, NY 12222

Dear Judge Smith:

  The defendant, <u>John Doe</u> completed the Aggressive Driving Course to which he had been sentenced on March 22, 2000:

    __x__ satisfactorily
    _____ unsatisfactorily

  If you have any questions concerning this matter, please feel free to contact me, Tara Galovski, at 442-4025. Thank you for your participation in our program.

Yours truly,

Tara Galovski, PhD
Treating Clinician

documentation to the courts; the attorneys; and, of course, participants. A participant was considered to have completed the program when he or she had completed the pretreatment assessment (all paper-and-pencil measures, interview, and psychophysiological assessment), four sessions of group therapy (timely, consistent attendance and responsiveness were required), a posttreatment assessment (paper-and-pencil measures, brief interview, and psychophysiological assessment), and a 2-month follow-up packet of questionnaires. At the 2-month follow-up point, we mailed the participant the questionnaires to be completed and mailed back to our center. Once we received the completed measures, we sent copies of the completion letter to the courts, to the defendant, and to the defendant's attorney.

APPROACHING COLLABORATORS

    Once the concept of the referral system had been established, it was time to contact potential collaborators. We wrote a brief cover letter describing the principal investigator's current position, research, and qualifications. A brief proposal was included that outlined the justice system's potential role in this endeavor and gave an estimation of the effort their participation would entail as well as the potential benefits such participation might afford them. The potential benefits to the general public are highlighted below.

    Included with the cover letter and brief overview of the proposal was a list of roadway behaviors that the literature had cited as aggressive. A

EXHIBIT 11.3
Examples of Aggressive Driving

Driving Behaviors

- Purposefully driving slowly with the intent to block another vehicle's passage
- Tailgating
- Improper passing (passing on the shoulder, passing on the right)
- Failure to yield the right of way
- Blocking another driver from merging
- Failure to keep right
- Horn honking
- Flashing high beams
- Deliberately using high beams from behind (keeping them on unnecessarily)
- Failing to signal properly
- "Racing" or competing with another driver (toll booths, stop lights)
- Obscene gesturing
- Verbal insults (overt)
- Throwing objects
- Physical assault (on another vehicle or individual)
- Giving chase to another driver

Subjective Feelings

- Verbal insults (covert)
- Feeling angry at another driver
- Wishing harm to another driver
- Feeling impatient at intersections
- Feeling upset at delays, other drivers, and so on

sample of this list is included in Exhibit 11.3. We included this list to ensure that defendants would be remanded to the program for appropriate offenses (i.e., aggressive driving rather than poor driving). Sample copies of the referral sheet and completion letter were also included so that the members of the justice system could ascertain exactly what their participation would entail.

A list of the town justices and the city court judges was secured from the DA's office, and we selected a few specific judges to invite to lunch so we could explain the overall program. A packet of the information described above was sent to all of the town justices in the entire county. Finally, the principal investigator presented the program to the DA and all of his assistants. We ironed out the remaining details, particularly those regarding confidentiality, as described below, and then we began the program.

Overall, the system worked well. The bulk of the referrals came from the assistant DAs, who were in the best position to identify qualifying individuals. We also received several referrals from private defense attorneys in the area who typically defended these types of drivers, so in establishing such networks in the future, it may be worthwhile to send out informational packets to defense attorneys as well. Potential defense attorneys who may be interested in the program could be identified by asking the DA for the names of local attorneys who typically defend driving violations or by using the telephone book and identifying interested parties on the basis of the content of individuals' advertisements. During the course of the program, the principal investigator regularly (every month or so) sent out a supply of referral sheets and flyers to all parties named above, both to restock any dwindling supplies and as a reminder to keep sending referrals. Finally, an update on progress was sent at both the halfway point and at the conclusion of data gathering as feedback on the program's impact and in consideration of the justice system's participation.

ADDRESSING THE ISSUE OF CONFIDENTIALITY

It is most often the case that when psychological services are provided to court-mandated patients, the court itself is typically considered the client. As such, the client does not have the same right to privileged, therapist–client communication as does a traditional psychotherapy client. For instance, court-remanded assessments often result in a full report of the findings being delivered to the court. The lack of confidentiality inherent in such situations is clearly detrimental to the therapeutic process. If the patient is concerned that his or her answers and comments will be relayed to the judicial system, then the likelihood of "faking good" for fear of reprisal is increased. In this study, a significant amount of data was collected for academic purposes, so it clearly behooved the science to ensure confidentiality of responses. As a result, the principal investigator arranged a system with the court by which the defendants' responses would remain confidential. Only the defendants' participation, or lack thereof as described above, would be relayed to the courts in the manner described (the completion letter). This arrangement was made clear to all court-referred participants, with the usual exceptions to confidentiality of instances of child abuse, suicidality, or homicidality. The arrangement was explained verbally and written explicitly into the informed consent. Prior to the pretreatment assessment, we gave the client an exact sample copy of the completion letter that would be sent back to the courts at the conclusion of his or her participation and then gave the defendant a completed copy at the end of treatment for his or her records.

Without exception, this arrangement worked well. Although the court-referred drivers were often wary about divulging potentially incriminating information, clearly underreported their overall driving behavior, and minimized their culpability for their arrest, as rapport increased their answers appeared to gain more veracity.

The institutional review board (IRB) at the University at Albany also addressed an additional concern for the welfare of these patients. The purpose of the IRB is to oversee the research conducted at the university and ensure the protection of the rights of all research subjects, regardless of how they are referred into a research program. In this case, the IRB was concerned that participation in the research was not voluntary and was, in fact, coercive. In other words, because of the punitive nature of the program, the patient did not have a choice as to whether his or her personal information would be included (albeit anonymously) in published research—in essence, in the public domain. To ensure that inclusion in the research was entirely voluntary, the following system was devised. All court-referred patients had to complete the entire program, including the assessments, as had been arranged with the courts. However, whether the defendant wished to include his or her data in the research aspect of the program was entirely voluntary. Thus, a patient could choose to have his or her responses removed from the data set and not included in any publications. The voluntary nature of participation in the research was both explicitly written into the consent form and verbally explained to each participant. None of the court-referred participants refused to take part in the research aspect of the program. A sample of the informed consent document used in this study is included in Exhibit 11.4.

HINTS FOR DEVELOPING FUTURE PROGRAMS

When approaching potential collaborators, the principal investigator invariably mentioned the benefits of participating in such a program. For the courts, this program provided a sentencing alternative to the usual fines and/or imprisonment that directly targeted dangerous roadway behavior. We equated this program to drunk driving and defensive driving courses and pointed out their success in targeting specific behaviors. We highlighted the fact that this service was offered free of charge to both the participant and the public (because it required no tax dollars) and thus was not overly burdensome to either party. We provided supporting traffic statistics to highlight the hazards of aggressive driving from a public health and safety point of view. If one cannot find local statistics, use national statistics or compare aggressive driving with drunk driving rates, as Justice Recardo Martinez did in an address to Congress (see National Highway Traffic Safety Administration, 2001). It should be noted that programs such as these are particularly beneficial to elected officials, especially if you can arrange it so that it does not involve tax dollars. This particular program generated a substantial amount of positive publicity for the DA. A DA from a neighboring county actually contacted us to find out how he could participate because of the positive feedback from the public and media about the program, but unfortunately, we could not accommodate his request. The Department of

EXHIBIT 11.4
Informed Consent

The research project that I am about to enter is concerned with studying the effect of a psychological treatment on aggressive driving behavior. I will be participating as either a volunteer or as a court-mandated participant.

I understand that the following things will happen to me or be required of me:

1. I will be asked a series of questions about my driving habits as well as about other aspects of my life and functioning.
2. I will be asked to complete a number of psychological tests.
3. I will be asked to monitor my driving behaviors on a daily basis for the period of 2 weeks. This monitoring will be done on paper-and-pencil diaries provided to me and explained by the CSAD staff.
4. If I meet criteria for an "aggressive driver," I will be asked to participate in a psychological treatment program for the purpose of reducing my aggressive driving behaviors. This treatment program consists of four group sessions held on 4 consecutive weeks. Sessions are 1.5 to 2 hours long.
5. At the conclusion of the treatment, I will be asked to complete a series of psychological tests and once again complete 2 weeks' worth of driving behaviors monitoring.
6. Two months after the conclusion of treatment, I will be contacted to see how well I am doing, to schedule a single follow-up appointment, to monitor driving behaviors one final time, and to complete one last series of psychological tests.

Risks

There are no risks associated with any of these procedures or treatment. However, I may be embarrassed by some of the questions.

Rewards

I further understand that I will receive the following rewards for my participation in the study:

1. I will receive a full psychological assessment and four treatment sessions free of charge. If purchased on a fee-for-service basis, these services would probably cost over $600.

Discontinuing Participation in the Research

I further understand the following concerning my participation in the research:

1. I may discontinue participation at any time. I should let the experimenter know about my stopping.
2. The experimenters may drop me from the study for any of the following reasons:
   - It is discovered that I do not meet criteria for aggressive driving.
   - It is discovered that I am not keeping usable records.
   - I fail to attend the group sessions without letting my supervisor know.

If I have any questions, they are written below.

_____

_____

_____

_____

_____

(continued)

EXHIBIT 11.4   *(Continued)*

Confidentiality

All information from the assessments and the treatment will be kept confidential and released to no one without my consent in writing. All professional reports of the results will have any information identifying me removed.

If I have any questions that are not answered, I may schedule an appointment with the experimenter, Tara Galovski, to discuss them.

If I have any questions about Human Subjects participation, I should contact the Compliance Officer, at 442-3510.

Subject

Date

Experimenter

Note. CSAD = Center for Stress and Anxiety Disorders

Motor Vehicles and the New York State Governor's Traffic Safety Committee also contacted the principal investigator to inquire about possibilities for instituting parts of her program into existing programs. The time-limited nature of the program did not allow implementation of this idea, but it may warrant some attention in the future.

The DA was able to generate enough publicity to greatly increase public awareness for the program and was most certainly helpful in recruiting the self-referred population. All told, the principal investigator appeared on several local news stations and conducted radio shows and interviews across the country and into Canada. For others interested in establishing such a network, we suggest starting with one DA's office and using the success of that program to open doors to other such offices. This book could also be used as supporting evidence for the potential success of such an endeavor.

Other potential collaborators are motor vehicle departments, including driver's education classes. Relationships could also be built with insurance companies; for example, driver participation could reduce insurance rates on completion of the program, as is often the case for defensive driving courses.

Because this program was conducted as research for a doctoral dissertation, the participants were treated free of charge. Private practitioners could not afford to conduct business in this manner. However, it would be interesting to test the potential for modeling a payment program on defensive driving courses that do charge for participation. Fortunately, this treatment appears to be successful in a group format; because such a format is more cost-effective than individual treatment, the cost may not be prohibitive for the average mandated driver. The returns, however, could be immeasurable.

REFERENCES

Adams, J. R. (1970). Personality variables associated with traffic accidents. *Behavioral Research in Highway Safety, 1,* 3–18.

Ajzen, I. (1985). From intentions to actions: A theory of planned behavior. In J. Kuhl & J. Beckmann (Eds.), *Action control: From cognition to behavior* (pp. 11–39). Berlin, Germany: Springer-Verlag.

American Psychiatric Association. (1968). *Diagnostic and statistical manual of mental disorders* (2nd ed.). Washington, DC: Author.

American Psychiatric Association. (1980). *Diagnostic and statistical manual of mental disorders* (3rd ed.). Washington, DC: Author.

American Psychiatric Association. (1994). *Diagnostic and statistical manual of mental disorders* (4th ed.). Washington, DC: Author.

Archer, J., Kilpatrick, G., & Bramwell, R. (1995). Comparison of two aggression inventories. *Aggressive Behavior, 21,* 371–380.

Arnett, J. (1990). Drunk driving, sensation seeking, and egocentricism among adolescents. *Personality and Individual Differences, 11,* 541–546.

Arnett, J. (1994). Sensation seeking: A new conceptualization and a new scale. *Personality and Individual Differences, 16,* 289–296.

Arnett, J. J., Offer, D., & Fine, M. A. (1997). Reckless driving in adolescence: "State" and "trait" factors. *Accident Analysis and Prevention, 29,* 57–63.

Averill, J. R. (1982). *Anger and aggression: An essay on emotion.* New York: Springer-Verlag.

Averill, J. R. (1983). Studies on anger and aggression: Implications for theories of emotion. *American Psychologist, 38,* 1145–1160.

Ax, A. F. (1953). The physiological differentiation between fear and anger in humans. *Psychosomatic Medicine, 15,* 432–442.

Bandura, A. (1969). *Principles of behavior modification.* New York: Holt, Rhinehart & Winston.

Bandura, A. (1973). *Aggression: A social learning analysis.* Englewood Cliffs, NJ: Prentice Hall.

Barkley, R. A., Guevremont, D. C., Anastopoulos, A. D., DuPaul, G. J., & Shelton, T. L. (1993). Driving-related risks and outcomes of attention deficit hyperactivity disorder in adolescents and young adults. *Pediatrics, 92,* 212–218.

Barkley, R. A., & Murphy, K. R. (1998). *Attention-deficit hyperactivity disorder: A clinical workbook* (2nd ed.). New York: Guilford Press.

Barkley, R. A., Murphy, K. R., & Kwasnik, D. (1996). Motor vehicle driving competencies and risks in teens and young adults with attention deficit hyperactivity disorder. *Pediatrics, 98,* 1089–1095.

Barratt, E. S. (1991). Measuring and predicting aggression within the context of a personality theory. *Journal of Neuropsychiatry, 3*, S35–S39.

Beck, A. (1987). Cognitive therapy. In J. K. Zeig (Ed.), *The evolution of psychotherapy* (pp. 149–178). New York: Brunner/Mazel.

Beck, A. T., Steer, R. A., & Garbin, M. G. (1988). Psychometric properties of the Beck Depression Inventory: Twenty-five years of evaluation. *Clinical Psychology Review, 8*, 77–100.

Beck, A. T., Ward, C. H., Mendelson, M., Mock, J., & Erbaugh, J. (1961). An inventory for measuring depression. *Archives of General Psychiatry, 5*, 561–571.

Beck, R., & Fernandez, E. (1998). Cognitive–behavioral therapy in the treatment of anger: A meta-analysis. *Cognitive Therapy and Research, 22*, 63–74.

Begg, D., & Langley, J. (2001). Changes in risky driving behavior from age 21 to 26 years. *Journal of Safety Research, 32*, 491–499.

Beirness, D. J. (1993). Do we really live as we drive? The role of personality factors in road crashes. *Alcohol, Drugs, and Driving, 9*, 129–143.

Beirness, D. J., & Simpson, H. M. (1988). Lifestyle correlates of risky driving and accident involvement among youth. *Alcohol, Drugs, and Driving, 4*, 193–204.

Berkowitz, L. (1989). Frustration–aggression hypothesis: Examination and reformulation. *Psychological Bulletin, 106*, 59–73.

Berkowitz, L. (1993). *Aggression: Its causes, consequences, and control.* New York: McGraw-Hill.

Berkowitz, L. (1994). Is something missing? Some observations prompted by the cognitive–neoassociationist view of anger and emotional aggression. In L. R. Huesmann (Ed.), *Aggressive behavior, current perspectives* (pp. 35–57). New York: Plenum Press.

Bernstein, D. A., & Borkovec, T. D. (1973). *Progressive relaxation training: A manual for the helping professions.* Champaign, IL: Research Press.

Blanchard, E. B., Barton, K. A., & Malta, L. (2000). Psychometric properties of a measure of aggressive driving: The Larson Driver's Stress Profile. *Psychological Reports, 87*, 881–892.

Blanchard, E. B., Hickling, E. J., Buckley, T. C., Taylor, A. E., Vollmer, A., & Loos, W. R. (1996). The psychophysiology of motor vehicle accident–related posttraumatic stress disorder: Replication and extension. *Journal of Consulting and Clinical Psychology, 64*, 742–751.

Blanchard, E. B., Hickling, E. J., Taylor, A. E., Loos, W. R., & Gerardi, R. J. (1994). The psychophysiology of motor vehicle accident–related posttraumatic stress disorder. *Behavior Research and Therapy, 25*, 453–467.

Blanchard, E. B., & Schwarz, S. P. (1988). Clinically significant changes in behavioral medicine. *Behavioral Assessment, 10*, 171–188.

Blanchard, E. B., Wulfert, E., Freidenberg, B. M., & Malta, L. (2000). Psychophysiological assessment of compulsive gamblers' arousal to gambling cues: A pilot study. *Applied Psychophysiology and Biofeedback, 27*, 251–260.

Boyce, T. E., & Geller, E. S. (2002). An instrumented vehicle assessment of problem behavior and driving style: Do younger males really take more risks? *Accident Analysis and Prevention, 34,* 51–64.

Brenner, B., & Selzer, M. I. (1969). Risk of causing a fatal accident associated with alcoholism, psychopathology, and stress: Further analysis of previous data. *Behavioral Sciences, 14,* 490–495.

Bryant, S. G., Felthous, A. R., & Barratt, E. S. (1993). Recruiting subjects for clinical aggression research. *Aggressive Behavior, 19,* 107–112.

Burns, J. W., Evon, D., & Strain-Saloum, C. (1999). Repressed anger and patterns of cardiovascular self-report and behavioral responses: Effects of harassment. *Journal of Psychosomatic Research, 47,* 569–581.

Bushman, B. J., & Anderson, C. A. (2001). Is it time to pull the plug on the hostile versus instrumental aggression dichotomy? *Psychological Review, 108,* 273–279.

Bushman, B. J., & Baumeister, R. F. (1998). Threatened egotism, narcissism, and direct and displaced aggression: Does self-love or self-hate lead to violence? *Journal of Personality and Social Psychology, 75,* 219–229.

Buss, A. H. (1961). *The psychology of aggression.* New York: Wiley.

Buss, A. H., & Durkee, A. (1957). An inventory for assessing different kinds of hostility. *Journal of Consulting Psychology, 21,* 243–248.

Buss, A. H., & Perry, M. (1992). The Aggression Questionnaire. *Journal of Personality and Social Psychology, 63,* 452–459.

Calvert, S. L., & Tan, S. (1994). Impact of virtual reality on young adults' physiological arousal and aggressive thoughts: Interaction versus observation. *Journal of Applied Developmental Psychology, 15,* 125–139.

Chase, L. J., & Mills, N. H. (1973). Status of frustration as a facilitator of aggression: A brief note. *Journal of Psychology, 84,* 225–226.

Chliaoutakis, J. E., Demakakos, P., Tzamalouka, G., Bakou, V., Koumaki, M., & Darviri, C. (2002). Aggressive behavior while driving as predictor of self-reported car crashes. *Journal of Safety Research, 33,* 431–443.

Clement, R., & Jonah, B. A. (1984). Field dependence, sensation seeking and driving behaviour. *Personality and Individual Differences, 5,* 87–93.

Clifford, F. (1989, October 4). The Times poll: Traffic or no, we love our autos. *Los Angeles Times, Orange County Edition,* Section 1, pp. 1–3.

Coccaro, E. F., Kavoussi, R. J., Berman, M. E., & Lish, J. D. (1998). Intermittent explosive disorder—Revised: Development, reliability, and validity of research criteria. *Comprehensive Psychiatry, 39,* 368–376.

Conger, J. J., Gaskill, H. S., Glad, D. D., Hassel, L., Rainey, R. V., & Sawrey, L. (1959). Psychological and psychophysiological factors in motor vehicle accidents. *Journal of the American Medical Association, 169,* 121–127.

Crancer, A., & Quiring, D. L. (1969). The mentally ill as motor vehicle operators. *American Journal of Psychiatry, 126,* 807–813.

Davies, M. C., Matthews, K. A., & McGrath, C. E. (2000). Hostile attitudes predict elevated vascular resistance during interpersonal stress in men and women. *Psychosomatic Medicine, 62*, 17–25.

Deaux, K. K. (1971). Honking at the intersection: A replication and extension. *Journal of Social Psychology, 84*, 159–160.

Deci, E. L., & Ryan, R. M. (1985). The General Causality Orientations Scale: Self-determination in personality. *Journal of Research in Personality, 19*, 109–134.

Deery, H. A., & Fildes, B. N. (1999). Young novice driver subtypes: Relationship to high-risk behavior, traffic accident record, and simulator driving performance. *Human Factors, 41*, 628–643.

Deffenbacher, J. L. (1999). Driving anger: Some characteristics and interventions. In *Proceedings of the 35th annual meeting: Prospective Medicine—The Tools, the Data, the Interventions, and the Outcomes* (pp. 273–284). Pittsburgh, PA: Society of Prospective Medicine.

Deffenbacher, J. L., Deffenbacher, D. M., Lynch, R. S., & Richards, T. L. (2003). Anger, aggression, and risky behavior: A comparison of high and low anger drivers. *Behaviour Research and Therapy, 41*, 701–718.

Deffenbacher, J. L., Filetti, L. B., Lynch, R. S., Dahlen, E. R., & Oetting, E. R. (2002). Cognitive–behavioral treatment of high anger drivers. *Behaviour Research and Therapy, 40*, 895–910.

Deffenbacher, J. L., Filetti, L. B., Richards, T. L., Lynch, R. S., & Oetting, E. R. (2003). Characteristics of two groups of angry drivers. *Journal of Counseling Psychology, 50*, 123–132.

Deffenbacher, J. L., Huff, M. E., Lynch, R. S., Oetting, E. R., & Salvatore, N. F. (2000). Characteristics and treatment of high-anger drivers. *Journal of Consulting Psychology, 47*, 5–17.

Deffenbacher, J. L., Lynch, R. S., Deffenbacher, D. M., & Oetting, E. R. (2001). Further evidence of reliability and validity for the Driving Anger Expression Inventory. *Psychological Reports, 89*, 535–540.

Deffenbacher, J. L., Lynch, R. S., Filetti, L. B., Dahlen, E. R., & Oetting, E. R. (2003). Anger, aggression, risky behavior, and crash-related outcomes in three groups of drivers. *Behaviour Research and Therapy, 41*, 333–349.

Deffenbacher, J. L., Lynch, R. S., Oetting, E. R., & Swaim, R. C. (2002). The Driving Anger Expression Inventory: A measure of how people express their anger on the road. *Behaviour Research and Therapy, 40*, 717–737.

Deffenbacher, J. L., Lynch, R. S., Oetting, E. R., & Yingling, D. A. (2001). Driving anger: Correlates and a test of state–trait theory. *Personality and Individual Differences, 31*, 1321–1331.

Deffenbacher, J. L., Oetting, E. R., & Lynch, R. S. (1994). Development of a driving anger scale. *Psychological Reports, 74*, 83–91.

Deffenbacher, J. L., Petrilli, R. T., Lynch, R. S., Oetting, E. R., & Swaim, R. C. (2003). The Driver's Angry Thoughts Questionnaire: A measure of angry cognitions while driving. *Cognitive Therapy and Research, 27*, 383–402.

Deffenbacher, J. L., White, G. S., & Lynch, R. S. (2004). Evaluation of two new scales assessing driving anger: The Driving Anger Expression Inventory and the Driver's Angry Thoughts Questionnaire. *Journal of Psychopathology and Behavioral Assessment, 26,* 87–99.

DePasquale, J. P., Geller, E. S., Clarke, S. W., & Littleton, L. C. (2001). Measuring road rage: Development of the Propensity for Angry Driving Scale. *Journal of Safety Research, 32,* 1–16.

Dimberg, U. (1983). Facial reactions to facial expressions. *Psychophysiology, 19,* 219–233.

Dimberg, U. (1988). Facial electromyography and the experience of emotion. *Journal of Psychophysiology, 2,* 277–282.

Dodge, K. A., & Coie, J. D. (1987). Social information processing factors in reactive and proactive aggression. *Child Development, 51,* 162–170.

Dodge, K. A., Lochman, J. E., Harnish, J. D., Bates, J. E., & Pettit, G. S. (1997). Reactive and proactive aggression in school children and psychiatrically impaired chronically assaultive youth. *Journal of Abnormal Psychology, 106,* 37–51.

Dodge, K. A., Price, J. M., Bachorowski, J., & Newman, J. M. (1990). Hostile attributional biases in severely aggressive adolescents. *Journal of Abnormal Psychology, 99,* 385–392.

Dollard, J., Doob, L. W., Miller, N. E., Mowrer, O. H., & Sears, R. B. (1939). *Frustration and aggression.* New Haven, CT: Yale University Press.

Donovan, D. M., Umlauf, R. L., & Salzberg, P. M. (1988). Derivation of personality subtypes among high-risk drivers. *Alcohol, Drugs, and Driving, 4,* 233–244.

Donovan, J. E. (1992). Young adult drinking–driving: Behavioral and psychosocial correlates. *Journal of Studies on Alcohol, 54,* 600–613.

Doob, A. N., & Gross, A. E. (1968). Status of frustrator as an inhibitor of horn-honking responses. *Journal of Social Psychology, 76,* 213–218.

Dukes, R. L., Clayton, S. L., Jenkins, L. T., Miller, T. L., & Rodgers, S. E. (2001). Effects of aggressive driving and driver characteristics on road rage. *Social Science Journal, 38,* 323–331.

Dula, C. S., & Ballard, M. E. (2003). Development and evaluation of a measure of dangerous, aggressive, negative emotional, and risky driving. *Journal of Applied Social Psychology, 33,* 263–282.

Eckhardt, C., Norlander, B., & Deffenbacher, J. (2004). The assessment of anger and hostility: A critical review. *Aggression and Violent Behavior, 9,* 17–43.

Eelkema, R. C., Brosseau, J., & Koshnick, R. (1970). A statistical study on the relationship between mental illness and traffic accidents: A pilot study. *American Journal of Public Health, 60,* 459–469.

Ellison, P. A., Govern, J. M., Petri, H. L., & Figler, M. H. (1995). Anonymity and aggressive driving behavior: A field study. *Journal of Social Behavior and Personality, 10,* 265–272.

Ellison-Potter, P., Bell, P., & Deffenbacher, J. (2001). The effects of trait driving anger, anonymity, and aggressive stimuli on aggressive driving behavior. *Journal of Applied Social Psychology, 31*, 431–443.

Engerbretson, T. O., Matthews, K. A., & Scheier, M. F. (1989). Relations between anger expression and cardiovascular reactivity: Reconciling inconsistent findings through a matching hypothesis. *Journal of Personality and Social Psychology, 57*, 513–521.

Evans, G. W., Palsane, M. N., & Carrere, S. (1987). Type A behavior and occupational stress: A cross-cultural study of blue collar workers. *Journal of Personality and Social Psychology, 52*, 1002–1007.

Evans, L. (2002). Traffic crashes. *American Scientist, 90*, 244–253.

Evans, L., & Wasielewski, P. (1983). Risky driving related to driver and vehicle characteristics. *Accident Analysis and Prevention, 15*, 121–136.

Felthous, A. R., Bryant, S. G., Wingerter, C. B., & Barratt, E. (1991). The diagnosis of intermittent explosive disorder in violent men. *Bulletin of the American Academy of Psychiatry and the Law, 19*, 71–79.

Ferguson, A. (1998, January 12). Road rage. *Time, 151*, 64–68.

Fillingim, R. B., Roth, D. L., & Cook, E. W. (1992). The effects of aerobic exercise on cardiovascular, facial EMG, and self-report responses to emotional imagery. *Psychosomatic Medicine, 54*, 109–120.

First, M. B., Spitzer, R. L., Gibbon, M., & Williams, J. B. W. (1996). *Structured Clinical Interview for Axis I DSM–IV Disorders, Version 2.0.* New York: Biometrics Research Department, New York State Psychiatric Institute.

First, M. B., Spitzer, R. L., Gibbon, M., Williams, J. B. W., & Benjamin, L. (1996). *Structured Clinical Interview for DSM–IV Axis II Personality Disorders (SCID–II Version 2.0).* New York: Biometrics Research Department, New York State Psychiatric Institute.

Foa, E. B., & Meadows, E. A. (1997). Psychosocial treatments for posttraumatic stress disorder: A critical review. *Annual Reviews Psychology, 48*, 449–480.

Fong, G., Frost, D., & Stansfeld, S. (2001). Road rage: A psychiatric phenomenon? *Social Psychiatry and Psychiatric Epidemiology, 36*, 277–286.

Foster, P. S., Smith, E. W. L., & Webster, D. G. (1999). The psychophysiological differentiation of actual, imagined, and recollected anger. *Imagination, Cognition, and Personality, 18*, 189–203.

Foster, P. S., Webster, D. G., & Smith, E. W. L. (1997). The psychophysiological differentiation of emotional memories. *Imagination, Cognition, and Personality, 17*, 111–112.

Fridlund, A. J., Kenworthy, K. G., & Jaffey, A. K. (1992). Audience effects in affective imagery: Replication and extension to dysphoric imagery. *Journal of Nonverbal Behavior, 16*, 191–212.

Fumento, M. (1998, August). Road rage vs. reality. *Atlantic Monthly, 282*, 12. Retrieved April 29, 2005, from http://www.fumento.com/atlantic.html

Furnham, A., & Saipe, J. (1993). Personality correlates of convicted drivers. *Personality and Individual Differences, 14,* 329–338.

Galovski, T. E., & Blanchard, E. B. (2002a). The effectiveness of a brief, psychological intervention on court-referred and self-referred aggressive drivers. *Behaviour Research and Therapy, 40,* 1385–1402.

Galovski, T., & Blanchard, E. B. (2002b). Road rage: A domain for psychological intervention? *Aggression and Violent Behavior, 275,* 1–23.

Galovski, T. E., Blanchard, E. B., Malta, L. S., & Freidenberg, B. M. (2003). The psychophysiology of aggressive drivers: Comparison to non-aggressive drivers and pre- to post-treatment change following a cognitive–behavioral treatment. *Behaviour Research and Therapy, 41,* 1055–1067.

Galovski, T., Blanchard, E. B., & Veazey, C. (2002). Intermittent explosive disorder and other psychiatric co-morbidity among court-referred and self-referred aggressive drivers. *Behaviour Research and Therapy, 40,* 641–651.

Greenwood, M., & Woods, H. M. (1919). *Preliminary reports on special tests.* Sacramento, CA: Department of Motor Vehicles.

Gulian, E., Debney, L. M., Glendon, A. I., Davies, D. R., & Matthews, G. (1989). Coping with driver stress. In M. G. McGuigan & W. E. Sime (Eds.), *Stress and tension control* (Vol. 3, pp. 173–186). New York: Plenum Press.

Guyll, M., & Contrada, R. J. (1998). Trait hostility and ambulatory cardiovascular activity: Responses to social interaction. *Health Psychology, 17,* 30–39.

Halderman, B. L., & Jackson, T. T. (1979). Naturalistic study of aggression: Aggressive stimuli and horn-honking: A replication. *Psychological Reports, 45,* 880–882.

Hankes-Drielsma, M. P. (1974). *Driver aggression and frustrator identity.* Kingston, Ontario, Canada: Department of Psychology, Queen's University.

Harano, R. M. (1975). The psychometric prediction of negligent driver recidivism. *Journal of Safety Research, 7,* 170–179.

Hartos, J., Eitel, P., & Simons-Morton, B. (2002). Parenting practices and adolescent risky driving: A three-month prospective study. *Health Education and Behavior, 29,* 194–206.

Hauber, A. R. (1980). The social psychology of driving behaviour and the traffic environment: Research on aggressive behavior in traffic. *International Review of Applied Psychology, 29,* 461–474.

Hemenway, D., & Solnick, S. J. (1993). Fuzzy dice, dream cars, and indecent gestures: Correlates of driving behaviors? *Accident Analysis and Prevention, 25,* 161–170.

Hennessy, D. A., & Wiesenthal, D. L. (1997). The relationship between traffic congestion, driver stress, and direct versus indirect coping behaviors. *Ergonomics, 40,* 348–361.

Hennessy, D. A., & Wiesenthal, D. L. (1999). Traffic congestion, driver stress, and driver aggression. *Aggressive Behavior, 25,* 409–423.

Hilakivi, I., Veilahti, J., Asplund, P., Sinivuo, J., & Laitinen, L. (1989). A sixteen-factor personality test for predicting automobile accidents of young drivers. *Accident Analysis and Prevention, 21,* 413–418.

Houston, B. K., Smith, M. A., & Cates, D. S. (1989). Hostility patterns and cardiovascular reactivity to stress. *Psychophysiology, 26,* 337–342.

Isherwood, J., Adams, K. S., & Hornblow, A. R. (1982). Life event stress, psychosocial factors, suicide attempt, and auto-accident proclivity. *Journal of Psychosomatic Research, 26,* 371–383.

Iversen, H., & Rundmo, T. (2002). Personality, risky driving, and accident involvement among Norwegian drivers. *Personality and Individual Differences, 33,* 1251–1263.

James, L., & Nahl, D. (2000). *Road rage and aggressive driving: Steering clear of highway warfare.* Amherst, NY: Prometheus.

Jamison, K., & McGlothlin, W. H. (1973). Drug usage, personality, attitudinal, and behavioral correlates of driving behavior. *Journal of Psychology, 83,* 123–130.

Jessor, R. (1987). Risky driving and adolescent problem behavior: An extension of problem-behavior theory. *Alcohol, Drugs, and Driving, 3,* 1–11.

Joint, M. (1995). *Road rage.* London: Automobile Association. Retrieved April 29, 2003, from http://www.aaafoundation.org/pdf/agdr3study.pdf

Jonah, B. A. (1986). Accident risk and risk-taking behaviour among young drivers. *Accident Analysis and Prevention, 18,* 255–271.

Jonah, B. A. (1997). Sensation seeking and risky driving. In T. Rothengatter & E. C. Vaya (Eds.), *Traffic and transport psychology, theory and application* (pp. 259–267). New York: Elsevier Science/Pergamon Press.

Jonah, B. A., Thiessen, R., & Au-Yeung, E. (2001). Sensation seeking, risky driving, and behavioral adaptation. *Accident Analysis and Prevention, 33,* 679–684.

Kassinove, H., & Eckhardt, C. I. (1995). An anger model and a look to the future. In H. Kassinove (Ed.), *Anger disorders: Definition, diagnosis, and treatment* (pp. 197–204). Washington, DC: Taylor & Francis.

Kassinove, H., & Sukhodolsky, D. G. (1995). Anger disorders: Basic science and practice issues. In H. Kassinove (Ed.), *Anger disorders: Definition, diagnosis, and treatment* (pp. 1–27). Washington, DC: Taylor & Francis.

Kenrick, D. T., & MacFarlane, S.W. (1986). Ambient temperature and horn-honking: A field study of the heat/aggression relationship. *Environment and Behavior, 18,* 179–191.

Klepp, K. I., & Perry, C. L. (1990). Adolescents, drinking and driving: Who does it and why? In R. J. Wilson & R. E. Mann (Eds.), *Drinking and driving: Advances in research and prevention* (pp. 42–67). New York: Guilford Press.

Knee, C. R., Neighbors, C., & Vietor, N. A. (2001). Self-determination theory as a framework for understanding road rage. *Journal of Applied Social Psychology, 31,* 889–904.

Knowles, E., & Elliott, J. (Eds.). (1997). *The Oxford English dictionary of new words.* New York: Oxford University Press.

Kontogiannis, T., Kossiavelou, Z., & Marmaras, N. (2002). Self-reports of aberrant behaviour on roads: Errors and violations in a sample of Greek drivers. *Accident Analysis and Prevention, 34,* 381–399.

Krahé, B., & Fenske, I. (2002). Predicting aggressive driving behavior: The role of macho personality, age, and power of car. *Aggressive Behavior, 28,* 21–29.

Lajunen, T., & Parker, D. (2001). Are aggressive people aggressive drivers? A study of the relationship between self-reported general aggressiveness, driver anger, and aggressive driving. *Accident Analysis and Prevention, 33,* 243–255.

Lajunen, T., Parker, D., & Stradling, S. G. (1998). Dimensions of driver anger, aggressive and highway code violations, and their mediation by safety orientation. *Transportation Research Part F,* 107–121.

Larson, J. A. (1996a). Driver's Stress Profile. In *Steering clear of highway madness: A driver's guide to curbing stress and strain* (pp. 25–28). Wilsonville, OR: BookPartners.

Larson, J. A. (1996b). *Steering clear of highway madness: A driver's guide to curbing stress and strain.* Wilsonville, OR: BookPartners,.

Larson, J. A., Rodriquez, C., & Galvan-Henkin, A. (1998, May). *Pilot study: Reduction in "road rage" and aggressive driving through one day cognitive therapy seminar.* Paper presented at the New York State Symposium on Aggressive Driving, Albany.

Lawton, R., & Nutter, A. (2002). A comparison of reported levels and expression of anger in everyday and driving situations. *British Journal of Psychology, 93,* 407–423.

Lawton, R., Parker, D., Manstead, A. S. R., & Stradling, S. G. (1997). The role of affect in predicting social behaviors: The case of road traffic violations. *Journal of Applied Social Psychology, 27,* 1258–1276.

Lawton, R., Parker, D., Stradling, S. G., & Manstead, A. S. R. (1997). Predicting road traffic accidents: The role of social deviance and violations. *British Journal of Psychology, 88,* 249–262.

Lion, J. R. (1992). The intermittent explosive disorder. *Psychiatric Annals, 22,* 64–66.

Loo, R. (1979). Role of primary personality factors in the perception of traffic signs and driver violations and accidents. *Accident Analysis and Prevention, 11,* 125–127.

MacDonald, J. M. (1964). Suicide and homicide by automobile. *American Journal of Psychiatry, 121,* 366–370.

MacMillan, J. (1975). *Deviant drivers.* Lexington, MA: Lexington Books.

Maiuro, R. (1998, Summer). Rage on the road. *Recovery, 9*(2). Retrieved April 29, 2005, from http://www.icbc.com/library/recovery/volume9/number2/rageon theroad/index.html

Maletzky, B. M. (1973). The episodic dyscontrol syndrome. *Diseases of the Nervous System, 34,* 178–185.

Malta, L. S. (2004). *Predictors of aggressive driving in young adults.* Unpublished manuscript, University at Albany, State University of New York.

Malta, L. S., & Blanchard, E. B. (2004, November). *Predictors of aggressive driving in young adults*. Poster presented at the 38th Annual Convention of the Association for the Advancement of Behavior Therapy, New Orleans, LA.

Malta, L. S., Blanchard, E. B., & Freidenberg, B. M. (in press). Psychiatric and behavioral problems in aggressive drivers. *Behaviour Research and Therapy*.

Malta, L. S., Blanchard, E. B., Freidenberg, B. M., Galovski, T. E., Karl, A., & Holzapfel, S. R. (2001). Physiological reactivity of aggressive drivers: An exploratory study. *Applied Psychophysiology and Biofeedback, 26*, 95–116.

Mattes, J. A., & Fink, M. (1987). A family study of patients with temper outbursts. *Journal of Psychiatry Research, 21*, 249–255.

Matthews, G., Desmond, P. A., Joyner, L., Carcary, B., & Gilliland, K. (1997). A comprehensive questionnaire measure of driver stress and affect. In T. Rothengatter & E. C. Vaya (Eds.), *Traffic and transport psychology, theory and application* (pp. 317–324). New York: Elsevier Science/Pergamon Press.

Matthews, G., Dorn, L., Hoyes, T. W., Davies, D. R., Glendon, A. I., & Taylor, R. G. (1998). Driver stress and performance on a driving simulator. *Human Factors, 40*, 136–149.

Mayer, R. E., & Treat, J. R. (1977). Psychological, social, and cognitive characteristics of high-risk drivers: A pilot study. *Accident Analysis and Prevention, 9*, 1–8.

McElroy, S. L. (1999). Recognition and treatment of DSM–IV intermittent explosive disorder. *Journal of Clinical Psychiatry, 60*, 12–16.

McElroy, S. L., Soutullo, C. A., Beckman, D. A., Taylor, P. Jr., & Keck, P. E. (1998). DSM–IV intermittent explosive disorder: A report of 27 cases. *Journal of Clinical Psychiatry, 59*, 203–210.

McFarland, R. A. (1968). Psychological and behavioral aspects of automobile accidents. *Research Review: A National Safety Council Publication, 12*, 71–80.

McFarland, R. A., & Moseley, A. I. (1954). *Human factors in highway transport safety*. Boston: Harvard Public School of Health.

McGarva, A. R., & Steiner, M. (2000). Provoked driving aggression and status: A field study. *Transportation Research, Part F, 3*, 167–179.

McGuire, F. L. (1976). Personality factors in highway accidents. *Human Factors, 18*, 433–442.

Meadows, M. L., Stradling, S. G., & Lawson, S. (1998). The role of social deviance and violations in predicting road traffic accidents in a sample of young offenders. *British Journal of Psychology, 89*, 417–431.

Mednick, S. A. (1977). A biosocial theory of the learning of law-abiding behavior. In S. A. Mednick & K. O. Christiansen (Eds.), *Biosocial bases of criminal behavior* (pp. 1–8). New York: Gardner Press.

Meichenbaum, D. (1986). Cognitive behavior modification. In F. H. Kanfer & A. P. Goldstein (Eds.), *Helping people change: A textbook of methods* (pp. 346–380). New York: Pergamon Press.

Michalowski, R. J. (1975). Violence on the road: The crime of vehicular homicide. *Journal of Research in Crime and Delinquency, 12*, 30–43.

Miller, M., Azrael, D., Hemenway, D., & Solop, F. I. (2002). "Road rage" in Arizona: Armed and dangerous. *Accident Analysis and Prevention, 34,* 807–814.

Miller, N. E. (1941). The frustration–aggression hypothesis. *Psychological Review, 48,* 364–368.

Mizell, L. (1997). Aggressive driving. In *Aggressive driving: Three studies.* Washington, DC: AAA Foundation for Traffic Safety. Retrieved April 29, 2005, from http://www.aaafoundation.org/pdf/agdr3study.pdf

Monopolis, S., & Lion, J. R. (1983). Problems in the diagnosis of intermittent explosive disorder. *American Journal of Psychiatry, 140,* 1200–1202.

Murphy, K., & Barkley, R. A. (1996). Attention deficit hyperactivity disorder adults: Comorbidities and adaptive impairments. *Comprehensive Psychiatry, 37,* 393–401.

Naatanen, R., & Summala, H. (1976). *Road user behavior and traffic accidents.* Amsterdam: North Holland.

Nada-Raja, S., Langley, J. D., McGee, R., Williams, S. M., Begg, D. J., & Reeder, A. I. (1997). Inattention and hyperactive behaviors and driving offenses in adolescence. *Journal of the American Academy of Child and Adolescent Psychiatry, 36,* 515–522.

National Highway Traffic Safety Administration. (1999). *Aggressive driving and the law: A symposium.* Retrieved November 8, 2003, from http://www.nhtsa.dot.gov/people/injury/aggressive/symposium/introduction.htm

National Highway Traffic Safety Administration. (2001). *National aggressive driving action guide: A criminal justice report* (DOT HS 809 351). Retrieved November 8, 2003, from http://www.nhtsa.dot.gov/people/injury/enforce/dot%20aggress%20action/index.html

Neighbors, C., Vietor, N. A., & Knee, C. R. (2002). A motivation model of driving anger and aggression. *Personality and Social Psychology Bulletin, 28,* 324–335.

Norris, F. H. (1992). Epidemiology of trauma: Frequency and impact of different potentially traumatic events on different demographic groups. *Journal of Consulting and Clinical Psychology, 60,* 409–418.

Novaco, R. W. (1975). *Anger control.* Boston: Lexington Press.

Novaco, R. W. (1979). The cognitive regulation of anger and stress. In P. Kendall & S. Hollon (Eds.), *Cognitive–behavioral interventions: Theory, research, and procedures* (pp. 241–285). New York: Academic Press.

Novaco, R. W. (1986). Anger as a clinical and social problem. In R. Blanchard & C. Blanchard (Eds.), *Advances in the study of aggression* (Vol. 2, pp. 1–67). New York: Academic Press.

Novaco, R. W. (1991). Aggression on roadways. In R. Baenninger (Ed.), *Targets of violence and aggression: Advances in psychology* (pp. 253–326). Oxford, England: North Holland.

Novaco, R. W., Stokols, D., Campell, J., & Stokols, J. (1979). Transportation, stress, and community psychology. *American Journal of Community Psychology, 7,* 361–380.

Parker, D., Lajunen, T., & Stradling, S. G. (1998). Attitudinal predictors of interpersonally aggressive violations on the road. *Transportation Research Part F, 1,* 11–24.

Parker, D., Lajunen, T., & Summala, H. (2002). Anger and aggression among drivers in three European countries. *Accident Analysis and Prevention, 34,* 229–235.

Parker, D., Manstead, A. S. R., & Stradling, S. G. (1995). Extending the theory of planned behaviour: The role of personal norm. *British Journal of Social Psychology, 34,* 127–137.

Parry, M. (1968). *Aggression on the road.* London: Tavistock.

Perry, A. R. (1986). Type A behavior pattern and motor vehicle driver's behavior. *Perceptual and Motor Skills, 63,* 875–878.

Perry, A. R., & Baldwin, D. A. (2000). Further evidence of associations of Type A personality scores and driving related attitudes and behaviors. *Perceptual and Motor Skills, 91,* 147–154.

Pfohl, B., & Zimmerman, M. (1989). *Structured Interview for DSM–III–R Personality Disorders.* Iowa City: University of Iowa College of Medicine.

Pitman, R. K., Orr, S. P., Forgue, D. F., deJong, J. B., & Claiborn, J. M. (1987). Psychophysiologic assessment of posttraumatic stress disorder imagery in Vietnam combat veterans. *Archives of General Psychiatry, 44,* 970–975.

Powch, I. G., & Houston, B. K. (1996). Hostility, anger-in, and cardiovascular reactivity in White women. *Health Psychology, 15,* 200–208.

Raikkonen, K., Matthews, K. A., Flory, J. D., & Owens, J. F. (1999). Effects of hostility on ambulatory blood pressure and mood during daily living in healthy adults. *Health Psychology, 18,* 44–53.

Reason, J. T., Manstead, A., Stradling, S., Baxter, J., & Campbell, K. (1990). Errors and violations on the road: A real distinction? *Ergonomics, 33,* 1315–1332.

Richards, T. L., Deffenbacher, J., & Rosen, L. A. (2002). Driving anger and other driving-related behaviors in high and low ADHD symptom college students. *Journal of Attention Disorders, 6,* 25–38.

Rimm, D. C., DeGroot, J. C., Boord, P., Heiman, J., & Dillow, P. V. (1971). Systematic desensitization of an anger response. *Behaviour Research and Therapy, 9,* 273–280.

Roberts, R. J., & Weerts, T. C. (1982). Cardiovascular responding during anger and fear imagery. *Psychological Reports, 50,* 219–230.

Rosenman, R. H., Swan, G. F., & Carmelli, D. (1988). Definition, assessment, and evolution of the Type A behavior pattern. In B. K. Houston & C. R. Snyder (Eds.), *Type A behavior pattern: Research, theory and intervention* (pp. 8–31). New York: Wiley.

Rogers, C. R. (1951). *Client-centered therapy.* Boston: Houghton Mifflin.

Ross, H. L. (1940). Traffic accidents: A product of social–psychological conditions. *Social Forces, 18,* 569–576.

Salzinger, K. (1995). A behavior-analytic view of anger and aggression. In H. Kassinove (Ed.), *Anger disorders: Definition, diagnosis, and treatment* (pp. 69–78). Washington, DC: Taylor & Francis.

Scarpa, A., & Raine, A. (1997). Psychophysiology of anger and violent behavior. *Psychiatric Clinics of North America, 20*, 375–394.

Schaeffer, M. H., Street, S. W., Singer, J. E., & Baum, A. (1988). Effects of control on the stress reactions of commuters. *Journal of Applied Social Psychology, 18*, 944–957.

Schreer, G. E. (2002). Narcissism and aggression: Is inflated self-esteem related to aggressive driving? *North American Journal of Psychology, 4*, 333–342.

Selzer, M. L., & Payne, C. E. (1962). Automobile accidents, suicide, and unconscious motivation. *American Journal of Psychiatry, 119*, 237–240.

Selzer, M. L., Rogers, J. E., & Kern, S. (1968). Fatal accidents: The role of psychopathology, social stress, and acute disturbance. *American Journal of Psychiatry, 124*, 46–54.

Selzer, M. L., & Vinokur, A. (1974). Life events, subjective stress, and traffic accidents. *American Journal of Psychiatry, 131*, 903–906.

Shaw, L. (1956). The practical use of projective personality tests as accident predictors. *Traffic Safety Research Review, 9*, 34–72.

Shinar, D. (1998). Aggressive driving: The contribution of the drivers and the situation. *Transportation Research Part F, 1*, 137–160.

Shinar, D., & Compton, R. (2004). Aggressive driving: An observational study of driver, vehicle, and situational variables. *Accident Analysis and Prevention, 36*, 429–437.

Shope, J., & Bingham, R. (2002). Drinking–driving as a component of problem driving and problem behavior in young adults. *Journal of Studies on Alcohol, 63*, 24–33.

Shope, J., & Patil, S. M. (2003). Examining trajectories of adolescent risk factors as predictors of subsequent high-risk driving behavior. *Journal of Adolescent Health, 32*, 214–224.

Siegman, A. W., Anderson, R. A., & Berger, T. (1990). The angry voice: Its effects on the experience of anger and cardiovascular reactivity. *Psychosomatic Medicine, 52*, 631–643.

Sinha, R., Lovallo, W. R., & Parsons, O. A. (1992). Cardiovascular differentiation of emotions. *Psychosomatic Medicine, 54*, 422–435.

Slomine, B. S., & Greene, A. F. (1993). Anger imagery and corrugator electromyography. *Journal of Psychosomatic Research, 37*, 671–676.

Smith, G. T. (1994). Concepts and methods in the study of anger, hostility, and health. In A. W. Siegman & T. W. Smith (Eds.), *Anger, hostility, and the heart* (pp. 23–42). Hillsdale, NJ: Erlbaum.

Smith, T. W., & Alfred, K. D. (1989). Blood-pressure responses during social interaction in high- and low-cynically hostile males. *Journal of Behavioral Medicine, 12*, 135–143.

Spielberger, C. D. (1983). *Manual for the State–Trait Anxiety Inventory—STAI (Form Y)*. Palo Alto, CA: Consulting Psychologists Press.

Spielberger, C. D. (1988). *State–Trait Anger Expression Inventory: Professional manual*. Odessa, FL: Psychological Assessment Resources.

Spielberger, C. D., Gorusch, R. L., & Lushene, R. E. (1970). *STAI Manual for the State–Trait Inventory*. Palo Alto, CA: Consulting Psychologists Press.

Spielberger, C. D., Jacobs, G., Russel, S., & Crane, R. J. (1983). Assessment of anger: The State–Trait Anger Scale. In J. N. Butcher & C. D. Spielberger (Eds.), *Advances in personality assessment* (Vol. 2, pp. 161–190). Hillsdale, NJ: Erlbaum.

Spielberger, C. D., Johnson, E. H., Russel, S. F., Crane, R. J., Jacobs, G. A., & Worden, T. J. (1985). The experience and expression of anger: Construction and validation of an anger expression scale. In M. A. Chesney & R. H. Rosenman (Eds.), *Anger and hostility in cardiovascular and behavioral disorders* (pp. 5–30). New York: Hemisphere.

Spielberger, C. D., Reheiser, E. C., & Sydeman, S. J. (1995). Measuring the experience, expression, and control of anger. In H. Kassinove (Ed.), *Anger disorders: Definition, diagnosis, and treatment* (pp. 49–65). Hillsdale, NJ: Erlbaum.

Spitzer, R. L., & Endicott, J. (1977). *Schedule for Affective Disorders and Schizophrenia—Lifetime Version (SADS–L)*. New York: Biometrics Research Department, New York State Psychiatric Institute.

Stanford, M. S., & Barratt, E. S. (1992). Impulsivity and the multi-impulsive personality disorder. *Personality and Individual Differences, 13*, 831–834.

Stanford, M. S., Greve, K. W., Boudreaux, J. K., Mathias, C. W., & Brumbelow, J. L. (1996). Impulsiveness and risk-taking behavior: Comparisons of high-school and college students using the Barratt Impulsiveness Scale. *Personality and Individual Differences, 21*, 1073–1075.

Stanford, M. S., Greve, K. W., & Dickens, T. J. (1995). Irritability and impulsiveness: Relationship to self-reported impulsive aggression. *Personality and Individual Differences, 19*, 757–760.

Stokols, D., & Novaco, R. W. (1981). Transportation and well-being. In I. Altman, J. F. Woblevill, & P. B. Everett (Eds.), *Transportation and well-being* (pp. 85–130). New York: Plenum Press.

Stokols, D., Novaco, R. W., Stokols, J., & Campbell, J. (1978). Traffic congestion: Type A behavior and stress. *Journal of Applied Psychology, 63*, 467–480.

Suarez, E. C., Kuhn, C. M., Schanberg, S. M., Williams, R. B., & Zimmermann, E. A. (1998). Neuroendocrine, cardiovascular, and emotional responses of hostile men: The role of interpersonal challenge. *Psychosomatic Medicine, 60*, 78–88.

Suarez, E. C., & Williams, R. B. (1989). Situational determinants of cardiovascular and emotional reactivity in high and low hostile men. *Psychosomatic Medicine, 51*, 404–418.

Suchman, S. H., Pelz, D. C., Ehrlich, N. J., & Selzer, M. I. (1967). Young male drivers. *Journal of the American Medical Association, 200,* 102–106.

Tafrate, R. C. (1995). Evaluation of treatment strategies for adult anger disorders. In H. Kassinove (Ed.), *Anger disorders: Definition, diagnosis, and treatment* (pp. 109–129). Washington, DC: Taylor &Francis.

Tedeschi, J. T., & Felson, R. B. (1994). *Violence, aggression, and coercive actions.* Washington, DC: American Psychological Association.

Tillmann, W. A., & Hobbs, G. E. (1949). The accident-prone driver. *American Journal of Psychiatry, 106,* 321–331.

Tsuang, M. T., Boor, M., & Fleming, J. A. (1985). Psychiatric aspects of traffic accidents. *American Journal of Psychiatry, 142,* 538–546.

Turner, C. W., Layton, J. F., & Simons, L. S. (1975). Naturalistic studies of aggressive behavior: Aggressive stimuli, victim visibility, and horn honking. *Journal of Personality and Social Psychology, 31,* 1098–1107.

Ulleberg, P. (2002). Personality subtypes of young drivers: Relationship to risk-taking preferences, accident involvement, and response to a traffic safety campaign. *Transportation Research Part F, 4,* 279–297.

Ulleberg, P., & Rundmo, T. (2003). Personality, attitudes and risk perception as predictors of risky driving behaviors among young drivers. *Safety Science, 41,* 427–443.

Underwood, G., Chapman, P., Wright, S., & Crundall, D. (1999). Anger while driving. *Transportation Research Part F, 2,* 55–68.

U.S. Department of Transportation, Bureau of Transportation Statistics. (1998). *Transportation statistics annual report* (BTS 98-S-01). Retrieved December 15, 2001, from http://www.bts.gov/publications/transportation_statistics_annual_report/1998/

U.S. Department of Transportation, Bureau of Transportation Statistics. (1999). *Transportation statistics annual report* (BTS 99-03). Retrieved December 15, 2001, from http://www.bts.gov/publications/transportation_statistics_annual_report/1999/

U.S. Department of Transportation, Bureau of Transportation Statistics. (2002). *National transportation statistics* (BTS 02-08). Retrieved November 8, 2003, from http://www.bts.gov/publications/national_transportation_statistics/2002/

Waller, J. A. (1965). Chronic medical conditions and traffic safety: Review of the California experience. *New England Journal of Medicine, 273,* 1413–1420.

Weiss, G., & Hechtman, L. T. (1986). *Hyperactive children grown up.* New York: Guilford Press.

Weiss, G., Hechtman, L. T., Perlman, T., Hopkins, J., & Wener, A. (1979). Hyperactives as young adults: A controlled prospective ten-year follow-up of 75 children. *Archives of General Psychiatry, 36,* 675–681.

Wells-Parker, E., Ceminsky, J., Hallberg, V., Snow, R. W., Dunaway, G., Guiling, S., et al. (2002). An exploratory study of the relationship between road rage and crash experience in a representative sample of US drivers. *Accident Analysis and Prevention, 34*, 271–278.

West, R., Elander, J., & French, D. (1993). Mild social deviance, Type A behaviour pattern and decision making styles as predictors of self reported driving style and traffic accident risk. *British Journal of Psychology, 84*, 207–219.

West, R., & Hall, J. (1997). The role of personality and attitudes in traffic accident risk. *Applied Psychology: An International Review, 46*, 253–264.

Wiesenthal, D. L., Hennessy, D. A., & Gibson, P. M. (2000). The Driving Vengeance Questionnaire (DVQ): The development of a scale to measure deviant drivers' attitudes. *Violence and Victims, 15*,115–136.

Williams, A. F. (2003). Teenage drivers: Patterns of risk. *Journal of Safety Research, 34*, 5–15.

Williams, R. (1994). *Anger kills: 17 strategies for controlling the hostility that can harm your health.* New York: HarperCollins.

Wilson, R. J. (1991). Subtypes of DWIs and high-risk drivers: Implications for differential intervention. *Alcohol, Drugs, and Driving, 7*, 1–12.

Wilson, R. J., & Jonah, B. A. (1988). The application of problem behaviour theory to the understanding of risky driving. *Alcohol, Drugs, and Driving, 4*, 173–191.

Zillman, D. (1994). Cognition–excitation interdependence in the escalation of anger and angry aggression. In M. Potegal & J. F. Knutson (Eds.), *The dynamics of aggression: Biological and social processes in dyads and groups* (pp. 45–72). Hillsdale, NJ: Erlbaum.

Zimbardo, P. G. (1978). The psychology of evil: On the perversion of human potential. In L. Krames, P. Pliner, & T. Alloway (Eds.), *Advances in the study of communication and affect: Vol. 4. Aggression, dominance, and individual spacing* (pp. 155–169). New York: Plenum Press.

Zuckerman, M., & Neeb, M. (1980). Demographic influences in sensation seeking and expressions of sensation seeking in religion, smoking, and driving habits. *Personality and Individual Differences, 1*, 197–206.

INDEX

Antisocial traits, 124
Anxiety, 117
Anxiety disorders, 88–90, 93, 94, 96, 97
Arguing with other drivers, 10, 14
Arithmetic, 126, 130–134
Arizona, 7, 11
Assault, 7–9, 89
Assessing driving hostility, 16–17
Assessment procedures
    driving diaries, 56, 57
    initial, 55–56, 59–72
    interviews, 55, 57
    psychophysiological. *See* Psychophysi-
        ological assessment
Attention control, 156
Attention-deficit disorder, 89
Attention-deficit/hyperactivity disorder
    (ADHD), 30, 95, 99
Attorneys, 219–220
Audiotapes, 126–128, 130–142
Australia, 35
Automotive vigilantes, 41
Avoidant personality disorder, 92, 98
Awareness, 155
Axis I disorders, 88–91, 93–95, 97, 100
Axis II disorders, 88, 89, 92–94, 97, 98,
    100

Beck, A. T., 154
Beck, R., 156
Beck Depression Inventory, 107, 108,
    113, 116, 117
Behavioral change, 155
Behaviors, driving, 210
Belief systems, 148, 183, 208
Belligerence, 30
"Be my guest" strategy, 191
Binge eating disorder, 91
Bipolar disorder, 89, 95
Bipolar II, 90
Blocking other vehicles, 6–11
Blood pressure (BP)
    ambulatory measuring of, 143
    diastolic. *See* Diastolic BP
    systolic. *See* Systolic BP
Body dysmorphic disorder, 91
Borderline personality disorder (BPD),
    30, 31, 85, 86, 92–94, 97, 98
BPD. *See* Borderline personality disorder

Breathing, 180, 200
Bumping other vehicles, 6
Buss–Durkee Hostility Inventory, 107–
    109

Canada, 35
Candidness, 111
Cardiovascular disease, 124
Chronic externalizing disorders, 33
Coercive actions, 20
Cognitive and relaxation coping skills
    (CRCS), 149–151
Cognitive–behavioral therapy, 156
Cognitive behaviors, 40–41
Cognitive distortions, 154, 192–196, 211
Cognitive factors, 154–155
Cognitive treatment, 156
Colorado State University, 102, 149–151
Comfort of driver, 38
Comorbidity, 85–86
Competing factor, 105, 108–110, 112,
    118, 121
Competition-seeking behavior, 21
"Competitive drivers," 13
Competitive driving, 31
Competitor typology, 41, 206
Completion form, 217, 218, 220
Composite Primary Symptom Reduction
    (CPRS), 160–163
Conduct disorder, 30, 98
Confidentiality, 168, 220–221
Consent form, 49n.
Consequences of driving, 210
Coping strategies, 182–183, 190–192
Cost of therapy, 216
Court-referred (CR) drivers, 47–50
    and aggressive vs. reckless driving,
        22
    in Albany study, 158–159
    and confidentiality issues, 221–222
    denial of responsibility by, 56
    offenses incurred by, 48
    outcome in self-referred vs., 163–
        164, 166
    psychological characteristics of self-
        referred vs., 107–109
    sample description, 49–50
CPRS. *See* Composite Primary Symptom
    Reduction

Excessive accelerating when lights turn green, 8

Facial muscle activity, 124, 126
Failure to yield right of way, 5
Fatalities
    aggressive driving involved in, 5
    from MVAs, 4
Fear-arousing tape, 127–128, 130–133, 136–140, 142
Female aggressive drivers, 36, 37
Fernandez, E., 156
Flashing lights, 9
Flyers, 216, 217
Forehead electromyogram, 130, 133, 134, 142–143
Four-muscle relaxation training, 196–197, 200
Frustration–aggression driving aggression
    environmental factors in, 35–38
    personological factors in, 38–41
Frustration–aggression hypothesis, 28, 33, 34–41
Full disclosure statement, 49n.

GAD. See Generalized anxiety disorder
Galovski, Tara E., 158, 216
Galvanic skin response (GSR), 149
Gender
    and anger/aggression, 118–120
    and competing/punishing factors, 121
    DAS norms, 122
    and driver typologies, 42
    and honking, 37, 38
    and impatience, 120
    of samples, 50–52
Gender driving norms, 36
Generalized aggression, 32
Generalized anxiety disorder (GAD), 90, 93, 95
Gestural aggression
    measurement of, 102, 104, 108, 110, 114, 118
    and MVAs, 14
    and neighborhood status, 38
    prevalence of, 5–9
Giving chase, 6, 8
Greek drivers, 8, 9, 12

Green light phases, short, 38
GSR (galvanic skin response), 149
Gun brandishing, 7
Gun threats, 6

Headlight flashing, 8
Heart disease, 174
Heart rate (HR), 130–131, 134–136, 138, 142
Hierarchy list, driving situation, 182–183, 207
High-anger drivers, 32
Histrionic personality disorder, 92, 97
Honking
    and car status, 37
    prevalence of, 6–10
    in response to delays, 38
Hostile aggression, 19
Hostile competitor typology, 41
Hostile driving aggression, 21
Hostility, 15–16
    and aggression/anger, 23–25
    definition of, 17
    and IED, 109
    and psychopathology theory, 30
    psychophysiological assessment of, 124
Humanistic therapy, 154
Humor, 202

Idiosyncratic audiotapes, 126–128
IED. See Intermittent explosive disorder
Illegal driving, 102, 104, 108–110, 114, 118
Impatience, 105, 108, 110, 112, 118, 120
"Impulse expression" score, 31
Impulse noncontrol theory, 28, 31, 33
Impulsiveness, 31–32
Inappropriate "should" and "should not" statements, 194, 211
Informed consent, 221, 222
Injuries
    aggressive driving involved in, 5
    from MVAs, 4
Institutional review board (IRB), 220–221
Instrumental aggression, 19, 37
Instrumental driving aggression, 21
Insurance companies, 223

Intent, 21, 22, 173
Intermittent explosive disorder (IED)
    and aggressive drivers, 109–110
    in college students, 95–99
    descriptive studies of, 86, 88–89
    diagnosis of, 85–88
    interview for, 86–88
    need for assessment of, 100
    and psychopathology theory, 31
    and psychophysiological assessment,
        141–142
    in sample participants, 52–53
    and treatment results, 167
    in treatment-seeking participants,
        96, 97
Interrupting the script, 155
IRB. *See* Institutional review board
Israel, 9, 10

Jekyll and Hyde drivers, 41

Labeling, 193–196, 211
Larson, J. A., 148, 174, 180
Larson's key strategies, 183, 208
Local driving norms, 37

Magnification, 194, 195, 211
Major depressive disorder, 90, 93, 95
Male aggressive drivers, 36
Martinez, Recardo, 221
Meichenbaum, D., 155
Mental arithmetic, 126, 130–134
Mind reading, 194, 211
Mood disorders, 88–90, 93–95, 97
Motor vehicle accidents (MVAs)
    age-related, 98
    aggressive driving as risk factor for,
        13–14
    aggressive driving involved in, 5
    and court-referred drivers, 50
    and DSP score, 105
    and generalized aggression, 32–33
    and impulse control theory, 31
    and impulsiveness, 31
    and personal maladjustment theory,
        29
    and psychopathology theory, 29–31
    and risk behavior syndrome, 33

    and social maladjustment theory, 28
    statistics of, 4
Motor vehicle departments, 223
Moving violations, 50–52
Multiple lane changes, 9, 10
Murphy, Jim, 49
Muscle relaxation program. *See* Relax-
    ation training
MVA risk literature, 27
MVAs. *See* Motor vehicle accidents

Narcissism, 40
Narcissistic personality disorder (NPD),
    92, 94, 97, 98
Narcissist typology, 41, 206
National Highway Traffic Safety Adminis-
    tration, 5, 21
Negative triad, 154
Neighborhood status, 38
The Netherlands, 8–10, 12
News media reporting, 12, 20
Novaco, R. W., 155–156
NPD. *See* Narcissistic personality disorder
Number of drivers on road, 36
Number of vehicles on road, 12–13, 36

Obsessive–compulsive disorder (OCD),
    90, 93, 95
Obsessive–compulsive personality disorder
    (OCPD), 92, 94, 97, 98
OCD. *See* Obsessive–compulsive disorder
OCPD. *See* Obsessive–compulsive person-
    ality disorder
Operant anger, 17
Oppositional defiant disorder, 95, 99
Orange County (California), 12
Overall-lack-of-insight hypothesis, 168

Panic disorder, 90, 93, 95
Paranoid personality disorder, 92, 94, 97,
    98
Passing vehicles, 9, 10
"Passive–aggressor" typology, 41, 181, 206
Patient acknowledgment of driving behav-
    ior, 176–178
Pedestrians, 8, 10, 12
    anger directed at, 16
    delays created by, 37

ABOUT THE AUTHORS

Tara E. Galovski, PhD, currently holds the position of assistant research professor at the University of Missouri—St. Louis, where she has conducted research at the Center for Trauma Recovery developing and testing psychosocial interventions for trauma victims. Previously, she worked and published in the areas of behavioral medicine and trauma recovery in a motor vehicle accident population. It was this latter research and her interest in anger management that precipitated her work with angry and aggressive drivers. She received her PhD in 2001 from the University at Albany, State University of New York.

Loretta S. Malta, PhD, is a licensed psychologist who received her PhD in 2004 from the University at Albany, State University of New York. She worked with Dr. Blanchard and Dr. Galovski at the University at Albany Center for Stress and Anxiety Disorders, where she conducted clinical research on aggressive driving and stress-related disorders. After interning at the National Center for Posttraumatic Stress Disorders in Boston, she completed her postdoctoral training at the New York University School of Medicine Institute for Trauma and Stress. Dr. Malta recently joined the faculty of the Department of Psychiatry, Weill Medical College, Cornell University, where she works in the Program for Anxiety and Traumatic Stress Studies. In addition to aggressive driving, her research and clinical areas of specialization include posttraumatic stress and trauma-related disorders.

Edward ("Ed") B. Blanchard, PhD, ABPP, recently retired from the University at Albany, State University of New York, after a 27-year tenure and is currently Emeritus Distinguished Professor of Psychology. He has published extensively in areas of behavior therapy, behavioral medicine, and the assessment and treatment of motor vehicle accident survivors. His work with road rage and the angry, aggressive driver began with work initiated by Dr. Galovski and Dr. Malta. He received his PhD in clinical psychology from Stanford University in 1969.